MOTHERS
ARE MADE

MOTHERS ARE MADE

How One Mom Overcame
Perfectionism, Self-Doubt, Loneliness,
and Anxiety and Became a Better
and Happier Parent

Danielle Sherman-Lazar

alcove
press

Published in the United States by Alcove Press, an imprint of The
Quick Brown Fox & Company LLC.

Alcove Press and its logo are trademarks of The Quick Brown Fox &
Company LLC.

Library of Congress Catalog-in-Publication data available upon
request.

ISBN (hardcover): 979-8-89242-234-5
ISBN (paperback): 979-8-89242-036-5
ISBN (ebook): 979-8-89242-037-2

Cover design by Philip Pascuzzo

Printed in the United States.

www.alcovepress.com

Alcove Press
34 West 27th St., 10th Floor
New York, NY 10001

First Edition: April 2025

10 9 8 7 6 5 4 3 2 1

For my girls, Vivienne, Diana, Julia, and Charli. You are my strength. My heart. My muses. My everything.

Author's Note

I AM A PARENT to little people who I love more than anything, like most of you picking up this book. These are my personal experiences. If you're concerned about something with one of your children, please seek out a medical expert or a psychologist. They're the ones who can diagnose, prescribe, and help get your kid on the right path.

Additionally, to protect the privacy of certain individuals, some names and identifying details have been changed.

Finally, this book contains material that can be triggering for someone who is struggling with an eating disorder. If this is you, please read with caution and know recovery is possible and worth it. A great resource is the National Alliance for Eating Disorders Helpline at 1 (866) 662-1235.

Contents

Introduction

Mothers are Made

"WHY ARE YOU crying again? You just ate," I ask my firstborn, newborn baby, Vivienne, as I bounce her on my hip, shushing her, milk leaking through my shirt, frustration leaking through my mind. Her soft skin presses against my bare chest as we dance back and forth. I lay Vivienne down, change her, and pick her back up, then I sit back down in the rocker, burp her and feed her some more. I swaddle her and croon softly to her, but her newborn cries continue to fill the room as my nipples burn. First babies should come with some sort of caution sign: they will spend most of the day crying, and half the time, you won't know why. Leaning back, I close my eyes.

Moments later, I tuck Vivienne into her bassinet still crying, needing a quick break, and plop down onto the living room couch, shaking my head. I'm numb to the noise from hearing her persistent cries most of the day. A mirror on the opposite wall reflects my image, and I drop my head into my hands. I can't stand the sight of myself, the dark circles under my eyes, my hair in a high, messy bun. I can't even seem to get myself properly dressed; I'm wearing nothing more than mesh hospital underwear and a nursing bra. Plus, I smell of spit-up and sweat. Honestly, I don't recognize the person I see in the mirror, the one who still looks four months pregnant and is swollen, sore, and stretched.

There were so many overwhelming firsts that came with Vivienne's birth. It was my first time putting someone else's needs before my own every minute of the day. It was the first time I couldn't shower or have a meal, shave, or do any uninterrupted work whenever I chose. This was a new kind of exhausted, a new kind of emotionally and physically drained. The sense of total defeat was constant.

I lift my head at the sound of the front door opening, and while I feel a wave of relief upon seeing my husband, I can't manage a smile. Catching a whiff of his cologne, I can only think how much better he smells than me.

"Why is she crying?" Jonathan says as he loosens his tie and eyes the bassinet.

"I don't know. She probably hates me. I know she hates my boobs." I sigh heavily as I get up to retrieve Vivienne and begin bouncing her again.

"She doesn't hate you. I think you're OK until the teen years," Jonathan jokes. He sets down his briefcase, takes off his jacket and starts gathering up the mess of burp cloths and pumped-milk bottles on the table.

Vivienne's shrieks rise, assaulting our ears. Jonathan doesn't seem the least bit distressed, but all I can feel is a burning urgency inside of me to make it stop, to make her calm.

"I'm going to try to feed her again," I say, raising my voice. But looking down into Vivienne's tiny, contorted face, I realize I'm speaking more to myself.

Ugh, how am I going to do this?

I have no answer. I sit down with her again, this time on the couch, and try, throat tight with unshed tears, nipples burning. I might have known in my bones that I was born to be a mother, but the actual experience was turning out to be nothing like the fairytale I had imagined.

Rewind to three years earlier. I open my eyes to see my mom standing at my bedside. *Where am I?* I look around the sterile, cold, alien room that somehow feels familiar, warmed by my mom's presence. The mix of her emotions, love, and tenderness, contrasted with a cooler current of fear, envelops me. Her hazel eyes aren't twinkling like they normally do. I am afraid, too. Something is wrong. Very wrong. *What happened?* I want to ask, but I can't form the words. They are frozen on my tongue.

She must see the look of overall puzzlement on my face—my brows furrowing and wrinkles forming on my forehead.

She says, "You're in the hospital. You had a seizure. You fell off the kitchen chair and began convulsing. I had to pin you down. Somehow, I called 911. You were speaking gibberish. It was so scary."

She strokes my hair as she speaks. It feels nice, calming. Everything else aches. I hear my dad talking to someone. A doctor, I guess. But they are too far away, and I can't make out what they are saying. All at once, memories from the night before start to flash through my mind: me bingeing and purging, head in the toilet, quaking; lying in bed, sweating and shaking under a blanket; fighting a feeling that something was different than the other times—scarier, worse, not OK. *I was not OK.*

That night, just days before my twenty-sixth birthday, I hovered between wanting to live and a wish to let myself die already. At one point, my near-weightless body lay on the cold marble floor of my bathroom—dizzy, nauseous, and shivering. It was either death or changing my life because I couldn't do it anymore—I was miserable. I couldn't keep living with my eating disorder in the driver's seat, depression and anxiety sharing the front seat, and me squished in the back, being dragged along for the ride. I promised myself that if I was going to live, I'd have to get better. In some ways, I wanted to die, and that's why I had become so reckless with pills, booze, and self-imposed starvation.

But then, in the dark predawn hours, I felt some faint flicker of hope and chose life. I dragged myself into a sitting position and sent a text to my parents—just three words: *I need help.*

They came. In the hospital, with my mother at my bedside, I remember last night's shame-filled car ride to my parents' house and how I had vowed, in tears, to kill this sick version of myself once and for all. How had I let it go on until I was almost twenty-six years old? *I am a failure.* The thought was like a drumbeat through my mind. It kept up its dark rhythm even as I fell asleep in my parent's bed, wrapped in a blanket from my childhood, my mother close by.

I glance at Mom again, still figuring out how to respond to all the information she gave me.

"How am I . . . going to . . . do this?" I finally ask her, voice halting, tears falling down my cheeks as the reality of being hospitalized, about going into treatment, about not totally knowing what is going to happen next sinks in. My whole body aches, I can't move, and clearly I'm struggling with forming sensible speech. I didn't know it then, but the symptoms—forgetting words, even stuttering—would linger for a couple of days as side effects of my seizure.

I had finally hit rock bottom.

At age fifteen, frizzy curls tied up high in a ponytail, I jot down everything my high school teacher says. She asks a question. Silence fills the classroom. I know the answer; I did all the reading, and studied just in case we had a pop quiz. But I can't make myself raise my hand.

"No one remembers the answer from the reading last night?" The teacher scans the class.

I do. I do. I debate if I should answer her as my leg shakes below the desk. What if I'm wrong? Or worse, what if someone rolls their eyes because I'm such a dork? I can't raise my hand. I'm paralyzed by fear. So, I don't.

I lived the first two decades of my life just like that. Afraid to raise my hand—to follow my heart, to explore a passion I might fail at. Afraid of everyone's opinions of me. Afraid to color outside the lines.

I was the good girl who didn't make waves or take up space. The girl with an addiction to saying "sorry," who could never accept compliments. I was the girl who studied extra hard because anything below an A meant she wasn't good enough. The "sweet" girl who never stood up for herself. The doormat who let everyone stomp on her. Social norms supported and even encouraged me in my effort to be obedient—to be acceptable. It laid out a pattern for perfection, and I went along with it like the "good girl" I was.

I grew up thinking everyone else was perfect. My parents believed hiding their big feelings from me was the best way to protect me. It wasn't their fault; it's how they grew up. I believed they were perfect, and I had to be, too. I didn't want to be the one who didn't measure up, so I did what I was told, and worked hard to do it perfectly. I didn't want to be the *failure* of the family. The *disappointment*.

It was during the summer before third grade that I developed an eating disorder. My parents had signed me up for sleep-away camp, and I remember the panicked tears welling up in my eyes as the bus to camp pulled away. Looking around at my camp mates, no one else was crying, so I quickly wiped my face. I was always an anxious child, often overwhelmed by emotions I felt like I couldn't talk about, but that summer, a triggering event sent my anxiety into high gear.

The first day, when the counselor led us into the cafeteria for lunch, I tried not to mind all the overwhelming cooking smells. But I didn't like them. They made my stomach roil. I remember being overcome by all the food choices—mac 'n' cheese, hot dogs, grilled cheese sandwiches. At home with Mom close by, I didn't think twice about it—these were all things I loved. But suddenly, I was turned off. Eventually I picked up a peanut butter and jelly sandwich from a tray stacked with them. For whatever reason, that sandwich spelled comfort to me. And that's what I ate from then on, every day, for every meal, besides breakfast, which was a tiny cup of dry cereal. There was no deviation. All summer long.

Everything was new: living without my parents and meeting new kids. But the sameness of my food choices numbed me, taking the edge off my anxiety.

Each summer, I'd go back, and the same thing happened. My weight would go up during the school year, and then down at camp, and then back up by the end of the fall. But the summer going into seventh grade was different. I went into that summer comparing my new puberty-ridden body to the women and girls in my life—my stomach was too flabby, my hips wide, thighs were too muscly from sports, and the long list in my head went on. This is the summer I stopped eating. The camp grew concerned and started monitoring me to the point where I was miserable. They were talking about my issue in front of all my peers and making me stand on a scale to see my weight rise. I felt so much shame.

I went home on visiting day feeling like a failure with a shirt soaked with tears and my nose leaking like a faucet. All I knew was my body wasn't enough, like the rest of me. I wasn't enough academically, I had to study twice as hard as everyone else to do well; I was diagnosed with a processing issue in third grade, meaning it took me a little longer to absorb information than most students. I wasn't enough for the "cool" girls around me to want to be friends with, unless I pretended I was something I wasn't. I couldn't control what other people thought of me, but this, not eating, I could control.

Looking back, this was the summer I stopped living.

High school brought on laxative bulimia and, in college, the bulimia became even more severe and frequent. By the time I was in my twenties, my anorexia and bulimia were out of control. I didn't have a life outside of them and work. I became extremely depressed, anxious, and had crippling insomnia. So, to shut off the noise in my head, I turned to pills and booze.

This pattern went on for four years until that terrifying night when I texted my parents for help, just before turning twenty-six.

After my parents brought me to their house, Mom made me a turkey sandwich. Setting the plate in front of me, she said gently, "Come on, Dani. It's time to get better."

I sat at the table, staring at it, shivering, and not only because there wasn't enough meat on my bones to keep me warm. The mere thought of taking a bite of that sandwich made me shake. *How could I let it touch my lips?* To do so would only underscore the fact that I was a failure, packing on the pounds, sitting in it. "And to get better, you have to eat," Mom urged. She couldn't stand another moment looking at her sick child, now an adult, starving herself to death.

I nodded, my eyes downcast, cheeks flushed from embarrassment that I couldn't do something as simple as eat. Other feelings had come, too—shame and disgust. Words crashed and buzzed around my head—*calories, fat,* and *failure*—making me queasy. My stomach and entire body screamed in rebellion and yet, somehow, I managed to pick the sandwich up. I remember my heart pounding in my chest as I took that first bite. And then some indescribable feeling had overtaken my body—and suddenly, everything faded to black, and I woke up in the hospital.

I was dancing with death. And when you do that kind of dance, it's not too surprising to find yourself waking up in a hospital bed in a blue gown, asking your mom, "How am I going to do this?" Meaning, *How am I going to do this life without my eating disorder? How am I going to learn to live unafraid? How am I going to be happy and healthy?*

What became clear, not just the night before my seizure, but for awhile afterward, was that I'd not been experiencing life. It wasn't an epiphany. I was sick, stuck, and miserable—held back by my eating disorder and my fear of failure—I felt it every day. Most days, I wanted to die.

I wanted to go to an outpatient treatment facility, but because my weight was so low, and I had just had a seizure, my only options were hospitalization or residential treatment because I needed an around-the-clock program.

When I expressed how afraid I was to be sent away, we were given one more option: the Maudsley approach ("weight restoration"). It's an intensive outpatient treatment where parents are full members of the treatment process and an integral part of recovery. They would oversee preparing my meals and making sure I ate each bite. I'd move back to my childhood home at twenty-six. I would see a psychologist twice a week and an eating disorder therapist twice a week, too. Part of the agreement was that I'd go on antidepressants to help my depression and anxiety. If I wasn't making progress with my weight gain, I'd be sent to a hospital or residential program right away.

While it didn't feel like it at the time, I did get the best gift of my life that year—a second chance. A chance to wake up and live this life like it was meant to be lived. So, during treatment, I vowed I would learn to be unafraid—to be myself, to follow my dreams no matter how many times I failed—and to put myself out there even if I got hurt.

In my recovery, I found strength in overcoming impulses and triggers—a strength that I build on today, no matter how difficult my circumstances. A strength that has changed me for the better. Taking risks, failing, and overcoming difficulties has taught me resilience.

Because winning over my eating disorder was the hardest fight of my life. I was battling against everything my brain knew: two decades' worth of entrenched eating habits. The eating disorder voice had isolated me from my friends and family. It was hard to picture this life without my constant companion. I thought it was protecting me from getting hurt, but it was an abusive relationship. It was killing me.

When I finally sought help after I hit rock bottom and wound up in the hospital, the doctors were asking me to go against everything I knew. They were asking me to increase my eating and gain weight, and my anorexia was making me feel worse for doing that, not better. I had to go against my instincts. I needed to learn to call for help instead of purging or starving, and it felt impossible at times. I asked myself, "How am I going to do this?" at every single meal.

Something as simple as eating a sandwich would make my palms immediately clam up in a sweaty panic. I'd shake with each bite. It was as if my body was rejecting it.

Now, over ten years later, I don't think twice when I eat a sandwich. And I don't take this lightly. This took hard work, therapy, medication, and years of desensitizing myself.

But gosh, was it worth it. I do have days where I feel bad about my body, but it's easier to get past those thoughts now that I have four girls that look to me as a role model.

Resilience isn't something we're born with. Like being a mom, it's something we learn and develop. It's something we gain through hard experience. We all have issues, messes to overcome, whether it's addiction, a looming divorce, mental illness, or a past we're not particularly proud of. As humans, we're fallible and complex. But we're also able to choose, so instead of sitting in the mess of our story—if we can overcome our hurdles, our situation, and thereby help our children overcome theirs and gain resilience—that will become our greatest strength.

In the hospital—the first time I held my firstborn Vivienne skin-to-skin on my chest, the thump of my beating heart aligning with hers—she took my breath away. Like so many new moms, I remember that day being filled with so much pain and so much joy. I was exhausted and reeked of my own vomit, brought on by hard labor that included an epidural leak, but my brain quickly edited out all the bad moments after I met her. I looked into her big gray eyes that would soon turn brown and felt tears fill my own. She was the most beautiful thing I had ever seen.

"I am going to be so strong for you, always." My promise to her rose unbidden but sure, borne on the rising wave of some deeply felt maternal instinct. I paused, stroking Vivienne's peach-fuzz hair. "And you are going to be strong, too," I whispered to her, kissing her forehead.

And teaching her to be strong, for me, meant teaching her that no one is perfect. That she is enough and mistakes are a part of learning.

Years later, when Vivienne was seven, she said to me, "My friend Audrey says everything is perfect, and I told her she's wrong. Nothing is perfect, right, Mommy?"

"Yes, you're right." I answered.

It sounded dark, saying it out loud to a child. It would have been nice if I could have waited a little longer. If it were OK for my daughter to think the world was filled with unicorns and rainbows forever. But I know how important it is for my children to know nothing and no one is perfect. So, I started teaching them young.

When they were toddlers, and they spilled their sippy cup of water all over themselves, I'd say, "Mistakes happen, no one's perfect," as I scooped one or another of them, sodden, sometimes teary-eyed, into my arms.

I took them in my arms, too, when, in a bad moment, my Tarzan-like scream of "I CAN'T DO ANYTHING RIGHT!" pierced their ears, sobs shook my shoulders, and everyone started crying. Holding them, I apologized. "I'm sorry I yelled. I was frustrated with myself. I'm not perfect, but I love you guys more than anything." They needed to know how harmful it can be for Mommy to hide her mistakes and big feelings. How feeling your feelings and embracing imperfection helps you build the resilience you need in life.

From the moment Vivienne was born, I was her home. That revelation, my understanding of it, burst into my brain, and I knew that in the days and weeks and years ahead, I would have to be made of steel, which would ironically take so much vulnerability. Because being vulnerable is brave. That conviction would only grow with the addition of three more daughters. But it was in those first moments with Vivienne that I vowed to find my resilience in every step of motherhood. I would be resilient for her, and through example and encouragement, I would teach her to be resilient, too. The promise I made to my daughter holds to this day. If anything, with the addition of three more daughters, it seems even more vital, especially because they're girls, and I know all too well the difficulties they'll face given the pressure that role comes with.

It didn't take me long after Vivienne's birth to learn that no one needs more resilience than a mom. As a caretaker, you've got to be resilient even when you're not prepared. There are so many hard days, seasons, and phases to go through. And there's no quitting motherhood, no paid vacation, sick days, or promotion. You hit the ground running, 24/7, ready to jump up quickly, ready to kiss a boo-boo, make a meal, or stop a sibling squabble. Sometimes you find yourself doing all three at once.

But our love for our children is a huge driving force, isn't it? They are our everything. They are the world itself—a shining light on every cloud-filled day. There is nothing we wouldn't do to keep them out of harm's way, to protect them, and to empower them against any and all hurts.

Sometimes, though, it's hard to strike a balance, hard to let them go even as we don't want to deprive them of the life experiences that will shape them. The beautiful thing about our children is that they can be anyone and anything. They have so much potential but, to reach it, they must try and fail in their attempts to reach for the stars, and we have to let them. In the end we can't hold them back, as much as we will want to at times—so we teach them resilience. We make them strong by letting them see how we, in the hard times, the painful times, can pick ourselves up, and in doing so, we teach them they can, too. No matter how exhausted we are, no matter how tough everything seems, with our kids as motivation, we're going to keep going because they need us, and we'd do anything for them.

When we're in labor, pushing and grunting in our effort, when the pain of each contraction is dominating our entire being, even as we hold our partner's hand and can barely breathe, much less articulate a thought, the question arises: *How am I going to do this?* But we keep pushing until that baby is out—we do.

Or when we're struggling to get pregnant, have six failed IVF cycles, and start to look into other ways to have a baby, feeling remorse that our bodies won't do what we want them to. We go through the ultimate job interview for a chance to adopt, and then something looks like it is going to happen, but it ends in failure. Our heart is broken as we say, "How am I going to do this?" But we try again, we know there is a baby out there that will be a perfect fit for our family—we do.

Or when we are presented with the option of surrogacy and are faced with judgment. We hear that we didn't try hard enough, or we didn't want to "ruin our bodies." When it was one of the toughest decisions of our lives, filled with so many tears, hormones, and injections. We worry about everything from miscarriage to the embryo transfer failing to depending on someone else to feed our baby properly as we lay awake each night thinking "How am I going to do this?" But we give up that control, so we can have our baby—we do.

And however we get our baby here, days later, when we're in over our heads at home with a crying newborn and up every two or three hours, too exhausted to shower, and terrified, fighting exhaustion and our own tears that question returns, haunting us. Yet, we manage to get up anyway, and we get through it. It doesn't matter how sore in body, mind, and spirit we are or how inadequate we feel, having no idea what we're doing. We feed and love that baby—we do.

There are the moments that take our breath away. It feels so hard, like when our baby is premature or they have a complication. Our first view of our infant is through the wall of a glass box in the Neonatal Intensive Care Unit (NICU) with tubes shoved up his nose and monitors beeping. Or later, when we come face-to-face with a hard diagnosis for our child from the pediatrician. But with a heaviness in our heart and an uncertainty of our child's future, we show up day after day and sit by their side with so much unconditional love and support—we do.

Regardless of our personal crises or mood or situation, if we're depressed or our brain feels foggy from exhaustion, we still manage to get out of bed and do all the things, even if our actions are mechanical and we aren't emotionally present. It's rote: feed the baby, change the baby, rock and shush the baby to sleep. We care for our older children as well, seeing to meals, bedtimes, and homework, even though, at times, it hurts to get up and move—we do.

Mothers are made in such moments.

The first moment after her birth, as I held Vivienne in my arms, I didn't feel quite like a mom. At least not the type of mom I needed to or wanted to become. I had a lot of learning to do. Since then, I've come to the conclusion that moms aren't born when their babies are born. Sure, we're technically "moms," and that's "our baby," and we'd do anything for that little human—but pushing and grunting and sweating out our first baby, or however that baby came to be ours, doesn't automatically make us strong and wise as moms.

Mothers are *made* through time and experience. We are made through long nights that pass in a tired, overwhelmed blur into harder days. But it's exactly through these difficult experiences with our children that we are created.

My struggles with breastfeeding made me feel like a real mom. Then there was mothering through the excruciating pain from an episiotomy stitch that fell out. The days spent in agonizing discomfort, before my OB-GYN stitched me up, made me a mom. The everyday antics of my strong-willed child Vivienne, such as the way she never listens and breaks every rule I make, made me a mom. My two stays at the NICU made me a mom. The list goes on. I know you've got a list, too.

I must have asked, "How am I going to do this?" a thousand times, but then somewhere along the way at a point when life was just overwhelming—my second daughter, Diana was in the NICU, I'd contracted mastitis (an inflammation of my mammary gland), and I had 18-month-old Vivienne at home—it occurred to me the question was irrelevant. After all, hadn't I found the way through dozens, if not hundreds, of dilemmas? Hadn't I faced any number of calamities? And no, I didn't always get it right, but I got through. I thought maybe as a mother I didn't have to throw up my hands in defeat. Maybe it was pointless, really, to doubt or question myself, or my ability as a parent. Wasn't I doing it every day?

I told myself I wasn't going to allow the old panic to stymie me. I had handled it all so far, and understanding this, I was thrilled with how calm I felt. Something inside had shifted, and I knew that while I would continue to make mistakes upon mistakes, there would also be triumphs, big and small.

What if, as mothers, instead of asking, "How am I going to do this?" we trust ourselves to figure it out? I realize it's hard in every case, so yes, we can have our time to feel our feelings, but what if after that we took positive action? Suppose we took time to search out ways we could advocate or fight for our child and get the situation resolved, wherever the difficulty lies. Possibly it's an issue with a school bully, or maybe it's a sudden inexplicable and troubling change of behavior. What if we tried to stay calm and got right into action?

I know most of us moms have been taught since we were little not to make waves, not to fuss or be an inconvenience, or make others unhappy or uncomfortable. But we are the voices for our children. Even the shy mom will find her voice—asking questions, raising concerns, and asking for help. We will dig deep. We will figure it out, and we will persevere, because that's what mothers do, especially for our babies.

Within these pages, you'll meet my four daughters: Vivienne, my eight-year-old; Diana, my six-and-a-half-year-old; Julia, my five-year-old; and Charli, my two-year-old. As you journey with me, you'll witness the profound growth and evolution I experienced with each birth, both as a mother and as a human being.

I will show you how I found my resilience to rebound through all the stages of motherhood, and I hope I inspire you to find your brave, too. I will start with challenging pregnancies and labors, focused on my preterm labor with Charli while sick with COVID-19, which resulted in a 45- day NICU stay. I will then get into life after pregnancy and the struggles we face as new mothers, I'll cover topics including life postpartum, the judgment, the adjustment when we go from "me" to "we," the journey to feeling appreciated, conquering loneliness and body insecurity, finding boundaries and learning to listen to ourselves over expectations and opinions, and trying to find the balance with marriage and little children. As we grow and become confident mothers, we can start the rewarding task of empowering resilience in our kids. And we can do all of this because of our overpowering love for our children. It helps us become the mothers we're meant to be.

But most of all I hope this book will help you realize that, as you summon your resilience through each hard situation, it will become easier to handle motherhood's many ups and downs. My wish is that by sharing my own imperfect and ongoing journey, you'll take heart knowing you're not alone. That you, too, will find the courage to keep going through the uncomfortable parts of motherhood, knowing you'll get to the other side—as a better, happier, and stronger mom.

— 1 —

The Birth of a Mother and a Baby

WITH NINE-MONTH-OLD VIVIENNE still fast asleep in the crib beside my bed, I rub my tired eyes and walk on tiptoes to the bathroom. I grab a pregnancy test and sit on the toilet. I put the stick on the counter and set my phone timer for two minutes.

The wait. It is brutal. My pulse beats so loud I can hear it in my tired head. I'm nervous. Beyond nervous. I wipe, yawn, and flush. I organize anything and everything in the bathroom cabinet to distract my mind.

Jonathan and I have been trying to have another baby for six months, and I've been on Clomid, a medication used to treat infertility, for five months. All the ovulation tests, timed sex ending with lying with my feet in the air for ten minutes after to "hold everything in," and the side effects of Clomid—including mood swings and depression—has been making me feel all kinds of crazy. Despite it all, every month when I take a pregnancy test, it says the same thing: "Not Pregnant." And each time I see it, my heart splits in two a little more. I know I'm extremely blessed with

Vivienne and am fully aware of how many people truly struggle for so much longer than I have, but when you want another baby, and you are doing everything to get pregnant but it doesn't happen—it's hard no matter the timeline.

With Vivienne, we got pregnant on the second month of trying. It was Father's Day. I read "Pregnant" on the test, and excitedly picked it up, jumping up and down, "Oh my goodness! Happy first Father's Day!" I put my hands over my mouth in disbelief.

Jonathan picked me up and walked us backward toward the mirror in our apartment.

"Those people are going to be Mommy and Daddy," I smiled, pulling his face toward mine.

He kissed the corner of my mouth.

We told my parents at Father's Day brunch.

I remember Jonathan staring at me the moment we sat down, not being able to keep the secret—I could see it on the tip of his tongue.

Me, not being sure if I should break the news or he should, since we didn't discuss who should do it, but taking his lip curving uncertainly as my cue to talk.

I placed the positive pregnancy test in front of my parents on the table and said, "Happy Father's Day, Dad! You're going to be a grandpa!"

My parents popped out of their seats like they were both Jacks-in-the-box and wrapped their arms tight around us. So many tears of happiness were shed, as we dug into pancakes, egg frittatas, and pastries.

"My baby is having a baby," my mom said more than once.

No one would ever top this gift, I thought, cracking a half-hearted smile. I touched my stomach and my smile widened. I couldn't believe I was going to be a mom, especially after years of thinking that would never be a part of my story. That I was "too sick," "a bad role model," and that "everyone would be better off without me." I had given up on myself. I was glad I got this second chance to become who I was meant to be for my baby.

"My baby," I said out loud at the table while looking down at my stomach, taking it in one more time: the words and the visual.

I know, this scene is almost nauseating; it was like it was out of a Hallmark movie.

But this time, as I stand in the bathroom waiting for the results of my pregnancy test, I feel different. This time feels more similar to the realities of motherhood, because it's unpredictable, a roller coaster, surprises at every turn.

The timer on my phone goes off. I slowly walk over to the pregnancy test, cringing in anticipation. I pick up the test: "Not Pregnant." Again. I sigh. My eyes snap completely open, no longer hindered by sleep.

Jonathan walks into the bathroom, our eyes connect, and he knows what's wrong. I don't even have to say anything.

"Next month it will happen," he says.

"I was talking to Dr. Ng about trying a trigger shot of HCG. She said it would help my ovaries release mature eggs when I ovulate. I'm going to call and set it up with her." I pause and hear Vivienne stirring and let out a breath. *She is my strength.*

"Then why do you look so sad, if you and your OB-GYN have a plan?" Jonathan asked, crow's-feet forming at the corners of his eyes from frowning.

"I know we're so lucky to have Vivienne—we have a beautiful healthy baby—but it's just . . . the Clomid has been making me feel down on myself about everything." I wipe my runny nose with a tissue.

"I know; I have been living with you." He smiles, now so close I can feel his breath against my cheek.

"Plus, Vivienne is only nine months. They'll still be very close in age. Maybe this is a sign we needed more time, but it will happen." He touches his thumb against my cheek to catch a falling tear, then squeezes my hand.

Vivienne starts crying. "Duty calls. Maybe literally, too." I kiss his cheek and make my way to Vivienne's crib.

"No lips?" He questions, his smile fading.

"Morning breath. I can't put that on you." I smile wistfully.

I had always thought having two kids would be enough for me. I only had one sister, and we put my parents through a lot. But the moment I held Vivienne in my arms, something shifted inside of me. I knew I wanted four children. This was a decision of the heart. I wanted a big family so my kids could have not just me, but each other. This world is hard enough, and I didn't want them to ever feel alone in it. I wanted them to have built-in best friends they could call if they couldn't reach me. And if anything happens to me, I know they have each other.

I pick Vivienne up and hold her close until she feels safe in my arms: her home. I lay her down on the changing table, admire her Michelin arms and legs, and instantly a smile unfurls on my face. How can I not be OK? *Look at her.*

I am in Dr. Ng's office laying on the exam table, my knees placed in stirrups with just a sheet covering them. She's giving me a transvaginal ultrasound, which requires inserting a small, lubricated probe inside my vagina, to look at my follicles, checking their diameters to see if it's "go time." It's a little uncomfortable. I feel lots of pressure. I flinch and tap my hands nervously on the exam table.

This is the second time she's checked my follicles. I came in two weeks prior when I was supposed to ovulate. At that visit, I learned my eggs have sloth-like tendencies—they were taking their sweet time to mature and needed two more weeks at least to get there. My hope was she'd be able to give the trigger shot today.

"You have a good follicle. We can move forward with the shot!" She smiles wide.

"Yay!" I do a little dance with my hands as I feel excitement shoot through my body like wildfire.

I pick my clothes up from a pile on the corner chair and pull on my sweatpants, nursing bra, and t-shirt while Dr. Ng prepares the shot. When she's ready, I lift my shirt and close my eyes. I feel a pinch in my abdomen. It hurts but feels good at the same time—like a pinch of hope.

"Have intercourse with your partner for the next four days to be safe," she says.

"Jonathan will be happy," I smirk and massage the area on my stomach.

"OK, Danielle. Hopefully the next time I see you, you will be at your six-week ultrasound," she says happily, grabbing my hand.

"Gosh, I hope so, too. Thank you." I slip my hands away, placing my palms and fingers together in the air in prayer.

This would be the appointment that got me pregnant with Diana. Each child after, I'd have to use a Trigger shot to become pregnant, too.

She leaves me in the room. I take a look around. This was the room where we first heard the whooshing sound of Vivienne's heartbeat, letting us know she was OK. This was also the room where I learned a lot about stretching pains, discomfort, and what women go through to become mothers. This was the room where I worried and prayed—because this was not only the room where I grew in size but where I grew in character.

I was *becoming*, changing, with each appointment.

This was the room where I started my transformation from a woman to a mother.

I'll forever be grateful for this room.

My first pregnancy with Vivienne was blissful. Sure, I had terrible stretching pains, but nothing was scary. I lived unaware of how truly terrifying pregnancy could be. Though labor was hard, including the epidural not quite working, and I vomited from the pain, Vivienne came out on her due date perfectly healthy, six pounds, eight ounces, with a full head of hair.

At thirty-five weeks pregnant with my second-oldest, Diana, I couldn't stop scratching my skin. I was so itchy all the time, but it got worse at night. I scratched so much my skin bled. I slathered on lotion, and it never helped. There was no visible rash, but the itch was unbearable. I was about to get tested for something called cholestasis, a liver disease that reduces the flow of bile and can cause itching as a side effect, but right before the next appointment I went into labor. Diana was born early and the itching stopped.

At twenty-nine weeks pregnant with my third child, Julia, we went on vacation to Disney World. Walking around the Magic Kingdom and Epcot holding Diana or chasing Vivienne as she ran to a ride or to a character was exhausting. Standing hurt. I was that uncomfortable after two prior pregnancies, and we walked miles each day. On the flight home, Diana was sitting on my lap. I was bouncing her up and down. Jonathan was next to us in the window seat, showing Diana the clouds. Viv was sitting behind us with my mom and dad.

Suddenly, I didn't feel well. I was nauseous. I turned pale.

"Jo, take Diana. Something's wrong with me." I murmured and swallowed. He quickly grabbed her off my lap, and I involuntarily yawned, my eyes twitching, and that was it—everything went black.

After thirty seconds, I came to. Diana was crying and stretching her arms toward me, wanting to be back in my lap, but Jonathan was afraid I would faint again. All I wanted to do was comfort her.

Jonathan held my hand as tears filled my eyes. "You scared me. Your eyes rolled to the back of your head, and I only could see the whites of your eyes."

I was so upset and distracted by Diana's crying and Jonathan's worry that I didn't notice the group of people surrounding our seats, whom I soon found out were doctors.

Apparently, I chose the perfect flight to faint on because there were five doctors onboard returning home from a medical conference.

My cheeks turned red with embarrassment as they asked me question after question. I felt like I was naked, under a spotlight. I wanted to sink into the seat and disappear. I could feel my heart beating in the back of my throat. I drank apple juice, even though I hate it, and ate some Chex Mix. I still didn't feel well the rest of the flight.

On the car ride home from the airport, I was again, nauseous, I was going to puke, I started gagging. "Jonathan, stop the car. I need to throw up!" I screamed. I threw up on the side of the road. The cold air felt good against my overheated, shaking body. I was over being pregnant.

A week later, at thirty weeks, I tested positive for cholestasis, the same liver disease I suspected I had while pregnant with Diana. I learned that it could cause preterm labor, fetal distress, and stillbirths. The nonstop itching got worse at night, and it was unbearable. I scratched in my sleep and woke up with blood in my nails and scratches all over my body.

Dr. Ng said if I didn't feel the baby kick for two hours I should go to the hospital. I was frightened. I was uncomfortable, and I lived the rest of my pregnancy until I was induced at thirty-seven weeks just like that, waiting to finally be able to breathe normally again.

I no longer thought pregnancy was filled with rainbows and unicorns and that every mother would safely meet their healthy newborn. I didn't like being pregnant anymore.

It was hard on my body, mind, and soul.

Pregnancy is glamorized in the media. They show you a tall, skinny blonde woman with bright blue eyes who has the perfect bump. She's smiling from ear-to-ear—simply glowing. But being pregnant doesn't always look and feel like that. It can, but it's not a realistic expectation to live up to.

It's watching your body transform, and sometimes, in a not so glamorous way. My belly grew side-to-side, not out, so I called myself a potbellied pig. I always joked I was having a butt baby, too, because my butt got tremendously large. And though I wrapped my insecurities in jokes, it was hard for me to see my body that way. It was a struggle to feel good about my changing body, even though I was carrying a gift.

And I didn't love how I felt physically, either. I didn't love the itching, nausea, roller coaster of emotions, and the worry.

My first pregnancy, I sometimes felt guilty for having these feelings. I wanted this child. I was supposed to be filled with so much joy. So I never admitted them out loud, thinking that would make me a bad mother. But now that I'm a mother of four, I've realized I couldn't have been more wrong.

You can complain during pregnancy and still be grateful. You don't have to be happy all the time or pretend to be just because you're carrying a blessing. You're allowed to have good days and bad days. It doesn't make you a bad mom, not even close—it makes you human.

And pregnancy also becomes harder when you have other kids at home to take care of.

During my first pregnancy, I only had to focus on me—and Jonathan only had to focus on me. Mornings went a little something like this:

"Good morning," he said, giving me a kiss, and kissing my bump. It was 8 AM. We overslept.

"I'll never not be tired," I said, pulling the blanket over my head. He joined me under the blanket and wrapped his arms tightly around me.

"After you take a shower, you'll be more awake, or I can wake you up in other ways." His hand turned my face to his and kissed my lips, then my cheeks, and my neck.

"I am a little nauseous, and I'm already late for work as it is," I moaned, pushing the blanket off both of us.

"Are you sure? What's ten more minutes?" He kissed under my ear, on my neck.

"You're right, just ten more minutes," I kissed him back, his lips soft on mine as I placed the blanket back over our bodies.

During my fourth pregnancy, things were a bit different.

"Good morning, Mommy and Daddy." Six-year-old Vivienne marched into our room and lay down dramatically at the end of the bed, making it bounce. Scrunched between me and Jonathan was Julia. Her hair was wild, curls shooting in all directions, and her feet were pressed against my bulging stomach. I was too tired to move her.

I lifted my head, looking at the clock on Jonathan's side of the bed: 5:45 AM.

"Shush, Viv, it's still so early. Julia had a rough night and is still sleeping," I whispered. Julia's feet came pitter-pattering into our room at 2 AM, and she was wailing, big tears streaming down her face. I held her close as she stuttered out, between big belly breaths, that she had a nightmare. She fell asleep as my hand stroked her head, and she had been snuggled close ever since. I mean, snuggled in close while also kicking and punching me in her sleep throughout the night.

"I'm bored, though," Viv said, clearly not understanding how to whisper.

"Enough, come with me." I whispered harshly, my teeth gritting together. I was nauseous but wasn't sure if it was from lack of sleep or the pregnancy. I popped out of bed and carried her to her room, her legs just fitting around my growing midsection.

I got into her bed and snuggled myself under the covers. She jumped beside me, one arm draped over me and the blanket.

"Mommy, I thought you were going to play with me!" She whined, disappointed, trying to pull the blanket off me.

"You can play. I am just going to lie here for a couple of minutes." I was so tired I could hardly get out the words. I tried to sleep while hearing Vivienne play with her dolls in the background, using my big belly covered by a blanket as a slide for her dolls, and waking me up sporadically to help her put a shoe on or change their outfits.

And then, around 6:40 AM: "Mommy, I'm hungry."

"Ugh, five more minutes," I begged as an unpleasant soreness overtook my body.

"No, Mom, I'm so hungry. Please!" She took my hand and pulled my arm.

"Fine, but don't pull me." I rubbed my eyes, but everything was still blurry. I made pancakes, even though I was so tired my eyelids kept closing. I finished packing the girls' lunches and snacks. I set up breakfast for Julia and Diana. Now, it was time to wake up everyone and get them ready for school.

"Pick me up!" Vivienne pleaded, leaning into me so hard I had to catch the wall with my hand.

"Viv, I just don't have it in me right now," I said, glad I didn't topple over.

I took Viv's hand in mine, and we walked upstairs.

Pregnancy with other kids at home is hard, because the expectations as a mother are still the same, but you're doing it with half the energy.

And no one else is going to clean the house and tackle that huge pile of laundry or bathe your kids because your joints hurt, and your ankles are swollen, and you feel so much pressure in your pelvis.

And no one's taking care of all the things for you, so you're spending most of the day on your feet: playing chase, carrying everything and them, and keeping up with your elder kids' busy schedules.

And when one of your children is on the ground at the store having a fit, no one will lift him for you. They will just give you dirty looks and raise their eyebrows, which won't help. If your partner isn't there, you'll have to pull them over your big belly while they're kicking, crying, and screaming, all while trying to calm them down.

The truth is every part of mothering becomes harder when you're pregnant: mentally and physically. Pregnancy is a battlefield. Women must navigate so much as we're ambushed with so many scary changes and challenges. We are way too often left anxious between appointments and the possibility of miscarriage on top of feeling not-so-great from the symptoms that come with pregnancy.

But we get through. We make ourselves uncomfortable for our babies because their comfort comes first. And this comes with just the thought of them. We don't care how exhausted we are or how much pain it takes to get our children into this world—we will do anything to get them there. We will go through IVF, where we inject ourselves and are left constantly heartbroken. We will go through uncomfortable pregnancies, where we itch, are sick, and feel drained more days than not. We go through failed adoptions where the birth parent decides to parent the child or chooses another family instead. Or almost-failed adoptions that end in success, but getting there drains our souls. We go through failed embryo transfers to get a viable pregnancy to get our surrobabies.

Pregnancy, surrogacy, and adoption and the physical and emotional toll that comes with them are hard work alone, so when combined with parenting a child or children who are already here, it can feel like you're doing everything wrong.

It's OK to put your children in front of a screen so you can take a midday nap. It's OK to give them mini muffins or Pop Tarts as you rush them out the door for school because you overslept. It doesn't make you a bad mom. You're having a baby! You are doing it all! You're a rockstar.

Besides, your children won't remember what you didn't do during this time. They will remember the love they felt from you.

So, yes, I never loved being pregnant, but I'm grateful for my pregnancies—they gave me the greatest gift—my children. Nothing encapsulates the battlefield of pregnancy and childbirth more than the story of Charli's birth: that day, a rush of adrenaline took over the terror, and every muscle pushed me to do anything to get Charli out and into my care.

— 2 —

Laboring Against the Odds

*C*OUGH, COUGH, COUGH, *cough.*
 "Are you OK?" My mom flinches at the sound of my cough.

"I feel like I got hit by a car, then the car backed up through me, then went at me again. So, just great." I say in a raspy voice. My throat burns when I talk.

My back hurts so badly, I lie down on the couch and start hacking again. I can't stop. My throat aches, my ribs burn, and tears are welling in the corners of my eyes.

She shakes her head. "You need to go to an Urgent Care. I'll watch Julia."

"It's Tuesday. We have such a busy day after school." I drop my eyes.

"Dani, you have to go." Her tone is sharp, serious.

I nod, knowing she's right, as much as I'd rather rest with Julia in the two hours before I need to pick up Diana and Vivienne from school. *This is terrible.*

I walk into Urgent Care and they admit me right away. The doctor checks me out. He looks in my throat. He gives me a rapid test: I am COVID positive.

I'm thirty-two weeks pregnant with my fourth daughter, Charli. I'm extra uncomfortable this pregnancy. I'm itching like crazy. I'm so sure I have cholestasis again. My hoo ha feels like it's going to fall out by the day's end. I need to start iron infusions next week or I may need a blood transfusion during birth. I'm run down, and now I have COVID. I can hardly believe this is my reality.

I wear my N-95 mask and gloves to keep the kids from getting it.

I still do all the things. I cook all the meals. Tuck them in. Bathe them. All in a mask and latex gloves. I have no other choice. Jonathan is working, since he is saving days off for when the baby comes. The kids also want me—their mommy. They are used to me as the stay-at-home parent. So, I keep momming on.

Then, two days later, it's early Friday morning and I'm sitting in bed. It's 12:45 AM. I can't fall asleep; I'm hacking and I can hardly breathe.

"This cough is awful," I say.

"Why don't you try a cough drop?" Jonathan offers.

Cough. "OK." *Cough.* I put one in my mouth.

He gives me a look. He can't stand that I'm so sick while pregnant.

Suddenly I feel wet in the bed.

"Oh, no!" I lean back, my heart beating furiously.

"What's wrong?"

"Oh no, oh no. This can't be happening!" I chant.

"Dani, what?" He jumps up in the bed this time.

"My water broke!" I guffaw in shock.

"Are you sure you didn't pee yourself?" he says, placing his hand on my shoulder to try to calm me. I jump out of bed and run to the bathroom.

"I have done this three times before, Jonathan. Yes, I didn't pee myself. And gosh, it's still coming. Pee doesn't keep coming." A stream of water hits the bathroom floor.

I put on a pad and call my parents, hacking. "My water broke. And I haven't had iron infusions yet, and I have COVID. I'm scared, and the kids don't even know I am pregnant!" My voice quivers and I burst into tears. Yep—you read that right. I hadn't told my kids I was pregnant. I had my reasons—the big one being that Diana had just started a new school and was still adjusting—but I couldn't believe my water was breaking before I could tell them.

"We're coming over!" My mom hangs up the phone.

I throw sweatpants into a bag. Two nursing bras. Some old mesh underwear. My medication and a toothbrush. I look around. We hadn't done anything to prepare for our girl. The bassinet was still in storage and so was the Doc-a-tot. We hadn't installed the infant car seat. These were all items on my "to do" list that I hadn't gotten to yet.

Jonathan throws on a pair of sweatpants and laces his fingers through mine, leading me down the stairs. Something makes me not want to go. I stop. I haven't told the kids. They aren't used to me being gone. I'm worried about them. It's a lot to take in. Too much.

The front door bursts open. My parents storm through. My mom's usually soft footsteps are heavy like Dad's. I hug both of them, crying some more. My mom looks scared, and her usually bright eyes are dull and tired.

I look outside. The sky is dark and misty.

"I think I am going to soak through my pants in the car." I sniffle between words.

"Who cares? You are going to a hospital!" My mom clutches her heart, as if trying to keep it from breaking all together.

"You guys need to get going," My dad says. I want him to say something different, something that would flood me with relief. But he can't do that right now. He's too nervous, and so is my mom.

"Please call me when the first kid gets up, so I can explain what's going on." My face is covered in tears. My body doesn't want to go, but my brain knows I have to. I'm frozen in place. Jonathan takes my arm, slightly tugging forward, but I pull back. "What if I give birth in the car and die because I need a blood transfusion? I haven't gotten my iron infusions yet." I suddenly let out a bunch of stuttering sounds, and more hot tears stream down my cheeks. My mind is cycling through the worst possibilities. The thought of not being here for my kids, of something happening to me that would keep us apart, makes breathing difficult. I squeeze my eyelids shut to try to stop the tears like a dam, but it doesn't work. Nothing works.

"Gosh, Dani, that was dark," Jonathan's dark brown eyes look tense.

"That's where my mind goes. I can't help it. I'm afraid," I'm almost inaudible.

"Let's go." Jonathan calmly says. One of us has to stay calm, and it's not going to be me. Clearly.

My parents give us both a hug, and we are off.

I'm in the front seat nervously looking out the window. It's so foggy and dark, I can hardly see, but Jonathan is used to this weather from living in San Francisco, so he manages to navigate through it. We get to the highway, and it's shut down. There's yellow caution tape and a DO NOT ENTER sign in the direction toward Manhattan, to the hospital where I gave birth to my three previous girls.

"Are you kidding me? Maybe it's a sign we should go to a hospital around here." Tears start pouring down my cheeks again out of nowhere.

Jonathan calls Dr. Ng, but she doesn't pick up. I email her. No answer yet.

"I want you to deliver with her like you did with all of them." Jonathan decides and puts the address in Waze to find another way to Lenox Hill in Manhattan. I don't feel contractions, so I think that's a good sign. I am still leaking so much water. I swear I have an entire ocean coming out of my belly.

We get there in twenty minutes. Jonathan drops me off and goes to park the car.

I am escorted to the labor and delivery ward. I decline a wheelchair; my pride won't let me, even though my tired body wants it. I look around. I see a couple holding their new baby in an infant car seat. Their newborn looks so small in the big car seat. His little hands are in the air as he stretches and hiccups, peacefully sleeping through the surrounding hospital noises. The mom is staring at her newborn, not able to take her eyes off him, while the dad is following the nurse out the automatic doors. There's no one luckier than parents who get to bring a newborn home from the hospital. It's such a gift. I couldn't wait until I was that parent.

We go upstairs and I'm checked into a room where I'm told to change into a gown.

Water fills the entire floor. I apologize as the nurse comes into my mess.

"Well, I see your water broke. Don't you apologize; it's no problem." She smiles.

"Thank you. I will help you clean it up." I am trying to be helpful by grabbing some tissues—there are no paper towels in sight—but I am a visible mess. My shoulders are rising and falling between coughs and belly breaths.

"No, you let me clean you and the floor up." She can sense my fear, my pain, my worry.

"I am COVID positive, too," I let her know before she touches me. Goosebumps fill my arms and legs. I'm so cold and tired.

"Aw honey, you lie down and rest. You've had a hard night," she insists. I nod, give in to her kindness, and use the tissues in my hands to soak my tears. She makes me feel like she cares, speaking to me like I'm human. I matter. She's wearing scrubs and a mask, her long thick hair in a bun atop her head.

"Thank you." The knot in my throat makes it hard to speak.

It is April 8, 2022, but COVID is still ever-present. Most people had vaccinations by then, but it was still a bad illness to get, especially for a vulnerable population. Masks were no longer a requirement in school to protect people from spreading the illness, but in a hospital with sick, pregnant, vulnerable patients, they were a necessity.

Jonathan finds our room and barges in. His hairline is sweating, and he's out of breath. He must have run here.

By the time he gets there, a female doctor in full scrubs is examining me, and we find out my cervix is only two centimeters dilated.

"We want to try to keep the baby in until next Thursday, unless you go into labor naturally. We want to give the baby some time to develop more. We're going to give you steroid shots to help the baby's lungs develop quicker. We'll also give you iron infusions," the doctor said.

My heart feels like she just chopped it with an ax. Split, right down the center. Split with one swing.

"Wait. I have to be here for a week without my kids?" I ask stiffly. I'm trying to make sure I am hearing her correctly. My kids are never without me. I can't do that. I didn't prepare for that long. I didn't prepare them. Diana will be beside herself. They will all be so upset.

"Dan, if you need to be here a week, we'll make it work. The baby's health and your health are the most important things," he says as if he can see the tornado of thoughts in my mind.

I nod my head. That's all I can do. Nod my head and continue to cry.

Logically, I know that my baby's health and my health as her mother are the most important things, but my mind can't seem to wrap itself around the idea of being away from my other kids that long. I burst into tears again. This kept getting worse and worse, but as long as Charli would be alright, I'd of course do what the doctors said.

"Oh, and he can't stay with you, either, or he has to stay for a week, too." She points to Jonathan.

"What do you mean?" I manage to say.

"If your husband is here, he has to stay here, because it means he's exposed to you. He can't go home and come back—and come in and out." She says this without batting an eye like it's no big deal.

"Wow, this keeps getting better and better," I wipe my eyes. "Geez. OK, Jonathan. The kids need you more than me. I want you to leave right now and be with them when they get up. When I'm in active labor, I'll call you and you'll come back."

"Are you sure you're OK here alone?" Jonathan leans past me to grab the box of tissues to hand me one.

"Thank you," I wipe my nose. "The kids need any bit of normalcy. Please go home. I'll be fine." I assure him, my face red and puffy, snot leaking from my nose again. I blink against the sting in my eyes, nose, and mouth. My whole body feels like it's crying at this point.

Jonathan kisses my head, and cups my face with his hands. "I love you."

"I love you, too," I whimper.

I watch him as he walks out the door.

Am I really fine? Not one bit.

Friday night arrives in a blink. All day on Friday, nurses come in and out to examine me. I speak to the girls on

FaceTime as often as possible. I break the news to them one by one with Jonathan. Vivienne was excited and was convinced she came up with Charli's name, even though my mom put it in her head. Diana and Julia were having a much harder time, as I had expected. I do a little writing between tests. They give me my first steroid shot. They come up with a theory that the COVID cough made my water break. My dad tries to drop off dinner for me and visit, but they won't let him or the meal in. I officially feel like a prisoner.

I make Diana a video at bedtime because she is having a hard time falling asleep. I pull down my mask when no one is in the room, my hair wild. "Hey Diana, it's Mommy. I see you are having a hard time falling asleep. I hope you know I'm lying with you even though I'm in a different bed. I'm going to be in bed with you all night, and I'll be watching you on the camera. I love you so much, more than anything in this world. I can't wait to come home to you, and we are going to have lots and lots and lots of cuddles. Sleep well my love. I will talk to you in the morning." I break a little after I send it. I descend into sobs.

Then I watch a dating show on Netflix for a couple of hours to distract myself from it all.

And at 11 PM, I have never felt more alone. There's a dead quiet except for the monitors beeping. It's me, my thoughts, and the monitors—a bad combination.

I want to be with my babies.

I want to be in Jonathan's arms. I want him to play with my curls and tell me everything will be OK.

I feel like I am the little curly haired nine-year-old version of me at sleepaway camp. Homesick, and wanting to go home more than anything. To be with the people I love and who love me.

I toss and turn to try and get some sleep.

Suddenly, my heart starts beating fast. My shoulders rise and fall with each breath. I burst into tears, and I can't stop.

I call Jonathan. "I'm having a hard time. I'm just so sad. I don't know if I can do this for an entire week. I don't like being away from you guys." It takes me a long time to get the words out through sobs and coughs.

"Dani, I know this is hard. Maybe you should ask a nurse if you can take something to sleep."

"OK. I love you. I'll let you sleep." I start coughing to the point where my ribs ache.

"I love you, too. You're going to be OK." His voice is hoarse like he's been sleeping.

I hang up, still coughing.

I press the button near my bedside. A tall nurse with black hair comes in.

Emotions tangle my tongue, and I can't speak clearly. "Hi. I'm having a hard time. I think I need to take something to sleep." I then start weeping again.

"OK. I need to ask your OB-GYN." This nurse is all business. She sees tears streaked across my face, and she hears how distressed I am, but she leaves me there as quickly as she came in.

An OB-GYN from the practice, whom I have never met before, comes in shortly after. She has a smile on her face, but when she sees me, it fades away.

"Oh no, are you OK?" She asks, fully knowing the answer.

"No, I think I'm panicking a little. I'm never away from my family, and I miss them. I don't know how I won't see them for an entire week. I don't feel good, and I can't fall asleep. I can't hold myself together for some reason right now. I'm completely undone." I take a shuddering breath, trying to gather myself.

"I know, you're going through a lot right now," she says. "Let's give you some Benadryl to help you sleep." She strokes my arm, communicating that it will be OK.

"Thank you," I rasp, wiping my nose with a tissue followed by a couple of coughs. I can hardly breathe under my mask.

My throat tightens. This is hard.

The nurse comes back and hands me two Benadryl. I take them with a big gulp of water, and I fall asleep into a tear-soaked pillow shortly after.

It's 3 AM. I wake up to painful cramps that make it hard to sleep. I have to pee. I trip over wires on my way to the bathroom. I set off the fetal monitor that is on me to measure Charli's heart rate and rhythm. The nurse comes in, bursting the door open.

I hear myself apologizing to her but feel like I am watching myself in a hazy dream. She helps me to the bathroom, and then back into bed where she hooks me up to the monitors again.

I'm still uncomfortable. I can't sleep. Twenty minutes later, I feel like I have to pee again. In a dream-like sequence, I see myself get out of bed as carefully as possible, even though I'd rather stay cozy in bed. I hear the fetal monitor go off. *Not again*, I think, but I'm watching myself go to the bathroom anyway, ignoring the beeping.

After I use the bathroom, the nurse helps me back into bed again. I apologize profusely.

"I am so sorry. I'm in so much pain," I hear myself moan. "I can't sleep."

"You're probably in labor." She mumbles.

"No, they don't want me to have her for a week," I say slurring. I feel like a sorority girl after playing a couple of rounds of beer pong. *Thanks, Benadryl.*

"I think she has other plans." The nurse says, fixing my wires.

I am hooked back on to the monitors. One more hour of sleep and I am in an unbearable amount of pain again.

I get up to pee again. I keep telling dream me to hold it in, but I have to go, and am watching myself maneuver terribly yet again. I set the monitors off.

The nurse comes in again. She must think I'm the most annoying patient on the floor.

"Do you want an epidural?" she asks.

"I don't know if I should wait until I am closer to having her." I manage to slur.

"It can't hurt, so don't wait if you are in a lot of pain. It also takes a while to get the anesthesiologist, too." Her gaze darts my way.

"OK. I will do it. I could really use the sleep." I narrow my eyes. I am not even sure I'm in labor, but at this moment, my out-of-it brain wants comfort and sleep, and I'm listening to it.

At 6 AM, the anesthesiologist comes in while I'm sleeping.

I still feel like I'm dreaming. She's talking to me but what comes out of my mouth is inaudible. I am not sure if it's because of the lack of iron in my system, the fact that I'm sick, the Benadryl, or some combination.

I am now shaking in anticipation of the shot. She tells me to try to stay still. I do. I try. I start losing feeling in my body and it feels glorious. Finally, no pain. I feel warmth. I feel relief.

I come to and there's a male anesthesiologist above me now.

He's getting frustrated with me. I think. I don't catch his name.

I am confused.

I fall asleep and wake up as Darth Vader. I have an oxygen mask over my face instead of my N95.

"You keep passing out," I catch, then everything fades to black again. I am in and out of consciousness. I overhear chatter around me.

I apologize when I come to, again. An old habit. I think they're watching me. I fall asleep.

I wake up and am doing much better. I have an iron infusion hooked up to me.

I am finally having a quiet lucid moment when the fetal monitor goes off. A doctor on the floor comes in and looks at the screen.

"Is everything OK?" I wrinkle my forehead.

She doesn't answer me right away. I stare at the monitor, trying to see what she's seeing.

"Your baby's heart rate is low. We're trying to decide if it's just a low heart rate or if we need to get her out."

I freeze. "Get her out?" As in, out of my body? She's way too nonchalant with that news.

I call Jonathan and let him know. "I'm in active labor. They may have to do a C-section. Come now."

Doctors come in and out, chatting amongst themselves for the next half hour. There are three of them.

One finally comes in with an ultrasound machine. They huddle around my belly and we hear her heartbeat.

She just has a low heart rate. Relief.

My chest aches. My heart can't take this anymore.

As if he heard my thoughts, Jonathan walks in, hair gelled back, wearing jeans and a plain white T-shirt. He looks tired. And gosh, seeing him is the first time I smile. He looks dreamy; he looks like home. I can't handle all this alone anymore. It's been too much. He holds my hand and I never want to let go.

The rest of the delivery is just as chaotic, scary, and completely overwhelming. A blur of two more iron infusions, three blood transfusions, a different OB-GYN delivering than who was by my side with my three other children, and an epidural not in full effect, so it felt like my insides were being yanked out while I screamed "Get her out!" at the top of my lungs with a mask on while pushing.

Despite it all, Charli is born Saturday, April 9, 2022, at 8:21 PM. She's placed into my arms for two seconds—that's all I get. She's pink and crying softly on me. All four pounds, five ounces of her sit on my chest. One photo in my arms. I don't even get a chance to look at her face. Feel her. Take her in. I'm wearing a mask, so I have no idea what she smells like.

And in a blink, I see my baby put in a plastic enclosed crib and wheeled to the NICU.

"Can I visit her after this?" I ask. My vision blurs behind tears. My heart breaks for Charli, alone in the NICU, being examined. I want to follow her there and be by her side more than anything, to hear every word the NICU doctors say when they examine her.

But instead, I'm glued to the bed trying to rub the stress off my face.

"Of course, you can visit her in an isolated corner." The corner of the nurse's mouth twitches, and her eyes return to what she's doing. I feel some relief. This separation will be brief. I'll hold her later.

My whole body feels weak, and I'm shaking from exhaustion. I have never felt so tired in my life. I let myself melt into the hospital bed. We made it.

— 3 —

Postpartum Warrior

"YOU CAN'T SEE your baby."

My heart dropped to the pit of my stomach. This couldn't be real. I had given birth to Charli two hours prior. Now I was in a wheelchair, ready to be taken to the NICU. Ella, the delivery nurse, had originally told me I could see Charli in an isolated corner. But now, another nurse, whose name I was too upset to catch, told me I couldn't see her at all. Tears streamed down my cheeks. I was too shocked to catch them.

"I'm sorry, ma'am, but you have COVID, and we have to be really careful with babies in the NICU." This nurse fidgeted as she spoke, feeling the need to explain herself to my tearful and shocked response. Rationally, I understood. But when you tell a mother she can't see her newborn, she will be anything but rational.

"But our labor nurse told me I could see her . . ." I repeated, wiping roughly at my cheeks. "I need to speak to someone in the NICU, please." My heart was beating so loudly in my head that I could hardly hear the words coming out of my mouth. Jonathan grabbed my sweaty, clammy hand and held it tightly.

"Can Jonathan go?" I asked.

"No, it's too risky."

"Risky?" I asked, trying to understand her logic. "But he's not COVID positive!" I argued. "He needs to see our baby if I can't."

"Dani, it's OK. Let it go," Jonathan reasoned.

I couldn't take it. Any of it. I wanted to drop to my hands and knees, but between giving birth and being sick, I was in too much pain to move. I sat in the wheelchair, unable to fight back a fresh outbreak of tears. Even when it was just me and Jonathan in the room again, I didn't move. I was rooted in that chair.

I picked the name Charli because it means warrior. I wanted the littlest of my girls to be able to hold her own, a strong warrior in this tough world. I didn't know she would have to prove that name from the moment she entered the world.

Ten long minutes later we were told that Charli was doing well. I had been given two injections of corticosteroids while in labor to help her breathe on her own once she was born, and we found out they worked. They put a camera on her Isolette, the see-through enclosed crib that maintains a warm environment for a premature baby and isolates her from germs, so we could see her.

When I saw her on the monitor for the first time, I touched the screen, trying to feel her. There were so many wires extending from her little body. All I wanted to do was hold her in my arms. To take in her intoxicating newborn smell. To learn her hunger cues and feed her, then admire her milk-drunk look, where she's so content and sleepy that surplus milk dribbles from her tiny mouth. I wanted to let her nuzzle against my chest, skin to skin, and feel her little body rise and fall. And then, when it was time to sleep, I'd swaddle her and place her in the bassinet just an arm's reach away.

I wanted it—wanted her—so badly.

But all I could do at that moment was stare at an image of my four-pound, five-ounce newborn projected through the unfeeling eye of a camera mounted in a corner of an Isolette. And my heart couldn't take it.

She was just across the hospital, but it felt like we were worlds apart. It was a little past midnight, three hours since I'd given birth, when a NICU nurse finally appeared in my room. I tried to see if she was smiling, hoping for good news, but her mask made it hard to tell.

"Hi. I'm Nicole. I'm the Assistant Nurse Manager of the NICU. Charli is doing great for a baby born at thirty-two weeks. You'll be able to see your daughter in person," she said. "But not until Friday."

"Like next Friday?" Whatever hope I'd felt faded. I shifted my glance. "That's five full days from now," I said, glumly.

"Yes, I know, but we need to wait the required ten days from when you tested positive for COVID." Nicole patted my arm. "I know it seems like forever."

It didn't seem like forever. It *was* forever.

So, the first thing the following morning, I emailed my OB-GYN asking if I could go home later that day. I needed to be with my other children. I needed their warmth. And they needed me. Home would feed my soul and heal me so much more than staying in the hospital. It was too hard being in this sterile room without my baby. Without her cries or feeling her weight in my arms. I could hear the cries of other babies outside my door all day long and the sound shredded my heart. I was grieving that the experience was so different from what I had expected, and I wanted to grieve with my other babies at home.

My doctor agreed. "As long as your bleeding is under control," she instructed. "I'll be in to check you out one more time later in the morning."

I was relieved. No one wanted to come into my room anyway. Jonathan and I were the lepers of the hospital— the COVID patient and her too-close-for-comfort husband. The day dragged on. Other than my OB-GYN's visit to discharge me, no one else came near us. No lactation coach or NICU social worker. In my previous births, we had people in and out all day long, checking on me and the baby. This time, our room was empty.

Finally, around 8 PM, I was the mother who was leaving the hospital without her baby. I remember, as I was being discharged, filling out the mental health survey. I almost laughed when I saw the question, "Are you more sad than normal?" Because, of course, I was more sad than normal. My baby was in the NICU, and I couldn't even visit her. And then, when I eventually *could* visit her, I'd be "just a visitor" instead of a constant presence, and that's unnatural for a mother.

Even as the orderly wheeled me out the automatic door into the dark, tranquil April night—a respite from the chaos in my soul—I felt like a piece of my heart was being ripped out of my body. And it was—it was back in the NICU.

As Jonathan loaded the car, the reality of it hit hard. There was an extreme silence between us that spoke volumes. We were always talking about something. But right then, there were no words, just a shared grief, because our sweet newborn wasn't in the car seat. And as much as I tried to brace myself, you can never prepare yourself to be the mother who leaves empty-handed.

As we drove off, I couldn't help but feel jealous of Charli's NICU nurses. I imagined them in their blue scrubs, comforting my crying girl by holding her close.

I wondered if they knew they were holding my heart, that I felt like they were more like mothers to her than I was right now. As we drove home, I watched the passing scenery of New York City skyscrapers and crowded streets through a prism of tears. It all felt unreal. But then I thought of my other girls, and my heart eased. I couldn't wait to be with them, to mother them, to appreciate them more than ever.

It was way past their bedtime when we got home. My mom let us in.

"I'm so happy you're home." She put her arms around me. She looked exhausted. Her usually bright eyes were dimmed by fatigue. I could tell she hadn't been sleeping well. How could she? It had been such a traumatic couple of days.

"Thank you so much for everything," I managed to say. Mom was home for me. She always will be. And man, did it feel good to be home.

My dad came in so groggy he could hardly walk straight. He gave me and Jonathan big hugs. His curly black hair was a mess.

"Aww, were you sleeping?"

"Yes. Your kids are exhausting!" My dad yawned.

"And you and Charli almost killed us with worry," my mom added, hugging me again.

"It's been a rough few days," I said. "You guys are the best Papa and Mimi ever. I can't thank you enough." I paused, then said, "I'm going to check on them, OK? I missed them so much."

"Go right in," my mom said. "We're going home."

Going into each of my children's rooms, I gave them a kiss on their foreheads, admired their sleeping faces, and watched as their small chests rose and fell. As I was staring at my almost-three-year-old, her eyes opened and immediately flooded with tears.

Instantly, I bent to her. "Julia, baby, what's wrong? Mommy's here."

Shooting upright, she dove into my arms, tears streaming down her flushed cheeks. Putting my palm to her brow, I said, "You feel warm." Filled with misgiving, I took her temperature—101.2°F. I didn't need a test result to know she'd come down with COVID.

I slept with Julia that night, draping my arms around her little body, and she nestled right into me. It was so good to be at home with her, mothering her. Loving her. And that's what I did for the next four days. Because life doesn't stop when you have a child in the NICU. It keeps coming at you fast and furious. I took care of my sick child, keeping everyone else separate from her.

Though I was mostly recovered from COVID, I started having new, horrible symptoms—waking up to throbbing, pulsating headaches every night, interrupting my sleep, and plaguing me through the day. Dr. Ng thought I had an epidural leak, and that's why I had a persistent unbearable headache, making postpartum life more intolerable than with my previous three children.

Dr. Ng told me to drink caffeine and rest—which sounded almost comical a couple of days postpartum. Six-year-old Vivienne and four-year-old Diana were at home for spring break, Julia had COVID, and Charli was in the NICU, so rest wasn't an option, especially with my anxiety on high alert.

Lying down in a flat position helped, but that wasn't a practical solution.

The best solution: an epidural blood patch, a procedure in which a small volume of blood is injected into a patient's epidural space to stop a fluid leak.

So we planned to make a stop at the hospital on the way to see Charli on Friday to get the procedure done.

As if my plate wasn't full enough, I had to deal with my kids adjusting to the idea of having a new baby sister who was born, but not home, not visible. It was very confusing for them. Especially given that they hadn't known I was pregnant to begin with. It was a messy situation.

In the following days, I called the NICU multiple times, so often, in fact, that I had Charli's medical-record number memorized. The reports were always encouraging. She was holding her own, gaining ground. And while I was grateful and relieved, I struggled with feelings of anxiety, grief, and being overwhelmed.

Finally, the day came—Friday—that Jonathan and I could see Charli.

"What do you guys want for breakfast?" I said, hair in a bun, mesh shorts over mesh underwear, teeth still unbrushed, feeling not-so-great.

"Can I have a bagel with cream cheese?" Vivienne asked, playing with her pigtails.

"Please," I added the reminder automatically. "Yes, you can."

"Please," she chimed in, looking up from her iPad.

"And you, Ms. Julia?"

"Muffin, *pwwwease*," she answered, twirling her curls.

"Coming up, cute face." I smiled.

"And Deedee, how about you?"

"Nothing," Diana said in a low voice, her bottom lip jutting out.

"How about pancakes? You have to put something in that little tummy of yours."

"I don't want anything!" Diana then threw herself onto the floor like a toddler, flailing and pounding her fists, a tsunami of noise pouring out of her mouth.

"Hey, what's going on?" I came down to her level, trying to calm her.

"I don't want you to leave again, Mommy," she finally said through heaving breaths. She was an earthquake and now her whole body was trembling.

"I'm not leaving, baby." I held her close and stroked the top of her head. This had been a lot for her. My girl with separation anxiety. My sweet girl who hates change. My girl who is most like me.

"You said you were going to see Charli." She sounded so hurt.

"I promise I'm not leaving you, OK?" I reassured her. And I meant it. At that moment, I decided to spend the days with my children at home and nights with baby Charli in the NICU, so my home children would never know I was gone.

You know, in retrospect, I was doing that mom thing where you think about everyone else's needs and run yourself way into the ground. What I didn't know then was that, as a NICU mom, I'd be forced to choose between who needed me most at that moment—my children at home or my newborn at the NICU. And that's not a choice any mother should ever have to make. A NICU mother's other children should be homed in neighboring rooms as siblings usually are, and a mother should be able to go back and forth, tending to them all. When the family isn't under the same roof, seeing to everyone's needs becomes nearly impossible. And no matter what a mother chooses, she will likely feel guilty about not meeting every one of those needs.

After we put the girls to bed, leaving them in my parents' care, Jonathan and I drove into the city to see Charli. On the way, we stopped at St Joseph's Hospital in New Jersey to get my epidural blood patch.

While filling out the forms at the check-in desk, I felt my phone vibrate and saw a text from my parents, who were home with my three oldest girls. *Diana is having a hard time. She woke up and said she doesn't want to go to sleep again until you get home.* My heart dropped to my stomach. I felt terrible. I didn't account for her waking up.

"It's OK, she will be fine," Jonathan said as he grabbed my hand to comfort me. He was on the group text, too.

Tell her I'll sleep with her when I get home. When she wakes up tomorrow morning, I'll be right next to her. I promise. This sucks. I pressed send as I touched my chest. The ache in my heart suddenly spread through my hands, limbs, and all the way to my feet until the heaviness was everywhere.

I finished filling out the forms, guilt twinging through my body.

As soon as I had a chance to catch my breath, a nurse led us to a big, standard-looking hospital room. My nose wrinkled as I smelled antiseptic.

"Change into this gown, and take everything off except for your underwear. I'll be back when you're done." The nurse handed me the gown and left.

I took off my shirt and baggy sweatpants, folding them on a small chair beside me. It was freezing. I cupped my hands and blew into them to warm them, but it didn't work. Goosebumps formed on my legs and arms.

"I'm tired of hospital rooms," I said to Jonathan, shivering.

The anesthesiologist came in and introduced himself. "Hi, I'm Avi." He began to explain the steps to me. "First, I am going to take blood from your arm. Then I will inject the blood into your back where the epidural happened. The blood will then restore pressure around your spinal cord."

"Fun times," I said, as my stomach twisted. I pulled my mop-like curls into a ponytail so the doctor would have a clear view of my back.

I saw the big sharp needle and sweat slicked my skin.

I closed my eyes. *It will be done soon, and I will have Charli in my arms.* I repeated this in my head all throughout the procedure.

Before I knew it, it was over. "Lie flat for the next two to three hours and you should be starting to feel much better," Avi said. He explained that staying flat helped the blood coagulate and stay in the same spot where he injected it.

"I'm going to see my baby for the first time in five days," as crazy as that sounded coming out of my mouth, "so I'll lie flat until we get to the hospital and after, but while we're there I'll be sitting or standing, holding her."

Not being with Charli a full five days after she had been born was one of the hardest things I had ever done. Technically, a full six days, if you count, waiting for Diana to go to bed to leave Friday night. Everything that was going on had taken a toll on me not only physically but mentally. I had cried so many tears, felt sorry for myself, and moped around. I could barely get my head above the waves of shock. But finally, I was going to see her. *My Charli.* I felt myself treading water with hope. And as long as she was OK, there was nothing that could sink me.

I lay down in my reclined front seat the entire hour and a half to Lennox Hill in Manhattan.

I felt like I was sunbathing in the car, but there was no tropical scenery to take in or warm sun pressing against my skin. Instead, there was a plain black ceiling, and I felt carsick. But I promised I'd lie down the entire way, and I'm a woman of my word, especially when it comes to my children and my health. I had to be well for them. They needed me.

So many emotions wriggled in my gut. I looked up at Jonathan's dark brown and glossy eyes, focused on the dark road. He was tired. We were both exhausted from everything we'd been through.

"As long as everyone in our family is healthy, every-thing will be OK," I said to Jonathan, reassuring myself in the process, the corners of my mouth twitching. That's what I kept telling myself to get through. "But I'm just so nervous to see Charli. I mean, I'm so excited, but I can't get rid of this nervous feeling."

"There's nothing to be nervous about; she's doing great, my love." He covered my hand with his own, a gesture that was meant to reassure me that everything would be OK. But I couldn't shake the nerves. I'm Charli's mom, so of course I was anxious. Nervous for what she'd look like in person. What she'd feel like. *What if it was too late for us to bond?* But gosh, I was also excited to finally get to see her, hold her, love on her. To let her get to know me. My thoughts were interrupted as we parked the car. We had finally arrived.

Passing rooms where moms cooed and comforted their crying but otherwise healthy babies tucked safely within their arms, I smiled, because what a beautiful and chaotic wonder it is, the sound of the dialogue that takes place between a mom and her newborn. It is a sound that I will never take for granted again. Outside the NICU, Nicole instructed us to wash our hands and then buzzed us through the heavy doors.

Jonathan laced my fingers with his own as we fol-lowed Nicole along an aisle lined with other babies in bas-sinets and Isolettes to our own baby's room near the back. A whiteboard, bearing Charli's name, hung on the wall and caught my attention. Under a heading that read: "Goals for the day," Nicole had written in black marker, "to get lots of snuggles from my parents." My heart melted.

But then my eyes darted to a big glass box that con-tained a shockingly small baby. My baby. She looked like a doll. I couldn't stop staring at her. I didn't remember her being so tiny. Tears welled in my eyes as my gaze took in the tube coming out of her nose and all the other wires that snaked from different parts of her little body. It had not felt as real before, watching her through a camera. It had seemed more as if I was watching a movie of someone else's baby. Up close now, with the sound of monitors beeping on and off, it was a lot to take in.

"She's so tiny." It was all I could say. I was overcome with an urge to swoop her into my arms and make everything better. But I knew she was exactly where she needed to be, that there was no one better than the doctors and nurses to make sure my baby would get home safely to me.

A nurse named Laura checked my medical ID bracelet and matched it to Charli's. Then, meeting my glance, she said, "Do you want to hold her?"

Did I want to hold her? *Did I want to hold her?* More than anything in the entire world. "Yes! I'd love to. I mean, I have to fulfill her goal for the day, right?" I smiled. I wanted Nicole, who was within earshot, to know how much I appreciated her sweet gesture.

Returning my smile, Laura delicately maneuvered wires, making it possible to safely give me our baby.

I held Charli close for hours, staring down at her, stroking her soft skin. Her hat and swaddle were so big on her. She was so alert, taking Jonathan and me in just as much as we were taking her in. Jonathan took a turn, but it wasn't long before I wanted her back. I needed to feel her, to hold my little girl. I was desperate to make up for the days when she wasn't with me, her mom, her world.

Just after midnight, Jonathan yawned. The time had passed so quickly, but I knew my parents needed to be at home in their own bed. They needed their rest. Reluctantly, I gave Charli back to Laura and said a final goodbye. "I'll be back tomorrow," I promised. I held my breath as we left Charli, something I'd do to stop myself from crying at the end of every visit for the next forty-five days.

The next morning, my postpartum complications continued.

I was chasing Viv up the stairs, Julia holding my hand, when suddenly I couldn't move my legs. "Something is wrong!" I yelled, as I caught Jonathan's eye. I couldn't make it up the stairs. My legs collapsed, and I fell to the ground. I felt so weak. My rib cage felt so tight I could hardly breathe. What was happening to me? Jonathan helped me up, steadying me, before he walked away. I was very unbalanced. Afraid I would fall again, I sat down on the top step, the rest of my body leaning against the door.

"You OK, Mama?" Julia asked, her smile fading.

"Of course, my love," tears glinted in the corners of my eyes, but I didn't let her see. She'd witnessed me cry way too much this week.

Jonathan called the anesthesiologist, and he said it sounded like I had spinal stenosis because he must have given me too much blood for my small frame, which made the extra blood place pressure on the nerves. He said it would balance out when the blood got reabsorbed. Jonathan repeated this to me casually like it was all no big deal.

"Spinal stenosis? Are you kidding me?" Tears welled up behind my eyes. "I'm surprised I still have tears left. What a week! At least I get to hold Charli again tonight. That is, if I can walk to her," the knot in my throat made it hard to speak as I felt myself melt into Jonathan. Sometimes I need to melt. His reassuring touch reminding me that I'm not alone can bring my soul back to life.

"But at least you don't have a bad headache," Jonathan said, kissing the side of my head.

I shooed him away, pushing his body away from mine, my gaze remaining dark and steady. I couldn't even tell him it was a bad joke. I was too burned out. I just shook my head.

Luckily, about forty-eight hours later, a full week from Charli's birth, I was finally feeling "OK-ish." Yes, my boobs were swollen, my ribs hurt, my body ached, the exhaustion was bone deep, and I still had a never-ending period, but that was normal life postpartum. Compared to what I had just been through between my scary delivery with COVID and the pounding headaches, it would be much easier to get through this familiar stage. Even with the added obstacle of Charli in the NICU, I knew I would. Because us moms? We push through. We keep going no matter what. Because our love for our children is our fuel.

And that's what I continued to do. My days became marked by routine. I'd spend the days with my kids, and after I put them to bed, when Jonathan was home from work, I'd make the trek into the city to be with Charli. We became two ships passing in the night—quick conversations and kisses stolen before I left for the NICU and before he left for work. That's all we had.

Driving home in those early morning hours, I'd pass groups of twenty-somethings running the streets after a night out. And the only way I could relate to them was that I felt drunk, too—from exhaustion.

During my initial visits, Charli was on a feeding tube, so I couldn't do much for her but cradle her in my arms, watching her as she slept. We stared at one another. I snuck kisses, pressing them onto her tiny face, in the hope that they would sink into her pores so she could feel me when I wasn't with her.

Then, finally, she was pronounced ready to nurse from a bottle. It was an arduous process, one that required practice and demanded patience, and I learned so much going through it. In your pregnant belly, at thirty-three weeks, babies begin to exercise sucking and swallowing reflexes, which are then fully coordinated by about the end of thirty-four weeks. Because Charli had arrived too soon to acquire the skills, it took her a long time to develop the proficiency that would enable her to thrive on her own. The doctors kept saying that with preemies like Charli, mastery would happen on their own time—that suddenly the instinct would click. So, I waited, and waited, and waited.

I drove back and forth, between the hospital and home, never having a chance to watch a television show, eat a sit-down dinner with my family, write, or read, while Charli and I trained through long night hours, learning a skill that is basic to life, one that would ensure my small daughter would get the most out of a feeding.

Each night while the doctors made their rounds, I couldn't help but think before they reached our turn: *What setbacks did we face today in her feeding journey?* And some nights I'd be happily surprised to hear she'd done better. This way, I wouldn't be disappointed if she didn't. Often, I'd come home and check on my babies as they peacefully slept. I'd sometimes make it just in time for nightmares or accidents. But then, when I'd finally get into bed, exhausted, I'd be so overcome by irrational thoughts that I'd get up to call the NICU.

"Hi, I just wanted to make sure Charli did OK in her last feeding."

"Hi, the nurse I left Charli with was having a bit of a rough time feeding her, so I just wanted to check on her."

"Hi, Charli didn't eat anything without the tube tonight, so I just wanted to make sure she was OK."

Whether it was 2 AM or 6 AM, someone was always there to put my mind at ease. But my emotions continued to be very up and down.

So, one moment I was smiling and out at the park with my older children, racing down the slides, and pushing them on the swings, or hearing that Vivienne had a great day at school and had received praise from her teacher for helping an upset friend, and the next moment, in my mind's eye, I'd see Charli crying in the NICU as clear as day—small and frail—and my own throat would constrict. One moment, feeling the warm embrace of little arms around me, I was at peace, and the next, I was calling the NICU and breaking into a million pieces because it all felt like too much.

And when I finally got to hold Charli in my arms each night, I couldn't help but feel blessed, yet guilty for not being there at every beep of the monitor or every time they changed her feeding tube.

But my kids at home needed me, too. And in some ways, during this time, they needed me more than my NICU baby. They were each struggling with their own things. Plus, Charli had all the care in the world surrounding her. People who, even though I hated to admit it, were better equipped to care for her than I was. Yes, no one would love her more than Jonathan and me. But, at this moment, she needed more than love. And even though I knew the day would come when I would bring my newborn home, I continued to ride an emotional seesaw while waiting.

The longer my sweet girl stayed in the NICU, the greater toll it took on my soul. I was going mindlessly through the days, doing what had to be done, just enough to get by. Sure, I'd smile when Julia said "I love you" or when Vivienne acted silly, but I was never totally OK. I wasn't feeling anything. There was never a break from the worry, the constant responsibility. I was always either tending to my kids, doing what little work I could, or with my baby in the NICU. I was running on adrenaline. Every day was a struggle. How could it not be, though, when you're holding your breath and leaving your baby every single day in the early hours of the morning?

But my children gave me so much strength—to get out of bed and face the day-to-day routine, then walk through the NICU doors yet again. They gave me strength on mornings when I was moping around feeling sorry for myself. They gave me the will every day to show up, no matter what. And because of that—their faith in me, their expectations, and belief in me—I did all that needed to be done for them. I made sure to love them in the way they needed to be loved, too. They are my resilience, my bravery, and my strength. Long nights, sitting with Charli in the NICU, waiting for her to learn to feed and thrive—I would think of Vivienne, Diana, and Julia, my other three girls, and how I would do anything for them.

Finally, after more than a month of ceaselessly traveling back and forth from home to hospital, it clicked: Charli's instinct to suckle and swallow and take enough to thrive kicked in. On that evening when I arrived in the NICU to visit her, Nicole greeted me with a question. Her eyes alight, she asked, "How would you like to bring in Charli's car seat for a car seat test?"

I clapped my hands to my mouth as my heart rose. "Really?" I knew that what Nicole was asking was NICU code for, "Your baby is coming home."

"Well," Nicole said, "You know she went through a whole long weekend of feeding without a feeding tube. We think she's good to go."

A few days later, the day of Charli's discharge arrived. I was so excited at the idea of having all my babies in one place—for them to meet at last.

And then, on the morning we were to bring her home, we got an email from Vivienne's kindergarten teacher. A child had tested positive for COVID, and Vivienne was a close contact. Testing her, we learned she was positive—of course she was. COVID was following us everywhere, popping in at the worst possible times.

So now I had to worry about keeping the baby totally isolated from Vivienne, which upset her. She so looked forward to meeting her new baby sister, but at least all my babies would be under one roof. I still couldn't wait for Charli to be home. I remember walking out of the NICU doors for the last time, carrying our tiniest daughter in her car seat. Neither Jonathan nor I could stop smiling. I could finally breathe. We were bringing our girl home at last after 45 days.

It was at that moment that my heart began to heal, because when your NICU baby comes home, the anguish and uncertainty lift. Away goes the heavy, clinging sense of how hard that time has been. It's carried off like a wave. The memory of all the weeks of traveling back and forth from home to hospital and all the late nights that ended in reluctant goodbyes at either place as you left either your family or your baby behind—all of that begins to dim. You are no longer haunted by worry over what will happen while you're away. And you will no longer get that sinking feeling when one of your children asks, "When's the baby coming home?" and you have to answer, "I don't know."

And now, as you carry your baby into her home at last, you realize you've become a different person. All because of this sweet baby girl. Because now that the clouds are lifting, and you can finally see the light—you also see your own strength. Because that baby has shown you how strong you are, and that kind of courage is a gift—one you can breathe into yourself, and your husband, and all your children. So that's what I did upon arriving home: I breathed in the miracle of having my family together and my heart nearly burst with gratitude for every imperfect second of it.

— 4 —

We're Not Letting Ourselves Go— We're Letting Ourselves Live

I REMEMBER MY FIRST look at my new body as a first-time mother. They don't tell you about the first time you see yourself in the mirror postpartum. I call it the first look. And boy, it can be a doozy, especially with your first baby. It's so shocking it pinches your chest.

It was just hours after I gave birth to Vivienne. I dragged myself from my hospital bed to the bathroom, my legs swollen and achy with each step I took. I closed the door and sat down on the toilet. Everything hurt. The trickle of pee mixed with blood burned so badly I could hardly walk. A couple of days later I found out that a stitch came out. I got a shot to numb the area so my OB could re-stitch it. I was completely awake on the examination table, dripping sweat, and screaming. I detached from my body in that moment. Nightmare.

I scrambled to my feet and looked in the mirror hanging above the sink. I could have sworn that I just had Vivienne in my arms, but she looked like she was still in my stomach. I looked a little smaller, probably five months pregnant instead of nine months pregnant. I had stretch marks and was swollen everywhere. I felt a gut-wrenching I-might-throw-up feeling. *Wow, I didn't expect this.* I flushed and walked out of the bathroom as fast as I could—running from my reflection.

"Jonathan! I look terrible. I feel gross, like I am wearing someone else's skin." A tear slid down my cheek.

"Babe, you look beautiful." He assured me.

"You're only saying that to me to make me feel better. I look deformed." I said.

The little voice in my head kept saying, "Get your body back!" and "Lose the baby weight."

I could see the titles of the magazine headlines in my head from the diet culture that had been inundating my brain ever since I was a little girl growing up in the nineties. Headlines like, "All my life I had a weight problem then with diet pills I lost 25 pounds," or magazines ripping apart celebrities if they didn't fit the super skinny image. Every one of them had an overwhelming focus on weight and size. The image of Kate Moss in Calvin Klein underwear hugging her hipbones will forever be etched in my memory. "Heroin chic" they called it, and that was considered beautiful. Everyone I knew was on a diet: from the Atkins craze to The South Beach Diet to SlimFast. "Nothing tastes as good as skinny feels," was a household phrase. The nineties was peak toxicity. We were told by everyone and everything around us that size was correlated with value, and it's hard to rewire that completely. I faintly heard the old voices that told me to fast, make myself sick, exercise for hours, and count calories. They hadn't been there in a while. I was determined not to let them win. But I had to honor my feelings.

Jonathan rubbed my arm in response. "You just had a baby," he shrugged, as if to say, *What do you expect?*

"Really? I didn't know that," I sassed, wiping my nose with the palm of my right hand because I couldn't find a tissue. "Everything about me right now is gross." I cried harder. "Sorry, I'm being so rude. I hate that that's where my mind goes, when I have a beautiful healthy baby in front of me—but I can't help how I feel." I looked down at Vivienne, peacefully sleeping, her chest rising and falling.

"Is there anything I can do, besides get you a tissue?" He squeezed my arm.

"No. Just let me have a moment." I took the tissue from his outstretched hand, and drew my knees into my chest, wrapping my arms around them. I needed a moment to mourn the loss of what my body had been.

A couple of minutes passed in silence until I heard newborn cries from the bassinet at my hospital bedside. Vivienne was awake. *My* baby was awake. It felt very surreal to realize that.

"My baby. My baby. My baby," I repeated. Saying it out loud sounded even more real. Especially with everything I went through with my eating disorder, I never thought I would have this. Have her—something so special. Be deserving of that kind of love. Be well enough to be a good role model. There were so many reasons why I was grateful then—and continue to be today.

I picked her up and held her in my arms. I took in her intoxicating newborn smell and tried to get her to latch. We struggled to find our rhythm. But all I could see was how perfectly imperfect she was. I took her in—her arms, feet, and squishy rolls. I heard her sweet gulping sounds after she was finally able to latch on. Then I stroked her soft hair until she had a content and sleepy look, with a half-smile and milk dribbling down her chin. She was "milk drunk." And I wanted my body image, everything, to be better for her.

Before I had Vivienne, I was in recovery and wasn't ready to confront the dark place that mirrors used to take me. So, I avoided them. I hardly looked at my reflection. Why go back to that place of so much hate and shame?

I spent way too many years hating the person who looked back at me in the mirror. It was a manifestation of never feeling good enough in other ways. I felt like I wasn't smart enough and didn't find myself particularly talented at school, but looking back, I was too afraid to try. That's because nothing academic came easily to me, mostly because of my processing diagnosis. My inner mantra became, "You aren't enough." It didn't help that students noticed how hard I worked to keep up with the naturally smart kids, and I was labeled an overachiever.

Any little reminder of my shortcomings would put me over the edge. I remember one time in sophomore year of high school during AP History class. Since I couldn't process what the teacher was saying during class, I overcompensated and wrote down everything he said to review later in my own time. My classmate Claire looked over at my notes and laughed out loud, signaling to the boy on the other side of me, Ryan, to look at something on my desk, and he broke out into laughter, too.

"If something is so funny, I think you should share it with the class," the teacher, looked at them both, annoyed.

"Dani wrote down the joke you made," Claire explained, and the entire class started laughing. My face turned beet red. My voice lost all its strength to speak but I forced myself to plaster on a weak smile. For a long moment the only sound was my pulse pounding in my ears, thankfully blocking out the laughter. I was humiliated.

I came home and stared at myself in the mirror. I was too big. Took up too much space. I wasted too much time body checking—obsessively checking my body—every time I saw a mirror. Lifting my shirt to see how flat my belly looked and pinching what I needed to get rid of.

Looking at my thighs and seeing big tree trunks with cellulite. I'd pray for a thigh gap and squeeze my inner thighs until it looked like I had it. And I'd leave that mirror with my eating disorder in full force every single time.

I had a hard time accepting what I saw looking back at me after my first two pregnancies and feeling this way was triggering. Because of it, I relapsed in my eating disorder behaviors after the birth of my second daughter, Diana.

Diana came a month early. We were not prepared. I was convinced I peed the bed, because with Vivienne I was induced—but then that "pee" kept coming and coming and coming.

Diana was in the NICU for 11 days, not because of her size, but because she started throwing up green bile. I remember my voice quavering as I asked them questions, my breathing coming in spurts, as they ran test after test to make sure she was OK. Then after all the tests came up fine, her body couldn't keep her temperature up, so we had to keep her in the NICU in an incubator until she could.

There were a lot of changes as it was. I had never been away from Vivienne, who was then eighteen months, and there I was in the hospital and away from her, my hormones out of whack, body aching and exhausted, and faced with the news that I wasn't going to be taking my newborn home. This sweet newborn with no hair and fair skin, who was the newest love of my life. I didn't want to leave her anywhere outside of my arms.

I also saw a new body again. A body that I didn't recognize. A body that was even more stretched and saggy than the first time. In my mind, I knew this body just gave birth, but between what I was seeing in the mirror and all the stress I was under, I felt like the weight of my body was suffocating me. I couldn't breathe in the uncertainty around me.

My schedule was extremely hectic: I was going to the NICU for Diana's first feeding before 5 AM so I could be back before Vivienne woke up. Then around 12:30 PM, after I'd put Vivienne down for her afternoon nap, I'd head back to the NICU for Diana's next feeding. Then to Vivienne around 3:30 PM to spend the rest of the afternoon with her until bedtime. Then after I put her down for the night, I'd go to the hospital until at least midnight. Between these visits, I was pumping around the clock, trying to get work done, and I wanted to put in quality time with Vivienne. Luckily, I lived a couple of blocks from the hospital at the time, but it was still a lot.

I was running around, so it was easy for me to skip a meal here and there. I am not a person who thinks about her hunger or herself first by nature, so it's very easy for me to miss those cues when I'm caught up in the stress around me. But as the days went on, the same routine continued.

Then when I had my two babies at home with me, I started missing those meals purposely—because it's easy to control your food intake when everything else around you feels so out of control. The hunger can be an addicting feeling in the hard times.

Until my mom looked at me juggling my two babies. I was following Vivienne as she toddled around. Her hair was wild. I hadn't had a chance to brush through it yet, between pumping, feeding, and making breakfast. I held Diana in my arms and let out a sigh.

"What a morning already," I said raggedly.

"You have to be well for them, too. I've noticed you've been stressed and not eating very much." She said in a quiet rasp. Her brown hair was blowing in her face from the breeze coming in from an open kitchen window. The sun was shining on her bowl of yogurt with fruit and granola in it.

"I'm in solid recovery, and I'm offended," I couldn't help but scoff, clearly in denial. "Just because I did it in the past doesn't mean I'd do it again. Plus, I'm pumping, so Diana depends on my breast milk. Do you think I'd do that to my baby?" But that's how strong eating disorders are; I was doing that to my baby. That was the scary thing: I was pumping, and my daughter needed the nutrients, but I wasn't giving myself anything.

Hearing myself say those words out loud freaked me out. That wasn't me talking.

So, after that interaction, I got back on the recovery bandwagon, not only for me, but for my daughters. I had come too far. I made sure I ate even when the stress of the world, of getting used to two babies under two, was weighing me down.

People don't want to talk about relapse out of shame. It's considered weak. But admitting you relapsed and picking yourself up again makes you very strong.

Going through this experience made me stronger in my recovery because I saw how quickly I could get myself back on track. I gave myself grace because there was such a learning curve in motherhood, and I didn't feel prepared like I did when I studied for a test. I didn't know everything about these two kids, how to juggle them best. I was learning as I went, and that bred insecurity.

By the time I had Julia, I finally realized that my body didn't need to become better, and I was much more confident in my motherhood. My body was perfectly imperfect the way it was, and so was my motherhood journey. My outlook on it was what needed shifting.

So, with each pregnancy after Diana, I learned to give myself more and more grace. I saw firsthand how amazing my body was through what it did and continues to do for each of my children daily. I also knew what to expect in terms of motherhood chaos by that point. And for someone who has struggled with her body and has been hard on herself most of her life, this perspective has helped me heal.

Because what our bodies do for not only us, but also our children, makes them amazing.

Take my arms. My arms do so much. They're my children's to wrap around themselves into a hug when they need comfort. They rock my babies to sleep, and push my kids on the swings in a silly way, their eyes flashing as they laugh.

And my legs. My legs are theirs to climb on the playground, and to chase them through the park as I'm choking from laughter. They hold me upright all day long and keep me going, no matter what.

My ears are for listening to coos and first words. They are used to help navigate my kids' problems, and to respond to the never-ending "Mommy, Mommy, Mommy!"

And now I'm able to look into the mirror for the first time in my life and be kind to myself. I am still not in love with my body, but I accept my body—and that's beautiful. I see a different person, and I'm much easier on her. She's the mother to my favorite people on the planet, so she's kind of great. Even in the early months postpartum, I reached an understanding that I just grew a baby and brought her into the world, so it's OK to look like I did both of those things.

For years, society had poisoned my understanding of what true beauty was, but today, my eyes are wide open, and I see the truth. Looking in the mirror and seeing my toddler wrapped around my leg smiling at her reflection is beautiful. My stretch marks, cellulite, and blemishes that brought my kids into the world are beautiful. Me, as a mother who keeps my babies happy, safe, and well, is beautiful.

So, if I could go back to that first time mom, having a hard time, I'd let her know it's OK to feel her feelings about her body, because it's a big change. Diet culture has made it hard for a woman to accept her body, even before a pregnancy. So, we can't expect her to feel amazing about it after. But I hope she can at least try to give it grace even if she's feeling self-conscious in her skin. And yes, it may take time and experience as a mother to get to a place of full acceptance but if she tries to stay neutral toward it and focuses on the love she has for the baby in her arms, she'll get there, especially when she sees all that her body does for her baby.

I say "acceptance" instead of "love" because it's a big jump from hate to love. Acceptance is a more obtainable middle ground. Obviously loving your body at every size and without thinking of it in terms of what it does for your children would be ideal, but embracing the body that you have right now is a good enough second as you walk toward love.

One big roadblock in the journey toward acceptance and love for our bodies is the way people think it's OK to talk about your body to your face. And it's hard to embrace your new body when it's constantly taking center stage in other people's eyes.

I remembered the comments I used to get after each kid.

"Wow, what did you do to lose the baby weight?" was the first thing my friend Karen said to me when she saw me postpartum after Julia's birth, giving me an awkwardly long once-over. She hadn't seen me since I was on my last few weeks carrying Julia and she was carrying her son, Brian. Their due dates were similar.

Her words hung in the air while I watched her take a sip of her spicy chai latte. She was wearing big golden hoops, jean shorts, and a trendy tank top. Her long brown hair was blown straight, wind rippling through it, which somehow made it look better. I was impressed.

My face got blisteringly hot, and my heart spiked. I wanted to turn the other way, but she was staring intently at me, determined. "I don't know. Just being a mother, I guess." The sunlight pressed against my skin. Sweat started to form on my forehead and palms. Gosh, I hated that question. I looked at her and instead of saying anything about her body that further perpetuated bounceback culture, I shifted the focus. "Oh my goodness, Brian is adorable. That little face. How are you feeling?" He was wearing a blue onesie, sleeping soundly.

"I'm exhausted." Karen tugged at her shirt as she started explaining her baby's latest sleep regression.

I listened while rubbing Julia's head tenderly. She was in my Bjorn, sleeping. Diana shyly hid behind my back, and Vivienne was on the ground drawing something resembling a heart using a stick and mud.

I was thankful to have changed the subject.

Because I hate how we're expected to look like we never had a baby at all the second after we give birth. I hate that because our bodies are changing people think it's an open invitation to comment on them. Newsflash: it's never OK. Women gain and lose weight, and it's never OK to talk about it, pregnant or not. A woman, a mother, is so much more than her body.

That's why if I run into you on the street, I want to hear about anything besides how you got your "body back."

You won't hear me saying: "Are you pregnant again?"

"You don't even look like you had a baby."

"You should try this diet—it worked for my friend."

These comments make a mother feel like she doesn't look how she's supposed to and that something about her body is wrong. But there's nothing wrong with her; everybody is different. A mother's worth has nothing to do with what she looks like.

So, I want to hear about how she overcame her mental health struggles like postpartum depression, how she was able to find her balance with a newborn and everything else, how she and her partner reconnected, and about her feeding journey. I want to support her through that, especially if she finds herself dabbing wet eyes more than leaky breasts.

Between bonding with her newborn and older children, learning to trust herself as a mom, taking the bad days in stride, and everything else that comes with being a mom, the least important thing about her is "how she got her body back."

Besides "the first look" and the nonstop comments about my body, there were so many changes with my body that I wasn't prepared for.

While they tell you how to care for a newborn—I learned things like the 5 S's (shushing, swinging, swaddling, sucking, and side position), and even took a class on how to breastfeed—I learned nothing about how to recover postpartum.

After giving birth to Vivienne, I didn't know that I was going to have vaginal aches from an episiotomy. Or how to recognize that a stitch fell out. My labia was hanging open for a couple of days, but I thought that was what it was supposed to look like after having a baby. Jonathan, too, until I showed my mom—and she turned paler than a ghost. "Call your doctor now!" Turns out it wasn't normal.

I didn't know my breasts would blow up like balloons when my milk came in, and they'd ache, too.

I didn't know that breastfeeding wasn't always blissful and beautiful. It doesn't always come easy, and feeling unsupported and guilty during that time is unfortunately normal.

I didn't know that you could get something called mastitis from a clogged milk duct and get a fever and feel like a truck collided into your boob in a hit and run. You didn't see it hit you, but gosh, you felt it! My breasts were angry and sore. The second time it happened to me with Diana, I felt so sick from the pain in my chest and the sudden 103-degree fever spike while visiting her at the NICU, Jonathan thought I was having a panic attack.

I didn't know I'd get the longest period of my life after each baby came, and I'd have to wear a pad for weeks.

I didn't know that while babies were brought to the doctor frequently for checkups that first year, I became an afterthought. I had one appointment after six weeks postpartum, and I didn't see the OB again until around the six-month mark—and only because I was struggling to get pregnant with Diana and needed to try Clomid and the trigger shot. While I was pregnant, I saw my OB every month, every two weeks, then every week up until delivery. This is after my body had been through hell and back. I also didn't know this was the norm for mothers.

I was in shock when I came home with Vivienne. I didn't expect to be in so much pain. I thought once the baby was out, I'd magically feel better. Instead, I was a pale swollen ghost of my former self.

There was so much I didn't know. A mother-to-be needs to be taught about life postpartum just as much as giving birth and caring for her newborn. Because moms need to prepare.

Moms need to know life postpartum is anything but easy or pain free.

It won't be her cleaning dishes when she can and emptying an overflowing diaper pail. It will be her engorged breasts aching as she bends over every time she performs those tasks.

It won't be her swaying her newborn to sleep. Instead, she'll feel like she's been in a car accident while attempting to rock her newborn to sleep with leaky breasts.

It won't be learning about her newborn with a twinkle in her eye. It will be tears as she's waddling around her house from a perineal tear or delicate incision site and the longest period of her life, white mesh underwear as her new best friend.

And she'll feel like more of a mess than a mother because she's exhausted and worn down. But she needs to know all of this, so when it happens, she won't think she's alone. Following each birth except Vivienne's, I knew what to expect, so when it was hard, it was more manageable because my expectations were realistic.

During this time, it becomes so easy to get swept away into a whirlwind of bottles, breastmilk, diapers, and baby cries. But as mothers, we need to make ourselves a priority, too. If we don't have our health, we don't have anything. We're no use to anyone if we're running on empty.

But I quickly realized it's hard to do this in practice. It's almost instinctual; if it's between me and any of my babies, I am going to pick my babies. If we are in a rush, I'll feed my child before me. I just will.

Because when you're deep in the hard of parenting little kids, self-care is easier said than done. And the phrase, "You really need to take care of yourself" puts more pressure on a mom. And it's not martyrdom, it's a reflex. Moms just need to know where the line is, where we can step back and get what we need before we crash. We do our best, and yes, we could do better. But this is most moms.

I used to have a hard time finding that line, especially in the newborn phase. After Charli's birth, I especially fell into a hole. It was the baby blues mixed with postpartum complications, managing the older kids' schedules and emotions, work, and Charli being in the NICU. It persisted past two weeks (which normally means you should speak to your doctor about postpartum depression), but it was more situational. I didn't have time to vocalize it between the back and forth from the NICU— but I wasn't OK.

I'd get texts asking how the baby was doing, but hardly any asking how I was. I know those people asking about the baby cared about me, too, and I appreciated their concern for Charli so much, but I could have used someone who wanted to really peel the layers back and let me be human instead of a robot on autopilot going through the motions.

It's not easy being the glue. The everything. As I continued to hold my family together for dear life, I was breaking at the seams—hanging by a thread.

I rubbed my eyes and continued going—because that's what moms do. Each day, for forty-five days while Charli was in the NICU, and the sad feelings continued for a little after she came home.

And I am not alone. I was in a toddler class and the topic came up about the struggles postpartum. What was so striking is how universal it is.

"I feel like everyone has had at least one traumatic delivery situation, and then they expect us to be mentally and physically OK postpartum, at least enough to care for a baby?" said Mel, an Australian mom with freckles dotting her face. She took a half step back and stroked her daughter's hair.

Six women nodded in agreement. We all had at least one traumatic birth story where we were nervous, afraid, or suffered an injury.

"You're right, and especially with your first baby. You have no idea what you're getting into." The teacher chimed in, her brows scrunched as she spoke, hair in perfect ringlets. She rested her elbow against the wall.

"Also, we must do it all ourselves with our hormones out of whack, breastfeeding around the clock. We aren't feeling well and have minimal help and sleep. We aren't overjoyed as mothers; we're overwhelmed," another mother said as she blew bubbles for her twenty-month-old who was dancing in circles trying to pop them. Her platinum blond hair was dancing with her as she giggled.

They were right; nothing prepares a mother for the first couple of weeks postpartum, and it will be anything but easy for her, especially because she'll always put her baby first.

I want to make a call to action regarding every woman postpartum: to hold the mother, not the baby.

Because even if she says she's OK, she could probably use the extra care.

The baby is being taken care of—fed, snuggled, and given all the love in the world—by not only the mother, but her partner, grandparents, siblings, cousins, and friends.

But the mother is going through so much. The mother is the baby's entire world and needs to be seen so she doesn't disappear into the postpartum fog of loneliness, mom guilt, and never feeling enough.

A mother agrees that her baby matters more. Nothing is more important to her in this world, but she's often hurting, sometimes gagged by society, while she's the person behind the baby, in the background, making it all happen.

So, right then in that moment, especially in the first couple of months postpartum, the mother needs your love. She will remember who held her up during this time. The baby won't.

So instead of "I'm coming to see the baby," try saying, "I'm coming to see you and meet the baby, too." It will mean a lot.

A few years ago, I ran into two other moms I knew from Vivienne's class. As we chatted, making the usual small talk, I was a little distracted by Julia, then two-years-old.

She would pull on my pants, and I would yank them back up. She went into my diaper bag on her own and took all my diapers, wipes, and change of clothes out to get a snack, making a mess. Typical toddler behavior. Once, digging in the mud, she cried over having her hands dirty, and as I was cleaning them up, one of the moms walked away to help her son scale a climbing wall.

"Wow, she really let herself go," the other mom whispered to me.

"Excuse me?" Straightening, I thought I'd heard her wrong. But unfortunately, when she repeated herself, I realized I hadn't. "Well, I think she looks great," I said, defending her.

Actually, she looked a lot like me. Hair up in a messy bun. Eyes dull from a sleepless night probably spent working and reworking an endless to-do list. She wore a big, baggy T-shirt, probably stinking of baby drool and whatever she'd made her family for breakfast that morning. Possibly there were a few stretch marks here and there; maybe she was carrying a few extra pounds, but none of that mattered.

That night, though, I couldn't stop thinking about those words, "Wow, she really let herself go."

They bothered me. I'd heard them before, most often directed at mothers.

Mothers whose bodies changed and became a home for their children.

Mothers who do everything for everyone and love them with their whole beings.

I've heard people say these words too many times. Casually, as if it's acceptable conversation. They say them with a slow shake of their heads, like it's the worst thing that could happen.

I've heard these words, too, when a woman gains weight. When her once slender figure takes up more space than it used to. When she doesn't have the time to dress up, do her hair, put on fake eyelashes—any of it. When she doesn't have even two craps to give about calorie counting or the scale. *Any of it!*

I was talking to Jonathan about these thoughts when something clicked in the middle of a sentence, and I knew that if I could go back to the park, I would've responded much differently.

I'd have smiled widely at that other mom, like I was letting her in on some big secret, and I'd have said, "She didn't let herself go. She's letting herself live, and that's the most beautiful thing that can happen to a woman."

Because that's what she was doing: living.

Because all I saw that day was that mom, laughing with her son, the look of love shining in her big blue eyes.

I saw her buying an ice cream cone for him, and they licked the drips and giggled as they shared it. I saw her running after her son in a game of chase, and when she caught him and scooped him up to tickle his stomach, his squeals of joy were loud enough to fill the entire playground.

I remember smiling over at her, because that kind of happiness is contagious.

So, all I saw was her happy and living. She was participating in life, and wearing clothes that made her feel comfortable doing those things.

And that's what we're supposed to do as humans.

So no, judgmental mom at the park, she didn't let herself go. In fact, she's done quite the opposite. She's letting herself live.

She's too busy making memories with her kids, sharing chicken fingers, and comforting their fragile hearts, to put on makeup and get her hair colored every time she sees a hint of gray. She's too busy enjoying life and those she loves to put that useless pressure on herself. And she's too busy enjoying her life as a mother to care what other people think. So instead, she's accepted the cellulite on the backs of her thighs and a stomach webbed with stretch marks as gifts from her babies. She's accepted her children aren't going to always behave perfectly, and she may get a few headshakes and whispers in her direction when out in public. They're badges of her strength as a mom.

So really, she's let go of all the things that don't matter.

She's let go of worrying about appearances.

And she's finally free of societal constraints, the pressure to be a certain weight and look a certain way. Dress a certain way. Parent a certain way. Act a certain way. The obsession with youth.

And she's become who she's meant to be all along: a happy, healthy mother.

So, the next time you hear, "She let herself go," look past her messy bun, and puffy eyelids, to her happy heart—and know that she's finally free.

And smile for her because you know she's never looked or felt better—felt more *her*.

— 5 —

I'm a Mom, Not a Superhero

I'M IN THE grocery store with two-year-old Vivienne and six-month-old Diana, who is babbling as she's strapped to my chest in my Bjorn. Vivienne waddles in front of us.

I'm browsing the fruit. I pick up a container of strawberries, see mold, put them back. I inspect another container. Looks good, I think. I place them in the cart, eyeing Viv.

She's ahead, wiggling as she walks. Diana moves her hands to my cheeks. I give her a kiss, and she kicks and giggles.

"Viv, do you want to come in the cart?" I ask, hoping she will say yes, so it'll be easier to watch her.

"No." She turns around, her eyes wide and alight as she takes a box of cookies off the shelf and tries to open them.

I kneel on the ground. "No, Viv, these aren't for you." I smile and take them away, placing them back on the shelf.

She picks up a bag of Cheetos and continues walking.

"Good choice, my love, but also not for now." I smile and take them away before she tries to open them, too.

We make our way to the row of freezers. I browse the popsicles.

Viv lights up. "I want!" Her chubby hand points to a colorful rainbow box of popsicles. I open the freezer door, the cold wind hitting my face as she grabs the first box. I quickly close the door.

"I want!" Viv demands again, this time pointing to a fudgsicle box, her other hand wrapped around the rainbow popsicles.

"No baby, you have these cool rainbow ones already." I take her hand to try to guide her away, but she resists.

"Vivie baby, come on," I plead. I don't open the door again. *She can't carry all of them!* I start walking away, hoping she'll follow, when suddenly Vivienne lets out a screech of "I want!" at full-volume and throws herself on the floor, smacking her head, which causes her face to distort and her screams and cries to increase.

I scramble to the ground.

Heat forms in every nook and cranny of my body as she fights me. I struggle to pick her up with Diana on my chest. My world feels like it's closing in on me.

I feel like I'm in a bad dream—my cheeks flaming red. I hope to wake up any minute soaking in sweat and in relief that none of this is real. That I am not this mom with a shaky voice trying to get her toddler off the dirty grocery store floor.

Vivienne is now army crawling her way to the freezer, her hair a mess from the ground, face red from screaming—she's inconsolable. I don't think she hears my voice when she reaches the freezer glass and starts pawing at it.

Diana starts crying in my Bjorn because of the noise. I try to comfort her by getting up and swaying from side-to-side, but it doesn't help.

An old man walks past us with an annoyed look across his face like something smells so bad, he's disgusted. I imagine he's thinking, "Control your kids!"

Color drains from my face. "Come on, baby," I beg, trying to calm Viv down so we can go, trying to reason with her. You can't reason with a two-year old, especially one stuck in a tantrum.

I pull her in my arms and place her in the cart, wheeling her away toward the front of the store as she continues screaming and banging on the cart like it's her prison cell.

I feel like the worst mom in the world. I want to cry as I stand in line trying to calm her down. Trying to calm Diana too. I place a bottle in Diana's mouth, only to have her push it away.

I can feel the stares. The eyerolls. The feeling like I am being filmed and this is my close-up, everyone waiting for me to continue to fail. To write a bad review. To rip me apart and tell me I'm doing everything wrong. I feel myself disintegrating under the weight of the embarrassment.

I am exhausted. My temper is short. I'm nervous I'm screwing up this whole motherhood thing. I panic. My heart starts beating fast . . . lub dub, lub dub . . . Sweat drips down my forehead . . . lub dub, lub dub . . . I see an older woman with wrinkles and soft white hair whisper something to her friend, then both of them cackle . . . lub dub, lub dub . . . I bolt.

I take Viv in my arms, on top of Diana, who's still in the Bjorn, leaving the groceries in the cart, and make my way out through the automatic sliding doors.

As the fresh air hits my skin, I let the tears fall down my face. My lashes are wet and my nose burns.

I put both the girls in their car seats and buckle their harnesses and chest clips. I get into the front seat and let out a sigh. I descend into sobs with my hands on the wheel. We're all crying, all three of us. I let out a laugh because this whole situation has been so terrible it's kind of comical. Then we cry the entire way home.

I felt so much shame after that trip. It was easy for me to feel shame in my early years as a mom. I was extra sensitive because I wanted to get this parenting thing right more than anything in the world—so much so that I became insecure in my ability as a mother.

So, when someone rolled their eyes at me, it cut deep. When someone laughed in my direction, I couldn't help but think they were laughing at me. It made me feel less than. Not good enough. It made me feel like I was failing.

Especially someone who is a recovering perfectionist and people pleaser. Before I had kids, I always felt like I didn't belong. That's why I turned to anorexia and bulimia. They kept me safe. If I was binging, purging, and safely studying, I didn't have to go to the high school party where I was sure to be judged for something awkward I'd do or say if I let my guard down. If I were at home binging on peanut butter on a cinnamon raison bagel, cereal, and anything I could get my hands on, I didn't have to try and try and try, even if it were only for a half hour. I already was studying twice as hard in school to do just as well as the naturally smart kids because of my processing issue. I had to be careful about everything I ate to be just as skinny as the naturally skinny kids. It was exhausting. I just wanted to breathe and not feel for a bit—bulimia was my breath.

By the time I had Viv, I was only two years into my recovery journey from eating disorders, so I still cared so much about everyone's opinions of me. And how people would think of me as a mother meant everything because motherhood was my most important role yet.

I followed a list of invisible rules that were supposed to make me a better mom. I had to breastfeed, to learn to cook even though it was never "my thing," and be attentive to my children 24/7 with no screens or breaks. Because if one person thought I was wrong, I was a bad mom.

I absorbed everyone else's opinions. I was so unsure of myself, a mom chameleon. If someone told me "I should give the baby a bottle already" when I was struggling to breastfeed, I'd cry that I was a terrible mom because I was starving my baby. I'd obsess over every decision. It was so easy to throw me off and make me question every choice I'd make.

Being a mom chameleon was causing me to live in a constant state of terror, thinking I was falling short, and that I needed to be better, somehow. It was filled with so much worry. And even when I followed all the rules, I still felt like I wasn't good enough. I wasn't good enough at getting the baby to bed, I wasn't good enough at cooking or cleaning. I didn't have my kids enrolled in enough baby classes. My kids didn't eat enough vegetables. I was a failure.

I would go to bed trying to hold back waves of tears.

This line of thinking led to a lot of sleepless nights. A lot of shame. A lot of time wasted doubting instead of enjoying my kids and learning who they were.

I always imagined myself as one of those mothers who would breastfeed as long as I could. I pictured myself sitting in the park on a nice summer day with a cool wind hitting my face with a baby gracefully nursing under my cover. There would be people around me, talking, laughing, and carrying on, but I wouldn't care, because I'd be in my own little nursing sanctuary.

I had looked up all the benefits of nursing, and it was hands down the way I was going. I only put bottles on my baby registry for backup. I believed in my heart that I was born to be a mother, so this had to come easy. It just had to.

Until it didn't . . .

When Vivienne was born, she came out screaming, covered in creamy white, and was placed on my chest. I wasn't sure what to do with her, to calm her. I read books, took a class, but wasn't sure what to do on the spot.

It was as if someone said "lights, camera, action," and now I had stage fright.

"Do you think she's hungry?" I choked out, everything around me feeling strange, dreamlike. I was shaking with nerves and exhaustion. This all didn't seem real. *I just gave birth to my baby.*

"You can try," said the nurse.

I had to feed my baby. I was trying to place her on my boob, but she was too busy wailing and wailing, newborn cries filling my ears. I felt clueless, tired, and my entire body ached. She was too upset to eat, probably exhausted and shocked from her intense transition into the world.

I stroked her back instead, taking her in. We both needed to rest.

After they cleaned both of us up and checked us, they gave her back to me. She looked adorable. I was completely enchanted. She was wearing her hospital hat, eyes sealed shut, wrapped in her swaddle like a baby burrito. I took her and held her close. Gosh, I couldn't believe she was mine. A couple of minutes later, she started to fuss. I assumed she wanted to eat but was not sure how to go about it.

"Can you please show me how to breastfeed?" I asked Tori, the nurse with a thin ponytail and a warm smile, in a low voice. I winced at how desperate, anxious, and uncertain I sounded.

The nurse started to show me how to do it. She walked over and brought Vivienne to my chest.

"Hold your breast in your hand and compress it to make a nipple sandwich." Her voice was husky. Her prominent blue eyes matched her blue scrubs.

"A nipple sandwich," I repeated, trying to visualize what that would look like. "Like this?" I asked, doing what I thought she meant.

"Yes, that's good." She maneuvered my hands only slightly.

"Aw that's kind of cute, you're going to eat a sandwich," I smiled at Vivienne, who scrunched her face and continued fussing.

"Then bring her to your breast." I do.

"Am I doing it?" I asked.

Hmm, was that a latch? I think she's sucking. Something hurts. Oh my gosh it hurts!

"Not quite. You know what? Let me call our lactation coach, Sarah." Tori left the room, leaving me with a not-very-happy Vivienne.

"Don't you worry sweet girl," I paused, admiring her small features, "Mommy is working on getting you some food."

Before I knew it, I had a small team huddled around me—a lactation coach, the nurse, and Jonathan—all trying to get Vivienne to latch as she fussed and fussed some more. They spent two hours helping me while I learned so much—like how the colostrum in my boobs was full of immunities and great nutrition but Vivienne didn't need that much of it. Her stomach was only the size of a marble. I felt relief that was all I had to feed her, since I was struggling.

I was told to try the football hold, where she was tucked under my arm and lying along the side I was feeding on, which was met with "She's getting there."

And then the cradle hold, where she lays across my lap, facing me, received an "Oh, so close."

After failed attempt after failed attempt, I dropped my face into my hands. "My baby's going to starve!" I said, voice cracking, as they comforted me.

Then she finally latched. We had one good feed on one side. Victory.

But it was a battle every single time I fed her. It never came easily when Vivienne and I were alone. I went to extraordinary lengths to try to make it work. I kept trying and trying. I got nipple shields because one of my nipples was inverted. I wanted her to bond with me. To feel the special connection that breastfeeding babies have. To give her antibodies. To be considered a good mom. To not feel like a complete failure.

Two lactation consultants, hundreds of dollars, cuts on my nipples and shooting pains, my mental health plummeting, and so many tears later, Vivienne still wasn't getting it. It was anything but magical. We weren't bonding at all. We were clashing.

I eventually hooked myself up to the pump, fearing that was the only option. My baby hated my boobs.

This way Vivienne would still get all the antibodies. And yes, it took more time, but I felt like it was my only option. I then spent the next six months exclusively pumping, hooked up to a machine, plugged into a wall, that took my nipples and squeezed milk out of them into little bottles connected to them. I had a to-go pump too. I have pumped everywhere: in a taxi, in a bathroom stall on a dirty floor, in a car, and at a work desk in the nook of my apartment.

I dreamed about being done. I hated every second I heard the "wah-oh, wah-oh," as the pump suctioned my milk, but I still did it. It was pumping and bottle-feeding followed by washing bottle parts and storing bags in the freezer all day and night. My nipples were cracked, but I kept going until I hit six months because that's what the American Academy of Pediatrics recommended. Because that's what good moms do, right? And when I stopped, I felt instantly guilty and selfish. I immediately regretted my decision. It was hard for me to escape the societal pressure of "breast is best" even when I secretly felt so much freedom and much happier.

The first time I poured Vivienne a bottle of formula out in public after running out of stored breastmilk, I felt eyes staring at me, death glares from some (at least in my mind), as if trying to look through me to see what's wrong with me that I wasn't breastfeeding. Because everyone knows "breast Is best"; countless studies on the benefits exist. My heart stuttered as I could only imagine those people thinking I was lazy or a bad mom. I couldn't escape the feeling of failure, like I let Vivienne down. I hid when feeding her on every outing after that.

When Diana was born, I tried breastfeeding again, but when it failed after one lactation coach, I went straight to pumping exclusively, knowing it wasn't in the cards for me. But that time I spent the next fourteen months pumping because of my insecurity to be seen with formula, to be judged, to be made to be felt less than as a mom. And I hated every minute I was on that pump and not holding Diana or playing a game with Vivienne.

The time spent plugged in was even more challenging with two kids under two vying for my attention. I pumped while watching two-year-old Vivienne spin around and try to pull out the plug. My "Noooo" was met with a mischievous smile.

I'd pump as I'd see Vivienne sneak toward Diana on her tip toes.

"Vivienne," I'd warn, the corners of my mouth twisting downward, letting her know I was watching her every move.

But Viv (being Viv) didn't care—that "no" only motivated her to keep going. She kept walking toward six-month-old Diana in her baby bouncer and held her hand out palm facing downwards and opened it.

"Vivienne, you better not hit her head!" My heart clanged as my voice rose.

I'd then hear a sharp blow and Diana's loud cries as I'd scream "Vivienne Lazar!" and stop pumping to calm Diana down and try to teach Viv that her attention seeking behavior wasn't OK.

I had so much milk that I'd wake up leaking and engorged. As much as I hated it and how time consuming it was, I had a hard time stopping.

I only gave myself guiltless permission to stop at fourteen months because I was pregnant with Julia and wanted some time without pumping in-between.

With Julia, I was induced in the early morning. She came so slowly, and then all at once. Suddenly at 9:30 PM she was coming, and it felt like my insides were a Slip 'n Slide. She slid through and it felt like she ripped everything apart on her way down. I was in so much pain, screaming, as sweat glistened on every surface of my body. I felt everything. I clenched the sides of the hospital bed and pushed once, and there she was in Dr. Ng's hands.

She was placed on my chest, and I cried from happiness and from the pain of my entire midsection and insides throbbing. My brain felt like it was sloshing around. I held her close. My shoulders melted with relief that she had arrived and was healthy. The love I had for this baby was so big already, it was all consuming. I knew I would forever feel as if I was pulled by a magnet toward her. I then looked into her eyes, and broke eye contact, blinking rapidly, caught up in my thoughts.

I didn't know how I would pump and take care of three kids under three. I had planned for it, had my pump all ready. But as soon as I held her in my arms, I felt unsettled and overwhelmed when thinking about it.

It struck me suddenly. I knew by now that Julia wouldn't latch. I never had the magical experience of a newborn feeding at my breast and sleeping sweetly in my arms, so pumping was my only choice.

That night I got to experience Julia as a baby, too. She wasn't calm like Diana. That first night was sleepless—she was up, angry, crying, red faced, and wanted nothing but to be held.

I leaned my back against the hospital bed and let out a deep breath.

"What's wrong?" Jonathan asked.

My stomach flip-flopped. I didn't want to admit my thoughts. Tears welled in my eyes.

"Dani, what's wrong?" Jonathan repeated. His tired eyes were filled with worry.

"I just don't think I can pump, on top of taking care of Diana and Viv, working, cooking, cleaning, laundry, and keep doing mommy and me classes, and playdates." My voice crackled and fell apart.

His mouth softened. "Dani, you don't have to pump. You can use formula. It's OK. Weren't you a formula baby?"

"Exactly, I'm all sorts of messed up." I let out a laugh through the tears.

"But seriously. Fed is best. You'd never judge another mom for using formula. You'd know she had her reasons." He now had his hand in my hair, stroking it.

"You are right. I just want to do what's best for Julia." I said, looking at her, sleeping peacefully in my arms.

"What's best for Julia is what's best for you. She wants to spend time with you. She doesn't care if she's on formula or breastmilk." He pleaded with me.

"I care. She'll get my antibodies. But I see what you mean." I said blinking back tears.

"I'm just telling you things you have said to me about people formula feeding." His brows pinched. The moment held as I took in his words that were my words. I must give myself the grace I gave and continue to give other moms.

"I'm glad you listen." Jonathan and I exchanged a look.

"Well, listen to yourself." He slung an arm around my shoulder.

"Touché," I said swiping the tears from under my eyes.

So, I fed Julia formula, and it felt like a weight had been lifted. She was happy and thriving. And this time, I fed her formula everywhere. I didn't care if anyone was staring at me. Part of the reason was, who had time to care? I had three kids under three. Another reason is, I finally realized that breastfeeding was not what made me a good mom.

So, I fed her formula at school pickup and didn't care if all the other moms were looking. I fed her in the park on a beautiful sunny day, watching her older sisters and helping them off the slide. I fed her in a car on the way to a play space as she'd sink against her car seat. I fed her at my desk while doing work. I fed her out in the middle of a mall while breaking off buttery pieces of soft pretzel for my older kids. And I didn't care what anyone thought.

My logic was flawed by shame. Society gives us a deep desire to breastfeed because we are made to feel like if we don't, we're a failure. Even the nurses at the hospital push it on us. We know the benefits, so it's hard to say no. But breast isn't always best for every family, and that's OK, too.

There are many ways to feed a baby and every parent's journey is different. All parents have a reason for what they choose to do. Some only breastfeed. Some breastfeed and bottle-feed pumped milk. Some only use formula and some use a combination of all of them. Because a fed baby is best.

I also came to the realization that someone would always disagree with how I did things as a mother. People would always be looking to tear me down to make themselves feel better or validate their own beliefs. Because in our society, a mother suffers guilt no matter what she does.

If she's on top of her kids making sure everything's OK, she's called a helicopter mom, and if she lets them run around as she sits on the side talking to a friend, she's neglectful.

If she prefers cooking from scratch and organic everything, her kids are "going to go crazy on junk food when they go to someone else's house." And if she feeds them donuts and muffins for breakfast some mornings because she's in a rush or just because, then her kids are unhealthy.

If she breastfeeds and doesn't produce enough milk, and her baby isn't thriving, then she's a failure. But when she adds formula, she's more of a failure for not giving her baby all breast milk.

If she stays home with her kids, she should be working—"How can her family financially keep up?" But if she's working, she's met with "They're only little once."

If she hasn't lost the postpartum weight, "Gosh, she let herself go." But if she did, "Wow, she must not eat, spend hours working out, and neglect her children."

And the sad thing is most of that judgment comes from other moms.

And it happens all the time. Just the other day I had a mom over who had a little girl Charli's age, around two years old. Charli was watching Mickey Mouse Clubhouse eating Cheez Doodles. Her Cheez-Doodle-orange-stained hands touched everything around the kitchen, making imprints.

"Wow, I'd never let my toddler eat those," Dahlia murmured softly. Her hair was long and brown with streaks of honey and she wore a perfectly put-together Brooklyn inspired hip outfit. A crop top, jeans with rips, and a red and black flannel. Her toddler was holding onto her leg, eating a squeeze pouch fruit and veggie blend while watching Charli dance to the "Hot Dog" song. Dahlia was systematically dismantling an orange, her face serious.

"It wasn't my top choice. Viv was eating them one day and she just screamed nonstop for them. I finally gave in and now she's on a Cheese Doodle kick." I said defending my parenting choice.

"I mean, you don't have to give in," she said placing a slice of orange into her mouth. *I mean, you don't have to be so damn judgmental,* I wanted to respond. Because we'll see how well she does when she has four kids. She was all high and mighty with her one mild-mannered child. But instead, I stayed silent. My pulse speeding up.

"Daisy seems to really like Mickey Mouse Clubhouse," I said, noticing her eyes transfixed by the television.

"Well, she never watches screens, so this is a treat for her." Another jab. I didn't know if she meant for it to be or was just stating facts, but it was a stab to my heart.

We fell into an uncomfortable silence.

Charli was dancing again. Her Cheese Doodle hands waved in the air. I let out a cackle because this was Dahlia's worst nightmare, but to me it was normal life.

This mother was not my people. Clearly. But this kind of judgment is commonplace with moms of little kids.

Moms are the hardest on each other. We're the ones going after each other in mom groups, at pick up, in the grocery store, on social media, everywhere. We're breaking each other's spirits. We can't hide our beliefs in public like our religion and politics, so we're out in the open, bottle feeding or breastfeeding and giving our kids cookies or cut up fruit at 10 AM. Most of the times I have been shamed it was by other moms. And they've given me their opinions, and it didn't matter if I had no interest in hearing them. You'd think that we would understand each other best because we know how hard motherhood is, but it's mostly not the case.

We need to change this, and instead of assuming the worst, we should assume we are all doing our best. If a friend shows up late, we should know better than anyone it's because she let the baby who was up half the night teething nap longer, or she couldn't find her son's shoe, and then while looking, he knocked his milk on his lap and needed to change his clothes, or her youngest had a tantrum. And we shouldn't be mad if she doesn't answer our text immediately—she's not ignoring you. She read it, and then the toddler had a tantrum, and she had to calm him down, or her kids got into a screaming match, or the potty-training child had another accident, and she forgot to respond. In motherhood, there are always unavoidable incidents that are out of our hands.

Women used to be pitted against each other. When I was a teen in the early 2000s, all I heard about was Britney Spears vs. Christina Aguilera, Selena Gomez vs. Miley Cyrus. It was a race to the top, and every woman for herself.

But that mentality has thankfully changed, and women are now supporting each other to the top. This needs to be seen more in mommy world. Especially when there's no right way to mother.

We all have reasons we do things the way we do. There's no one size fits all. We all come from different places, have different personalities, different backgrounds and have experiences that influence the way we think, and the choices we make as parents.

We need each other's support. We are on the same side—we all want to raise good humans. So, we need to speak our imperfect truths that our toddler ate a blue crayon or our three-year-old decided it would be fun to pee in the bathroom garbage. Because no one's motherhood is perfect, and we're not alone in our day-to-day chaos. To me, there's something so comforting about that.

Because no family is good at everything.

Take my house. We aren't the house of homemade baby food. We aren't the house with babies who sleep through the night and in their own rooms from day one. We aren't the house of no screens. We have screens everywhere, and I'm happy to turn one on if it can help avoid a fight or I can make dinner. We aren't always organized. We have rushed mornings where we're often running late.

But we're also a house that shows so much love through hugs and kisses, and by saying "I love you" all the time. We are a house that's good at having hard conversations. We are a "play date" house that always has friends over. We are a house that supports passions and dreams. We are a house that's good at saying sorry, to name a few.

There is no right way in parenting. Parenting is complicated. It's not about reading every book and studying like you are taking a test. It's hands-on, and about loving them, trusting your gut, messing up, and trying again.

In a society that knows "everything" and places too many expectations on moms, if we listen to everyone else, we're always going to fall short. We're going to waste too much time doubting ourselves and trying to be something we're not—when our kids just want us. Because no one loves our kids better or knows them better. So, just by being ourselves, and loving them, we're the mom our kids need—and by realizing this, we'll become better moms.

"Do you want me to carry something?" Elise, a mother from Vivienne's second grade class asks. She has open hands and is getting ready to grab one of the backpacks I'm carrying from my girls.

"Oh, thank you so much but I got it. I am used to it." My mouth says, as I graciously answer her. But my brain says, *Why can't you take the help?* I feel my nose running from the cold wind. I am holding two backpacks on one arm, a diaper bag weighing me down on my back, and a complaining Charli in the other arm. But I do this five days a week at my girls' elementary school pick up.

She frowns, "OK, you are truly supermom." And walks ahead with her daughter.

"No, I'm not. I'm very much human and feel it." I say this loud enough so my kids can hear, as they trail me.

Superheroes have superpowers that they use with little effort. While I have to walk all the way to the car with my bags and kids, Superman could fly to the car like it's no big deal, and Mister Fantastic could stretch all the way to the car. But here I am walking, step by step, my back aching, and out of breath. My "superpowers" take too much effort and time for me to be considered a superhero.

I don't want my children to think they have to be superheroes, too. I want them to know mommy is human, so they don't aspire to be this unattainable superhero, but can be human with all the mess that comes with that. I want them to know they don't have to hold it all because it's impossible to hold it all, all the time.

There are many days where I can't hold it all.

Where I'm walking to the car, and I start dropping things.

Maybe Charli's having a fit or there's just too much for my hands with added art projects, jackets, a hat Diana decided she didn't want to wear, on top of the backpacks, and a diaper bag.

So, sometimes I'll drop things along the way, a hat, a pair of gloves, a jacket.

Sweet Julia will say, "I got it, Mommy," and bend down and hold it until we get to the car.

Other times I'll ask Viv or Diana, "Can you pick up that hat, please?" or "Can you take your bag?" My arm roped with backpacks starting to fall over.

"Yes." They will take their backpacks and place them on their backs.

But at the same time, I have been conditioned since I was little to not be a burden and to feel like asking for help is a weakness, even though I now know otherwise.

So, I am often a mom who pushes and pushes and pushes some more. Because I'm supposed to be "Mommy." And I don't want to admit that I need help being mommy sometimes, because it sounds like I'm admitting defeat. I am the one who carried each of my kids for nine months. I am the one who wanted four children—not my partner or strangers asking to give me a hand, me. I don't want to ask people to stop their lives when I am the one who wanted this. There have been times where I felt like I needed help but haven't asked for it because of the false belief that I'd be a burden or can't handle my own kids. And when it comes to motherhood, we all will run ourselves into the ground to prove that we can handle it.

I have also heard people being judgmental to moms who have extra help. I have heard, "Oh, well she has help at home," when talking about a mother who lives with her own parents or has hired a nanny. It's an attitude where the help somehow dismisses all that she does each day, and it's not OK.

And truthfully, part of the problem is I want to do it all. I want to be able to be everywhere for everyone, holding all the things, and getting all the snacks, all at once. But I am human, and it's impossible.

I am now at a point in my motherhood journey where I accept help and will ask for it if I'm in a bind. I still feel guilt for "burdening other people," even though I know that's a false self-limiting belief. I am not perfect, and this is something I need to work on in my own motherhood, but I am a work in progress and have gotten better about it.

I remember a time recently where Charli woke up next to me sounding like a seal with a barking cough. Her nose was raw and her cheeks were bright red. She couldn't stop coughing as she struggled for breaths in-between barks.

"Oh, my goodness, my poor baby," I heard more barking noises, and Charli had so many tears dripping down her face, leaking onto her pajama top, hands spread out rasping "uh" between barks, because she didn't have the "p" sound to form "up" yet.

She puked all over her clothes and on the floor, making Jonathan gag. I carefully took off the sour smelling clothes and comforted her. I picked her up and brought her to the bathroom, turning on the bathtub faucet. I squirted two pumps of soap as I heard Charli's seal barks and cries.

"You poor sweet girl," I kissed her forehead, and wiped her tears off her cheeks with a towel.

A second later, Julia came into the bathroom, "Mommy!" she said, tears forming in her eyes. She was completely flushed, barking like a seal, too. Her curly hair messy from sleep. I pressed my lips to her forehead. She had a fever.

"Come on!" I heard. At first, I didn't know who shrieked it. I turned around.

Me. I did.

"Oh no. You poor things. This is terrible." My voice lifted three full octaves as my heart twisted with agony and disbelief. The both of them. *Really?*

Charli was in my arms with Julia wrapped around my legs so I couldn't move. Both were crying between coughs as the water filled the tub. They both needed my attention, but I'm only one person. My skin tingled under everyone's grip. *How was I supposed to help get the older two ready?* My whole body got hot thinking about it.

"What's wrong with Julia and Charli?" Diana came in, still in pajamas, rubbing her eyes. Her hair was wild, sticking straight up. I still hadn't woken Viv up for school.

"This is not good." I mumbled to myself. My ears rang with everything happening.

I called my mom, and screamed into the phone so she could hear me over the girls' cries, "I am going to call the doctor at 8:30 to get an appointment, but I need you to come with me. Charli and Julia have croup." Diana placed her hands over her ears.

"Oh no, of course. Let me know what time to be over." She said. "Is that them crying like that? I'll be over soon."

It was so loud and chaotic, I couldn't even scream goodbye. I just hung up.

My mom came and helped me that day, which didn't only help me get through, but helped my kids. I couldn't have given them enough care alone for how sick they both were. With my mom coming over, I was able to be a better mom to each of them. I could hold one, while my mom held the other, and whoever needed me more had my full attention while the other one had my mom's love. That day taught me that sometimes asking for help is better for my kids, too.

But I have learned to outsource some things, like using a cleaning service and ordering school hot lunches for Viv. Because no matter how much we'd all love to do everything, we can't, because mommy is human.

So, it's OK if you need "help being a mom."

It's OK, if you call your mom, a friend, a trusted-someone for their opinions on big decisions and small ones when it comes to your kids because they all seem important. It's OK if you hire a babysitter so you and your partner can finally get a night out, or a professional cleaner once a week, so you aren't constantly cleaning up messes. It's OK if your partner does bedtime duties most nights, and if you need to buy premade dinners or rely on school lunches.

No matter how hard we try to do it all, the weight of all things—the pressure parenting puts on your entire being and being only one person with so many hats—is impossible to do totally alone.

So, we should never feel wrong for asking for help in the first place. It doesn't matter if we're a working mom, a stay-at-home mom, or a combination, or whether we have one child or five. Because the truth is, we all need help with being a mom sometimes, so no one should judge anyone else for what they do.

When I was little, I remember sneaking into my parent's room when I had a nightmare, and tip toeing past my mom to my dad's side where I'd tap on my dad's shoulder.

"Can I sleep with you? I had a nightmare." I'd whisper, afraid to wake my mom, knowing she'd send me back.

My dad would startle awake. "Oh, come lay down," he'd say, his voice warbled and low.

He'd fall fast asleep again as I snuggled in close.

My mom was very strict about me sleeping in my own bed. So, when I became a new mom to Vivienne, I knew that she would start in a bassinet in our room and then move to a crib in her own room. *That's what good moms did,* I thought.

So I would make sure to wake up when I couldn't hold my heavy eyelids open anymore, even when she was over a year, and I didn't have to fear her slipping from my exhausted grip. Also, the American Academy of Pediatrics cautioned against it. They say that cosleeping increases the chance of sleep-related fatalities such as sudden infant death syndrome, accidental suffocation, and strangulation. I never thought about cosleeping—I was afraid of both the judgment and the risks.

But when I gave birth to Diana, things changed. I had more on my plate juggling two kids, and I kept her in our room, in a crib, for over a year. Every child after, the time in our room increased more and more, and I let them into our bed earlier and earlier.

Now, two years since we brought Charli home, we still cosleep with her in between us each night, and I don't plan on moving her out anytime soon. And every night I hear our bedroom door creak open and see the outline of curly hair sneaking in. It's Julia, coming in like clockwork, and as she gets closer, I prop my head up and squint through the darkness until I can make her out in the pitch blackness. Her smile lighting up the dark.

I lift the blanket and move over to let her in. I kiss her on her head and snuggle her in close.

I hold her close all night. I feel her heart beating against mine and the slow inhale and exhale of her breath.

I have Charli on one side of me and Julia on the other, and I can't think of a better way to sleep.

I received the same judgment when I admitted to lying down with my kids before they went to sleep. People warned me against it: "They won't be able to fall asleep at night without you." I have heard, "It's a bad habit." And now that I do it, I will never go back.

"OK Julia. It's bedtime, sweet girl," I said, so excited to finally start getting all the things on my to-do list finished. Vivienne, eight, and Diana, six, can entertain themselves and each other, but if Julia and Charli are up, it's impossible to get anything done.

"Can we do one more page of Waldo?" she asked me.

"One more and then it's bedtime," I whispered, as I narrowed my eyes on her.

"OK," She smiled, scrunching her cute button nose. Her head scanned the page in front of her. "I found him!"

"I think that's just a look-alike," I pointed out. This Waldo imposter had a ponytail.

"Oh, there he is," She jumped back in her bed, confident she chose the right one.

"Good job. It's not easy to find Waldo." I reached over to high-five her, and she met my hand with a loud smack. I took the book off her bed and put it on her dresser and turned on the shusher, a soothing "shush" sound machine, right behind it. The "shhhhh" of the shushing sound played as I went to shut off the lights.

I went up to her, giving her a big kiss on her forehead. "Goodnight, I love you so much." I kissed her two more times on her cheeks as she giggled.

I was about to leave the room. I had my hand on the doorknob when I heard, "Mommy, can you lie with me?"

"Yes," I glanced over my shoulder at her and took a steadying breath, because everything inside of me wanted to say NO. I unfolded my arms and made my way back to her bed. We talked about her day. She poured her heart out about every detail as I felt her warm cheeks against my chest. And then when she was drifting between wakefulness and dreaming, she nestled against me, and I held her close until she fell asleep.

I want to parent my way. To me this isn't a bad habit. I know soon I'll miss these days where my closeness was the comfort Julia needed to feel safe enough to drift asleep.

I know they'll all eventually go on and have their own lives. They are supposed to! They'll come home and want to go to their room, then their apartment, then their home. I'll no longer be the center of their universe, only a supporting role. But I'll be happy knowing every moment spent with them has built our relationship into a trusting one, where they can call me when they fall, where we accept each other's differences and support them, a relationship of mutual respect and love where they can always come home—back to their safe space, me, their sisters, and their father, where they'll be endlessly supported.

I'll take the judgment if it comes with all that any day.

I was in the grocery store recently, each of my three girls squeezing my wrists or elbows, Charli in my Bjorn. We needed cupcakes for Mimi's birthday.

Viv grabbed a bag of Ruffles from one of the aisles, "Oh we need these!" She handed them to me.

"We have two bags at home already, let's stick to cupcakes." I said, placing them back on the shelf. Charli started whining and pointing to a box of Teddy Grahams. I grabbed them and handed them to her.

"That's not fair. Why does she get something?" Vivienne pouted.

"She's a baby. I'm not buying them. It will just keep her quiet for a couple of minutes." I smiled at Charli as she wrapped her arms around the Teddy Grahams, protecting them, her eyes twinkling as she smiled.

We finally got to the bakery section. Diana and Julia perused the black-and-white cookies, the rainbow cookies, chocolate fudge cookies, and then we got to the cupcakes. Diana picked up vanilla cupcakes with rainbow sprinkles. Julia and Viv picked up chocolate cupcakes with chocolate sprinkles.

"Let's get one pack of vanilla cupcakes, and one pack of chocolate cupcakes." I paused, "I think we are ready to go. Good job girls." I placed my hand out for a high-five.

The girls each took a swing, slapping until my hand tingled.

Charli threw her box of Teddy Grahams on the floor and now was pointing to the cupcakes saying "Mama, Mama." I picked up the Teddy Grahams and handed her vanilla cupcakes. She smiled for two seconds, and then threw those to the ground, pointing at the cupcakes Julia had in her hands.

"Charli. I can't take Julia's from her." She started pointing and whining some more. I handed her some of her own chocolate cupcakes. She immediately threw them to the floor. I inhaled deeply through my nose.

"OK, let's go. Charli is being a brat." Charli was throwing a fit in my Bjorn, but I wasn't going to give her Julia's cupcakes, and I didn't care how loud she was or how many looks I got. She was not going to get her way. She screamed and wailed and wailed some more.

I saw people look at me with disbelief for letting her carry on as I went to self-checkout and scanned my items.

"Mommy, this is embarrassing," Viv's cheeks turned red, and she started fidgeting uncomfortably. "Can you get her to stop?" She moaned.

"She's a toddler having a fit, how is that embarrassing? It will stop soon. This is what toddlers do. Stop caring about what people think, Miss Viv." I said as I placed my credit card into the machine and picked up the cupcakes.

"Ugh, just make her stop, Mom." Vivienne moaned again.

Also, what is me getting angry or embarrassed going to do? Kids will be kids. They are not meant to be quiet, still, and neat. They're meant to be messy—they're still learning. Besides, she's not having a meltdown, flailing, and screaming to give me a hard time, she's just having a hard time. Her outburst is her not being able to handle her big emotions and not being able to tell me why she's upset.

A couple of years back I'd be a walking, breathing bottle of seltzer, panic tucked inside of me all bottled up. Instead, my own snort-laugh surprised me as I thought about how ridiculous my toddler was being and Viv's teenager-like reaction.

On the way out I shivered as a breeze slipped down my shirt.

"Julia, Viv, and Diana, hold on to me when we cross the street." I said, as they grabbed onto my diaper bag and jacket as we started crossing to the minivan.

Charli looked up at me. I handed her a bottle and she put it in her mouth, taking big calming gulps. I inhaled deeply. My heart stopped beating so fast, only because the sound of her crying is like nails on a chalkboard. But I couldn't care less about what anyone around me thought. I knew I was a good mom, and it had nothing to do with how my kids behaved for a moment in time at the grocery store. They were just being kids. My eyes used to get watery with shame when this happened in public, but today they remained clear and focused on my children throughout. I was brave and confident. I was a mom.

— 6 —

Earlier Isn't How You Win Parenting Gold

WHEN VIVIENNE WAS six months old, I heard from a friend about a magical unicorn of a class on the Upper East Side in Manhattan that would have my child speaking sooner. People swore by it.

"We need to do it!" My closest mom friend at the time, Patricia, said. She was holding her seven-month-old son close, a pacifier in his mouth. Her blonde hair was tied up into a neat ponytail. Her cheeks were rosy from the August sun.

I narrowed my eyes. "What do they do to get them to speak? Viv only babbles and says Dada, but she doesn't seem to associate it with Jonathan." I wrestled with my diaper bag, looking for a teether. I felt sweat forming on my hairline. Vivienne was in the stroller looking around. She was playing with a toy, but I could tell she wanted something to gnaw on.

"We will see. But it's worth a try." She placed her son in her stroller as I gave Viv a banana teether.

"Yes. Sure."

That night I got a text: "Get ready to sign up. Remember there's a waitlist."

"I'm ready!" I texted back.

I signed her up, even though it was a bit pricey, but I justified it because it was going to help her language development.

The first class, we walked to a beautiful church made of red brick on the Upper East Side. I saw the stroller parking and parallel parked my stroller next to a pink UPPAbaby Vista and a Bugaboo. I picked Vivienne up and placed my diaper bag on my back.

After I walked into the church, I was told by a tall, bearded security guard to go downstairs. I followed his pointing hand to a hidden staircase behind another door.

I walked down the yellow stairs. I felt like I was Dorothy and Viv was Toto, and we were following the Yellow Brick Road, walking into the unknown. I pushed open a big white door to an all-yellow room. There was another mom standing there. She had freckles and perfectly curled bright red hair. I was amazed she had time to use a curling iron. She was wearing a Lily Pulitzer dress with purple and red flowers and big hoops hanging from her ears. Her son was walking around.

"Hi, I'm Danielle. Who is this little guy?" I asked. I was wearing black champion shorts and a baggy t-shirt covered in sweat.

"This is Jaeger," she smiled.

"So cute. Hey buddy," I waved his way and he smiled back, two teeth revealing themselves, his strawberry blonde hair wild. "Have you heard anything about this class?" She snapped her fingers at her son, who was holding something gross from the ground. He dropped it and smirked mischievously.

90 Danielle Sherman-Lazar

"Oh yes. My Jaeger has been in it since he was six months. He knows about twenty words already." She said matter-of-factly, a cloud of Skinn by Titan hitting me in the face.

"Wow. Ten months and twenty words." I nodded my head, completely impressed. I would be impressed if Viv could say mama and not just babble dada by then.

"Well, I am a speech pathologist, too." Of course, she was. "I work with him all the time." Of course, she did.

"He's like a walking advertisement for you," I smiled at him. "Speaking of walking, look at him go like a pro." It was weird for me to see such a little baby walking. I couldn't even imagine Viv walking so young. She hardly sat up without falling straight back and almost slamming her head every time. I catch her right before she hits. Usually.

"He never crawled; he just went straight to walking." Of course, he did. He was obviously a very advanced child. I couldn't help but feel like Viv and I were falling behind. Were all the other babies in class going to be like Jaeger? The waiting area started to fill. I saw a baby with cherub cheeks with a couple wisps of brown hair in a bow. I saw another with darker skin and black curly hair, his eyes so big they took up his whole face. Another was crawling around babbling, his mother in a sundress with heels, glued to her phone.

Other nannies and moms started coming in, babies in hand. Then Patricia came running in with Aaron in her arms.

"I thought we were going to be late. Aaron had a poop blowout right before we left our apartment. I had to change his entire outfit." I smiled. My person had arrived.

"Aw, Aaron, did you do that to Mommy? That wasn't very nice," I said in a baby voice. Aaron's gummy smile was on full display.

A woman opened the door and let us into a blue room with a big black rug in the shape of a circle on the floor.

"Did I miss anything?" Patricia asked.

"Nope. We just met the next Bill Gates, Jaeger. Twenty words at ten months and walking." I whispered as we walked into the class.

"Oh, I see . . ." She smirked.

"Sit around the circle, everyone. Caretakers, we don't want you on your phones because we don't want you to distract the babies. So please answer your last message now and turn off your phone." The teacher said in a booming voice.

"Wow, there's some FBI classified stuff going on," I whispered to Patricia, putting my phone on vibrate and placing it into my diaper bag.

"Seriously," she cackled, answering one last text before putting her phone away, too.

Viv suddenly got upset so I rocked her back and forth, cooing, "It's OK!" and handed her a pacifier. "Viv, you are not going to be invited back to this elite class with this behavior." I whispered to her, laughing to myself at the ridiculousness of all of it. I settled her and then sat back down.

The class started.

"Buh buh ball," the teacher pointed to a ball. A puppet Elmo started talking about the "buh buh ball." This went on for about forty-five minutes. Viv clapped her hands together at times. At others, she was fussy, and I fed her a bottle.

They did the same routine each week for twelve weeks, the same exact class because that's how they learn language—"through the repetition." And yes, I'm sure it helped some babies. But I came to loathe it, continuing only because I paid way too much money for it. That class made me feel like I wasn't doing enough, and we were falling behind. I'd leave every week thinking I wasn't a good mom.

Now that I'm a mom of four, my perspective has shifted significantly. I have learned something that has been life-changing: reaching developmental milestones earlier doesn't always mean better, and it doesn't make you a better mom.

It shouldn't matter if one mom's kid walked at one year, and yours walked at eighteen months. Or if her kid potty-trained at two years old, but yours didn't potty-train until four years old. Or if her kid recognized all his letters and numbers before pre-school but yours had no interest until almost four. Or if her kid was sleeping through the night by three months but yours wasn't sleeping through the night until two years old. None of that matters.

Reaching developmental milestones early means nothing about a child in the long run. A college professor won't wonder how old her students were when they could count to one hundred or spell their names. He won't care what age they started preschool. And no one will know or care if the Harvard graduate or the CEO had a pacifier or didn't potty-train until five years old.

I came to that realization for a combination of reasons. One of them was when Diana wasn't speaking at eighteen months. Diana had a speech delay coupled with bad anxiety, and that didn't make me a bad mom. I was actually a good mom for being proactive about getting her the help she needed. It also didn't make Diana any less smart or less of an amazing kid. She just has had to work harder on it because it doesn't come naturally to her like most kids. That extra work, the three days a week of speech therapy, and overcoming her anxiety daily to get her comfortable in a school environment, teaches her resilience at a young age.

At six years old, she's no longer difficult to understand; her speech isn't perfect, but she's getting there, and that's all that matters. This experience helped me let the pressure go. Everyone goes at their own pace. I'm no longer rushing through their childhoods and making them miss out because I'm too worried and overwhelmed trying to make them meet milestones.

Charli at two years old has a speech delay, too. Even with the perspective of Diana and her speech delay, it's hard not to notice how behind she is. We hang out with a little girl her age with platinum blonde hair who speaks like she's fifteen years old; it's funny hearing the big vocabulary that comes out of her sassy little mouth. We also hang out with an eighteen-month-old who speaks much better than Charli, too. There's a constant voice whispering in my ear: *she's so behind.* But there's a louder voice combating it with *she will get there.* It gives my brain something else to focus on: her progress. We work with a speech therapist weekly, and I know she will get there, and that's all that matters.

Another reason was my experience with potty training. Potty training my kids wasn't easy. Vivienne was two years and nine months old when I decided it was time. In my mind, she was already behind and getting too old for diapers. The average age kids potty train is twenty-seven months, according to Google, but from the perspective of a now experienced mom of four, that sounds extremely young. There is such a huge range though. I based it mostly on Vivienne's classmates; most were already wearing underwear and using the potty. I was very pregnant with Julia and felt so much pressure about potty training Viv that my chest pinched when anyone mentioned something about it.

To start, we set a timer, and every ten minutes I placed her on the toilet. If she peed on the toilet, she would get an M&M. The first day was a mess—she peed everywhere: on a Barbie doll, on a couch, and on every inch of the floor, except the toilet. I remember lying on the pee-stenched floor trying to gather myself after that long day. I held my pregnant belly and declared to Jonathan, "If I knew what potty training was going to be like, I wouldn't have gotten pregnant with our third."

Jonathan's gaze dropped, "Seriously. This is terrible." He lay next to me and studied me for a second, and then laughed, followed by a groan.

The second day was a little better. We at least had some successes mixed in with the accidents. This went on for a few days until something clicked. A week in she was fully pee trained. The lingering problem was pooping on the toilet. My stubborn child refused to do it. She'd scream and thrust her body with such force that wisps of hair would blow across her face as she pleaded for a diaper.

This battle with poop went on for two and a half years. I tried everything to get her on the toilet. She would hold it in for an unhealthy amount of time until we just wanted her to let it out, so we gave in to a diaper. I had to give her countless suppositories and MiraLAX. I was humiliated that I couldn't get her to do it as much as I tried to force it. The summer before kindergarten it finally happened. I got her to do it with a trick I found on Scary Mommy. First she pooped on the potty in a diaper. And then I eventually cut a hole in the diaper, and she pooped through it. Then I took her diaper off, and she was pooping on the potty. She got a prize at each step. It magically worked.

I now know the fear of pooping on the potty is very common for children. I have a friend going through it right now with her daughter. I offer her support and encouragement daily because I know how much she needs it! It's so hard when you are going through it—your day centers around their need to poop or how they're not pooping. They are miserable because they're constipated. You are miserable because you're stuck in with a cranky constipated child. It's a terrible cycle.

I didn't rush Diana to start potty training after my experience with Vivienne. I waited until she was three and a half and seemed ready. She was fully peeing on the potty in two days, but like Vivienne, she refused to poop on the potty. Diana picked up on how bothered Viv was by the toilet, so her anxiety took that on and amplified that fear. We were calmer this time around, knowing she would get there eventually, but nothing could motivate her. I tried the technique that worked with Vivienne, and she hid, cried, and screamed until I touched her elbow and said, "we don't have to do it today." Diana's main problem was fear, whereas Vivienne's was control.

It got to the point where Diana would poop in her sleep because that's when she was relaxed. I even took her to a poop therapist. Yes, I spent a stupid amount of money on a therapist who promised me to get Diana pooping on a potty. I was desperate.

Months and months went by using this therapist, and there was no improvement. I was getting worried she would go to kindergarten and have a poop accident in school. She's the type of kid who would never want to go back to school. I finally tried the same way I did with Vivienne, with the added pressure of having to be ready for kindergarten, and this time it worked but not without tears.

I remember screaming with joy, "Diana, you pooped on the potty. You did it!" as she wiped off her sweaty face and took a big breath out to calm down. She saw she could do it, and each time after would get better and better.

Julia was fully potty trained by four, which is late for most, but for our family that was a record. I know we aren't alone in our late-to-be-completely-toilet-trained struggles. Diana had a playdate with a little boy in her kindergarten class recently who was still potty training.

"I want Arlo to sleep over!" Diana pleaded. I looked at his mom. She was wearing a summer dress, her short blonde hair styled in a bob and down.

"He's not old enough yet. Besides, he still wears a diaper to sleep." She started laughing, and so did Diana.

Arlo's lips parted, came together, and parted again. "Mom!" He loudly rasped, shaking his head.

"I only said that because he told Diana already," she took Arlo into her arms, embracing him in a big loving hug.

I smiled, "Well, earlier doesn't mean better. He will get there." I cleared my throat and told her about our potty-training struggles.

They all do get there, and the struggle shapes them and us.

Today, I can't believe all the time, energy, and money I wasted worrying about poop—but it becomes all-encompassing when you're in it. All my girls were behind the curve, but that means nothing in the scheme of their lives. And if you saw them now, you would have no idea how much they struggled with it.

The pandemic was another lesson learned. Before, I believed that Vivienne and Diana needed to be in different Mommy & Me classes each day to socialize them with other kids and gain new skills. I packed their days with activity after activity. What my babies were accomplishing and how I was helping them get there was the measure of how good I felt about myself as a mom at that point in my motherhood journey. They were giving me minimal verbal feedback, so I only went off how I was "measuring up." How long I pumped or breastfed, how many vegetables I could get them to eat, how many words they were saying etc. I felt a lot of pressure.

Vivienne was in the pool at three months old taking swim lessons with an instructor. I remember her wearing a cute pink one-piece as Jonathan blew in her face, saying "bubbles," and submerging her in the water as my heart fell to my stomach. Because we were told the earlier we had her in the pool, the better swimmer she would become. So, I continued those lessons even though my heart screamed every time she went underwater.

But the pandemic changed everything for me. During the lockdown, my three under three and a half were stuck inside. We couldn't go to a class each day. Everything was shut down. Jonathan still went to work. Vivienne was no longer going to preschool—they were doing "virtual school," which consisted of three-year-old Viv making funny faces in a class Zoom meeting and laughing at herself. We didn't go to stores. We had to rearrange our lives to isolate from everyone and everything, learning words like "self-isolation" and "social distancing." We were forced to slow down. We spent the days with each other, dancing, singing, and playing make-believe. We took long walks to a stream near our house and threw rocks into it. We painted. We played chase. We sought shelter in each other. It was simple, but I gained perspective. Those days filled with simplicity were equally filled with love.

I was not my best self, either. I was a mom in survival mode, a mom completely fatigued from wearing too many hats, frustrated and frightened by what was happening in the world around her, a mom who lost most of the social support she had, and a mom who didn't have anything together, not even her sanity on most days.

But I was a great mom not because of how many activities I did to better my kids, and if they excelled at them, or how many vegetables they ate. I was a good mom because I woke up each day and showed up, trying my best. I was getting us through a tough time and making them feel loved and safe through it.

Also, as I saw during COVID, none of those things that the mommy wars are about matter. It doesn't matter if Vivienne is the best athlete or reading by five. What matters most is the whole child—if they're healthy, happy, and a good human. So, I no longer measure my worth as a mother or their worth as humans based on their achievements. And I will always choose my kids' mental health over everything. They are not achievements but humans who deserve to be happy and loved.

Milestones are there to help kids get the extra help they need if they're falling behind and a doctor is concerned, and for early detection of other issues, so they are important in that respect. But they aren't supposed to be used as a way for moms to one-up each other in the race to find out who's the best mom.

Now I am the mother who doesn't have the heart to take away pacifiers or bottles, and who waits until they are "so ready" to make it less terrible to potty train. I am in no rush for them to grow up.

As my mom says, "They won't be walking down the aisle with a pacifier in their mouths."

And I always respond, "How cute would it be if they did?" Also, the thought of my daughters finding a partner that they're in love and happy with is so beautiful it makes my heart ache, I wouldn't care if they exchanged pacifiers at the altar.

She always rolls her eyes, the rest of her face calm. "Oh Dan, you're one of a kind."

But she's right: they won't be walking down the aisle with a pacifier in their mouth and wearing a diaper—though that diaper may be convenient in a big puffy wedding dress, too.

This is also true about rushing to find our children's passions.

My kids are not the best participators. Since they were little, between Vivienne's wild spirit, which had her running everywhere but where she was supposed to, and Diana's bad anxiety, where she would be afraid, crying behind my legs, I always stood on the outside, watching their classes with them instead of observing them participating with other kids. I always felt a tinge of jealousy for the parents who had kids who didn't give them a hard time and would participate in everything without a problem. The ones who tried everything and had fun. I signed up Vivienne for a bunch of activities. Her first soccer class when she was five years old, I watched her walk to the field, and then turn back jogging to me.

"What's wrong?" I huffed, knowing how she is at almost every activity.

"I don't want to play." She said, batting her head against my legs.

"Oh Viv, just give it a chance." I plead with her.

"Fine." She said like I just suggested the most miserable thing in the world to do.

She walked slowly onto the field, dragging her cleats through the muddy grass.

My heart sank as I saw all the other kids dribble their soccer balls around a grid in the field while Vivienne just slowly kicked and sulked.

The next practice when we were on our way I asked Viv, "Can you please try today?"

She shook her head from side-to-side. "No. I don't feel like sweating today." I studied her for a second, brow furrowed.

"Are you joking right now?" She was completely serious. She sat on the side, under a tree in the shade, playing with the dirt.

We ended up pulling her out of soccer after weeks of this pattern. I felt hopeless. Every other kid around her seemed to have a "thing" or "many things" they would do, but my kids didn't seem to have that or even want that. Viv seemed to like gymnastics, so we did that, but she wasn't passionate about it.

Toward the end of first grade, Viv started dancing around the house all the time. Every time I'd see her, she'd be making up routines and recording them. She stopped walking anywhere, she'd glide from place to place, or do cartwheels and land in a split.

"Viv, you should do a dance class." I swallowed, hoping she wouldn't reject the idea right away.

"Yes, I'll do it," she said.

"The only deal is you have to finish it. I am not paying for another class for you to bail on." She gave me a look I couldn't read, as if considering what I told her.

"OK," she said without much hesitation. I even sensed a bit of enthusiasm in her tone.

During the first class, the owner of the studio came up to me. She had bright red hair and a big cheery smile. "Are you Vivienne's mom?"

"Yes," I said, a tenderness around my mouth but concern in my brow. The blinds were closed on the classroom window so I couldn't see in and observe how Vivienne was doing. I pictured her sitting in a corner, fidgeting while everyone else danced, refusing to join.

"Can I speak to you over there for a minute?" *Oh man. What did Viv do?* I followed her down the hall, looking at the headshots of the instructors on the walls.

"You can sit right here." She pointed next to her on a black couch surrounded by white drapes. I sat down as anxiety gurgled in my stomach.

"So, I think Vivienne is very talented. She's a natural. I would love her on the dance team." She said as she started to explain the program and commitment.

My chest relaxed and was replaced by a pleased smile.

"Thank you. I will talk to her."

After the class, I told Viv about the team, and she was thrilled. Now, our life has been taken over by dance. She found her passion, and it's beautiful to see. Yes, it took until the summer going into second grade, but everyone finds at least one thing they enjoy eventually.

If your child isn't a participator or has a lot of anxiety and won't try anything—try not to worry. They will get there eventually. It's not a race. It doesn't make you a better parent if your child is enrolled in all the things or none of the things. Some kids just need more time, and that's OK.

So, the next time you are feeling the social pressure to have your kids excel—to hit all the milestones perfectly, or to do all the activities they're "supposed to do," or compared to their classmates—don't give your time or care to that competitive culture. Now you know the truth—your kids will do everything when the time is right. Once you learn this, you'll be able to relax more, worry less, and get to know the child you have without trying to push them to become something they are not. I now let my kids guide what I sign them up to do. I won't choose soccer just because I liked it. I listen to them and go by their interests. And that's how you truly win parenting gold.

— 7 —

Going From Me to We

"CRAP. WE WOKE up late again." I pop up in a glossy sheen of sweat. Charli is still sleeping next to me on one side while Julia is stretching on the other side of me.

"Hi Mommy," Julia purrs sleepily. She pushes her curly hair out of her eyes as she stretches.

I pull the warm covers off me and her and crawl through the middle of the bed. I make a cocoon of pillows around Charli so she doesn't roll off the bed. Julia follows my every step.

Briefly, I fantasize about going back to sleep, sinking into the nice warm bed, my cheek pressed into the pillow, and my body relaxed.

But as someone who isn't a morning person, this is my dream every morning. I turn on the shower, and behind me is Julia. Wide awake and smiling, a nice contrast to me.

"Let's go to the bathroom, baby. It's been all night." She grabs my hand, and we walk to the toilet. She sits down, as I twist my hair atop my head into a bun and brush my teeth, dancing to make her laugh. She moves her hands from the toilet.

"I'm done, Mommy!" Julia says, raising her hand. I place one finger up, mumble an inaudible "one second" and spit into the sink and rinse my mouth out under the sink faucet. I then head back to Julia to help her wipe.

"Mommy's going to hop into the shower for five minutes. Is that OK, sweet love?" I beeline to the shower door.

"I'll be here," she says, following me.

Of course, she will. She's my shadow. She follows me wherever I am throughout the day. I am constantly tripping over her or Charli because they're in my space. If I go to the bathroom, she does, too. If I'm in the kitchen getting a snack, she wants an apple with peanut butter, too. So every morning, she waits outside the shower until I am finished, vying for my attention over the shampoo and conditioner.

The shower door whines as I pull it open and heat billows toward me as I step in. I let the water fall over my head, hot water racing down my body. It feels good to have a moment alone in the steam. Time to myself to recenter. Until I turn around to Julia holding a towel with a smooshed face against the glass shower door. Water droplets cling to my brows as I smile.

This would be terrifying to most people, but not to me—or to most mothers. This is my life. Because there are no boundaries. No hiding in the bathroom or closet to get alone time. They'll cry or talk through the door until I let them in out of guilt.

Sometimes all I want is fifteen minutes. Fifteen minutes to get myself ready for the day. Fifteen minutes of quiet before my day of so much inescapable noise. The talking on top of each other, vying for attention, "Mommy, Mommy, MOMMY!" The ceaseless arguing and screaming at each other. The whining over being "so hungry," "so hot," "too cold," or "so thirsty." And when one sibling stops talking, another starts up again. Fifteen minutes to be just "me" without "them."

I try to coax her to her daddy. "Julia, why don't you go see what Daddy is doing? He has to get up for work." My hand furls against the glass.

"I want to stay with you." She blinks her eyes. Her dimpled smile doesn't fall as her gaze snags mine.

Ugh, I think, but I smile wide instead. She doesn't get one-on-one time often. When she sits on my lap or lays her head on me, Charli gets red in the face with jealousy and screams until she moves away. I've seen Julia act out lately to get my attention, not listening on purpose or pushing and hitting her sisters. She's very sweet, and gentle, so it's obvious she's looking for attention in any form. With three siblings, it's hard for her to get that. In a lot of ways, she's the least needy, so she can get lost in the mix.

As the water wraps me in a warm hug, my attitude changes. I draw a smiley face on the glass with my finger.

"Draw hair!" Julia excitedly jumps.

"OK, careful. I don't want you to slip on the water." I draw curly hair and a big bow.

"It's me!" Julia laughs, and plants a loud smooch on the glass, making the smiley have big lips.

"You're so silly!" I smile but don't think she can see it through the steamy door.

"How about this?" I write Julia in the condensation, but then realize that wasn't smart because she doesn't read.

"It says Julia!" She surprises me.

"Good job, baby." I say. She must recognize it from school. I am impressed. I rinse the conditioner out of my head and sing the "I'm going to shake my conditioner out," song to the tune of "Shake My Sillies Out" by Raffi.

Then she dances and I copy her. She moves her arms like a robot, and I follow. She waves her hands in the air. I follow. We both are laughing so hard my chest aches.

I shut off the water and open the shower door, feeling a brisk chill hit my body. I quickly grab a towel and dry myself off as goosebumps form on my arms and legs.

"Alright girlie, I'm going to get dressed, and we're going to get everyone up. Thank you for spending time with me." I finish drying off and put one foot into my black sweatpants, and then another. I throw on a nursing bra because they are comfortable, not because I am nursing anymore, and a T-shirt.

"You're welcome," Julia beams, taking a half-step back. I take her hand in mine, and we go to get her dressed, and then wake up everyone else.

While that morning wasn't what I expected it to be or initially wanted it to be, that's the beauty of motherhood. It gives you exactly what you and your children needed all along. I used to get much more disappointed when I didn't have time to immediately write down an idea for an essay, or finish folding the pile of clean clothes off my bedroom floor, or get to shower alone. But it will be what it will be, if I choose to accept it or not, so I learned that I might as well embrace the unpredictable and make the best of it.

But I didn't feel this way or gain this perspective until I had more than one child. The truth is that most mornings, it bothers me more than anything that I don't get alone time.

The other morning, I woke up with Charli on top of me, both of us soaked with sweat. The day before was filled with taking care of all my sick children, followed by a rough night of Charli coughing nonstop, and Julia and Diana joining us in bed. I was nauseous from exhaustion. Burnt out. I smelled like milk, pee, and sweat.

"Jonathan, can you please take the kids down for breakfast so I can have fifteen minutes to myself?" The blankets rustled as I stretched, and a cold breeze wriggled through. All I wanted to do was nestle myself back into the warmth of the covers, my face buried into a soft pillow, but I needed to get ready for the day. Another day of a sick and needy Charli.

"Dan, I need to get ready for work!" he said, frustration in his tone as a divot formed between his brows.

My stomach sank. "It's just fifteen minutes. Maybe even ten. We have over an hour until we have to leave. Please, smell me," I said lifting my arm in the air so he could sniff me if he wanted, equally annoyed. A silent conversation passed between us when he saw my desperation.

"Fine! Come on girls, let's go down for breakfast." He picked Charli up as she yelled for me, and Diana and Julia followed, Diana trailing way behind. I'd wake Vivienne after I was done with my shower. We still had time.

"Thank you! Thank you." I hopped out of bed and kissed his cheek.

"How about me?" Diana said, wrapping her hands around her chest.

"You can have kisses from me anytime." I kissed her on her cheek twice as she smiled.

Diana shut the door behind her, and I felt instant relief. To start the day with silence was truly a gift; I wasn't going to take it for granted. I turned on the water and as I was waiting for it to heat up, I pulled out my toothbrush and brushed from side-to-side, then rinsed and spit.

I took off my pajamas and opened the shower door.

"Daddy yelled at me!" Julia stormed into the bathroom, making my heart drop to the pit of my stomach like it was hit by a bowling ball. I wasn't expecting her.

"You scared me," I flinched, my heart beating fast. She dove into my arms.

"I didn't want eggs for breakfast," she sobbed.

"If you asked for them, and he started making them, and then you didn't want them, maybe he was a little frustrated, but that's OK. Let's try to calm down. Everything is OK." I pushed her hair out of her face and rubbed the palms of my hands over my eyebrows. Because when one of my kids is crying, it's a domino effect that forces me to shorten or skip my shower all together. So much for a little time for myself. I ran a cool washcloth over my face to wake myself up. I then threw my clothes on and tied my hair atop of my head in a messy bun.

I put Julia on my back. "Go horsey!' She screamed, as I brought her to her room and got her dressed for the day. I then went into Viv's room.

"Vivienne baby, it's time to get up for school." She yawned, eyes still closed as she stretched and scratched the back of her head. She slowly opened them and immediately made eye contact with Julia.

"Julia, get out of my room!" She screamed, her voice still husky from sleep.

"Viv, she's just with me. Don't worry, we are both leaving. Lose the attitude, please." I sighed as I shut the door behind me.

Diana ran upstairs and slammed her entire long body into me for a hug like she hadn't seen me in over a week.

"Dee Dee, you killed me with all that love. What did you have for breakfast?" I laughed against the top of her head. She looked up at me through her long lashes, her brown eyes on full display.

"Blueberry muffins and strawberries." She had strawberry on her face. I placed my finger in my mouth and wiped the strawberry stain off her with my thumb.

"Yummy, let's get you ready." Jonathan dropped Charli off with me while he went to get himself ready, and she followed us like a baby duck into Diana's room. I helped Diana pick out an outfit, a Royal Blue soft sweat outfit, and rainbow Aphmau cat socks. I then tied her hair half up, half down.

We talked about school, who she was excited to play with at recess, and laughed at Charli, who decided to put on too-big-for-her-face sunglasses. We went to the bathroom and then I yelled for everyone to come downstairs. I made Julia and Viv toasted bagels with cream cheese, as I continued trying to get everyone to move at the speed I wanted them to move—which was kind of like a person trying to herd cows on way-too-many drugs. No one was paying attention, and I had to do every little thing, even put their shoes and jackets on for them, and push them out the door.

The girls were sitting with their winter jackets on, staring at the television in a trance as Jonathan walked into the kitchen, heading straight for the Keurig. He was wearing a white T-shirt tucked into black slacks, with a freshly shaved face. His hair was perfectly slicked back. He looked clean and refreshed, and I envied him for that. I looked at the clock: 8:15 AM. I had ten minutes exactly.

Ten minutes to shower and get myself dressed.

Ten minutes to shave half of a leg and become somewhat presentable.

Ten minutes to throw gel into my hair.

I looked down at myself, still in last night's pajamas. I ran up the stairs, out of breath, sweat sticky on my skin. I turned on the shower water. I didn't wait for it to warm up. I closed my eyes as I stepped in, anticipating the cold water and immediately my eyes snapped open as the ice water hit me. Goosebumps filled my entire body and the back of my neck tingled. I put a glob of conditioner on top of my head and scrubbed quickly, too cold to wash it all out. I turned the shower off and grabbed my towel. Drying myself off, shivering, I saw I had six minutes left.

I threw clean clothing on and scrunched gel into my sopping wet hair. I ran into the kitchen with two minutes to spare. Charli's face was scrunched as she cried out for "Mama" nonstop. I picked her up, and she took a deep breath, calming down. My hair was still damp from my ice shower.

Jonathan pulled the lever up on the toaster and a Pop-Tart popped up. He complained about Charli's nonstop crying when I wasn't there.

"She's so overwhelming," I heard him say in slow motion. And I wanted to guffaw at his ten minutes of "overwhelmed," but I held it back.

Because *I* am overwhelmed. *I* am always a "we."

Me, who deals with the kids all day long, especially Charli.

Sometimes, no one seems to care about the time I need to myself. Jonathan gets his time, the kids get their time, and I only ever get ten minutes. If that. And most of the time one of my kids interrupts those ten minutes because "Vivienne said something mean" or "Diana isn't sharing" or "Julia is being annoying." All things they need to complain to me about, for some reason, instead of Jonathan when he's right in front of them. Because young kids don't get the need to be alone, not even when you are using the bathroom.

I used to be hard on myself for not loving these moments with my kids. Because I know one day soon, it will be different, and I'll miss the interruptions. But when you're in the thick of it all, it's hard to realize that. What I've come to learn is it's OK if you don't. Moms are exhausted. So, it's OK to be annoyed that one of our kids barged into our room in tears, ruining our alone time. It's OK to not enjoy when our toddler is screaming at us to pick her up as we're trying to put our clothes on. We don't have to love every second we're with our children to be good moms. There are times we do appreciate the interruption, like my morning with Julia, but most of the time, we'd rather be alone, and that's OK. We need to give ourselves grace for these very normal and human feelings. It's OK if we feel like we never have time, and most days, having a child enter the room during our rare peaceful moments gets to us.

Not having enough time to get my "to-do list" or work done used to really get to me, too. Before Vivienne was born, I went in to an office in Long Island City, where I'd spend the entire day doing all the behind-the-scenes operations to help run my family's business. I'd go in at seven in the morning and stay until seven at night. I was so used to going into an office and having at least ten to twelve uninterrupted hours to get my work done, work on any side passion projects I had going on, take a lunch break, and take personal breaks where I'd have time to grab a hot tea and browse People Online or talk to people in the office. I had nothing on my plate except for the work in front of me, and I'd still often feel overwhelmed.

When Vivienne was born, I continued doing the accounting work for our family business, and it was harder than I imagined trying to manage everything while working from home. I always thought I could do it all and do it all well. I was going to be one of those supermoms I heard about.

But the reality of working from home with a child to care for looked very different. I struggled to find the balance. Every time I'd try to get work done, I'd hear newborn Vivienne cry for milk or to be comforted. I felt like nothing was getting done. I was exhausted, and I mean absolutely spent, by the end of the day, and I didn't have time to finish the laundry, do much work, or make any healthy meals, and the apartment looked like a disaster.

I'd start adding numbers on my Ten Key calculator, an adding machine with a tape for proof that you have added columns of numbers correctly. I'd sit on my work chair in a nook in our apartment that I made into an office space. I'd be wearing a nursing bra with my mesh underwear, over a diaper (basically), and sitting on a bag of frozen peas. I didn't have time to shower. But I chose work over showering. I couldn't stop obsessing about how behind I was.

Five minutes would pass, and then I'd hear faint cries getting louder and louder. I'd pick Vivienne up and try to rock her back to sleep. When that failed, I'd try to nurse her, which would take at least an hour. Then her eyes finally would close in my arms, and I'd take in the smell of her skin as I'd carefully place her in her bassinet.

I'd sit back down at my desk and try to figure out where I left off with work to begin again. But my thirst would rise from a quiet bother to an incessant nagging. So, I'd go to the kitchen and open the refrigerator, grab a bottle of Diet Coke, and open the cabinet to see no cups. "Crap!" I'd then look to the sink filled with dirty dishes and cups. I'd start washing and loading everything into the dishwasher, realizing I'd been ignoring this build up for way too long.

Then newborn cries would pierce my ears, again.

"Ugh, you've got to be kidding me?" I'd cry, trying to swallow my frustration, which somehow made my words louder. I hadn't even taken a sip of Diet Coke yet. I'd take a swig from the bottle, take a deep breath in and roll my eyes at this cruel joke being played on me. I'd walk into the living room where the bassinet was and take in the scene: two finished bottles on the table, a burp cloth on the couch, and dirty onesies in a pile on the floor.

"What's going on, sweet girl?" I'd say, picking her up and holding her close. She'd start rooting again. I'd sigh. It would take me a full hour to get her to latch, and another forty-five minutes for her to fall asleep. I would never be sure if she was full or just exhausted from all our attempts.

My chest would ache with sadness. I'd feel so alone as I'd look around at the mess in the apartment. I'd feel like I was failing at everything.

This wasn't what I thought motherhood would look like. I just felt overwhelmed with all the things I'd have to do each day. Instead of crossing things off my to-do list, two new tasks would sprout up like weeds.

After days of this postpartum working pattern, I picked up my phone and dialed Dad, as the picture of him blurred with my tear-filled eyes, and my voice rattled as I told him I could no longer do the accounting work for our family business. Everything felt too overwhelming. I had no time. I was failing as a mother. The apartment was a mess. I couldn't seem to get it together. My heart stuttered as I apologized to him for being a disappointment.

The next day, when I had a clearer head, I admitted to being a bit irrational, hormonal, and bluesy and asked if I could have my job back. What I didn't realize at the time is that feeling overwhelmed is new-mom normal. Because it's normal to get nothing done with a newborn. To start a load of laundry but never finish it. To take a shower and have to jump out midway because the baby is getting upset. There are zero minutes in a day where the baby will be OK by herself. It's hard.

But now as a mother of four, I know it's temporary. I don't feel as overwhelmed as I once did, and if I do, I remind myself that I'm raising children. Everything else is second to that.

Yes, I still get overwhelmed at times. I'm human. But I give myself so much grace, especially in the newborn phase or when my kids are sick. On a typical day, not in the newborn phase, I work during my children's naptime; now that they're older, it's a rest time, and I mostly write at night. I text myself writing ideas when they come to me during the day. I was able to figure it out over time and with each phase. But of course, I often have to do work at night, too, before I can start writing. I never have found this magical balance; some days I feel it more than others. But I roll with the punches of each day of motherhood. Because it's unpredictable, so I've learned to be flexible.

But I embrace the mess now, and I now know how to cope. This is why I started to cherish my nights.

A lot of the time, the night is the only time I can get things done. It's the only time I don't need to tend to Charli. It's the only time I won't be interrupted by "Mommy, can you get me some strawberries please," or "Mommy, can you print me a picture of Pikachu to color?" I won't get Diana grumbling, "Vivienne hit my butt" and have to comfort her and tell Vivienne to keep her hands to herself. To sit and not have someone climbing on top of me and plopping down on my lap.

I can finally clean the house: load the dirty dishes into the dishwasher, fold the laundry, and pick up toys from the floor without them appearing in the same spot five minutes later.

I can finally cross things off my mental to-do list by making sure there's more peanut butter in the pantry, packing lunches for the next day with notes that remind my kids they are loved, and pay bills.

I can do work that I couldn't get done during the day or work on my writing. Or if I'm really lucky, but it's been rarer as my kids have gotten older, to spend alone time with Jonathan eating dinner together and commiserating about the day because adulting is hard.

And right before I go to sleep at 1 AM, I can lose myself in social media: memes, reels, all of it or get lost in a good book. Because sometimes I need to unwind and see what's happening outside my small world of me and my four kids. Or to scroll through the thousands of photos on my phone and tear up at how much my sweet babies have grown.

So, when a mom tucks reluctant children into bed, her day is just beginning. And there's a magic in those quiet hours, whether they happen before the sunrise at 5 AM or late at night after 11 PM. They're the reason mom has tired eyes and complains about not getting enough sleep even when her kids sleep through the night. But they're also the reason mom is able to keep going with a full and recharged heart.

This time's important for a mom's mental well-being, to pursue a career or passion, have an intimate conversation with a friend, and time to catch up on Netflix. It's time she can be herself.

Because the truth is, this quiet time fuels her in a way that sleep can't.

My quiet time brings me back to Dani. Not Dani from before kids. I will never be that Dani again. It brings me to a Dani who's fulfilled outside of her motherhood. Because through mothering, I've found a better me. This Dani has so much more purpose. She's more passionate about the world around her because she wants to make it better for her children. She cares about herself more than ever because her kids need her, and she knows she needs proper "me" time for her mental health to pursue those passions to be the best "we" possible. So, when you're no longer a "me" and become a "we," —it's life-changing for the better.

— 8 —

How Am I Lonely if I am Surrounded by Kids All Day Long?

I T'S ONE OF the many paradoxes of motherhood: feeling lonely while being surrounded by kids all day long.

It's a different kind of lonely. It's feeling invisible. When you feel alone in a room full of chaos, you trick yourself into thinking you don't matter. It becomes a drag on your soul. It happens in all stages of motherhood, but I felt it most when I had three kids under three and a half.

I remember one day in particular. I woke up after an exhausting night of spotted sleep between feeding three-month-old Julia, rocking her against my chest, and moving her legs because she was nonstop screaming with gas pains. I fed Julia as I made my way to Diana's room and took her out of her crib.

Julia fell asleep again in my arms, so I put her down in the bouncer.

What I noticed at the time was having three under three meant that I spent my days in meltdown prevention mode. I tried to be one step ahead, one snack ahead, one bottle ahead, one pacifier ahead, to avoid a meltdown. I predicted everyone's needs.

I went to the small upstairs fridge and handed twenty-two-month-old Diana her morning bottle as I changed her diaper and put a purple sweat outfit on her. She danced to The Wiggles. I heard Vivienne calling "Mommy!" through the monitor. I picked Diana up and took her to open Vivienne's door. I stepped into the room and said, "Good morning, sweet girl!" as she walked right past me. As I caught up to her, she looked over at me and said, "Milk please."

I handed her a sippy cup of milk when she got to the upstairs play area, and she sleepily sat on the couch watching The Wiggles, like she was sipping her morning coffee. Her face looked like what I'd imagine a "do not disturb" emoji to look like. I placed my hand on her arm, and she jerked it free. She woke up with anger shooting through her veins. She still wakes up that way.

I grabbed Vivienne a set of clothes and ran back into the room to find Diana crying and on all fours. I was gone less than ten seconds. Not even.

"Viv, what happened to Diana?" My voice rose as she dropped her head against her shoulder.

I could always see through her lies.

"Viv, what happened to Diana?" I repeated as I picked Diana up, trying to calm her down.

"She fell." She said with a grin on her face as I lifted my brows skeptically.

"She fell or did you push her? Or trip her with your leg? Viv, we don't do these things." I was angry. "It's not even 8 AM." I said out loud even though that meant nothing to a three-year-old.

I got Viv dressed. She was in the phase where she'd only wear dresses like a Disney Princess.

She spun around in all pink as I told everyone it was time for breakfast.

I placed Diana in her highchair, Viv in her booster seat, and Julia in a carrier so she remained sleeping and my hands were free to make eggs. I turned on Baby Bum, and then I grabbed the frying pan, opened the fridge, took out the butter and a carton of eggs, and got a mixing bowl.

"I need to clean these dirty dishes, and this counter is a mess," I sighed as I started washing the dishes, getting sidetracked.

"Mommy, I'm hungry," Viv moaned, a somber expression on her face.

"Eggs are coming," I put down a dirty dish and went back to breakfast mode.

I was stuck in the rush. I was rushing to get breakfast on the table. I was about to rush to take a shower after breakfast and then to get dressed. I was running to take care of someone at all times between tasks.

I cracked two eggs and started mixing as Vivienne decided to run around the kitchen. Each time she passed me, she tapped my butt. She was singing "Let It Go."

"Be careful please!" I cautioned as I saw her speeding up.

On her fifth trip around the counter, she fell on the wood floor, knocking a ceramic bowl with her head on the way down. She let out a wail as the bowl shattered into pieces onto the floor, a domino effect that scared Diana, who started wailing too. My heart fell to my stomach and my spine prickled.

"Are you OK?" I came down to her level and placed my hand on her back but couldn't scoop her up because Julia was in my baby carrier.

She had a big bump forming on her head. *Thank goodness none of the ceramic pieces hit her*, was all I could think.

"No one move!" I screamed, the tension around my mouth apparent, as I jumped into cleaning mode. I threw

the big broken pieces into a big garbage bag and vacuumed up the shattered mess left on the ground. Diana
and Viv were both still upset when I was done. Their
adorably pink cheeks were filled with tears, and their hair
was soaked with sweat and frizz.

I did a silly dance, moving my arms like a chicken and
hopping around like a bunny—a chicken-bunny—that
made Vivienne and Diana both start to laugh instead of cry.

"Now let's get you some ice, Viv." I forced a smile as I
helped Vivienne off the floor. I could tell tears still threat-
ened to come.

But: crisis averted. No one was going to pat me on the
back, so I patted myself.

I wanted to text or call someone to tell them about my
day so far. Jonathan was in a meeting, and so was my dad.
My mom was at tennis. And I didn't have enough time to
form a village outside them to conquer the loneliness
between work and dealing with the kids. At this point, the
connectedness I felt with the moms in my life was flimsy at
best.

I took a deep breath in followed by an exhale. I felt
lonely.

I went back to breakfast mode, as the eggs continued
to cook. I was taking them to a 10 AM music class, so I kept
checking the time. It was still early: 8:25 AM. Time moves
so slowly in babyland, especially when the day is hard.

I finally finished making the eggs and put them in
blue and orange suction bowls. I placed them in the fridge
to cool for two minutes. While that was happening, I saw
Diana getting restless in her highchair, so I went over to
her and played peek-a-boo. I took the eggs out of the
fridge and put them in front of the kids. Vivienne took a
bite and kept eating. *Victory.*

Diana did the same and made a grossed-out face, spit-
ting them out. She doesn't always eat them, and it was one

of those mornings. I cleaned the table in front of her with a paper towel and gave her some strawberries and cheerios instead.

I yawned and shook my head. I was exhausted already.

I don't do everything I do for praise. I do it because I love my children, but I am human, and sometimes the "not noticing" does get to me.

I did some version of this day in and day out. This same routine. And to this day, though now it's different, it's always about everyone else. Who needs something? What do I need to fix? Where do we need to go? I'm shuffling everyone from one place to another, making it all happen behind the scenes, so we don't fall apart.

And that can be extremely lonely, always giving and not taking. Not being seen. I don't even notice it myself at times, I'm so involved in the day-to-day.

I also have so many thoughts in my brain that I'm never completely paying attention to what's in front of me. I can be making a grilled cheese sandwich and look up and not remember making it because I was so deep in thought.

It's a bit terrifying.

Also, when I'm trying to focus, I'm interrupted every two seconds by, "Mommy, can you get me a snack?" or "Mommy, look at me!"

I am constantly questioning if I'm completely losing my mind.

I don't want to be late for this or that. I feed the baby again. I get more snacks. I change clothes that get dirty with paint. I put a load of laundry in the wash. I clean spit up. I do things like this again and again. I'm trapped in the routine.

Motherhood comes with constant worry and exhaustion. There's a lot of mental and physical drainage. And when you're running on empty, you start doing wacky things.

I recently went to the mall with my girls, pulled in, brought all our bags into the house, and I couldn't find my phone anywhere. I searched my entire minivan, between and under the seats. I called from the house phone, and still couldn't find it. I started to panic and remembered I had "Find My" on my computer. I immediately heard the beeping and started moving closer and closer. It was coming from . . . the trash? How could that be? I searched through the garbage bag to my Wetzel's Pretzels bag. I opened it, and lo and behold, there it was, beeping in pretzel crumbs.

But this is our brains on motherhood. We experience a tired that is unlike any tired we have experienced before. It's mom tired.

It's being tired of being the responsible one who never gets a mental break because if she does, nothing will get done.

It's throwing her hair up into a messy bun on top of her head because she has no energy or time to do anything else.

It's a bone-deep tired that lurks after a long day of doing everything for her kids, not even able to finish a conversation without someone jumping in, screaming "Mommy, look!" or tugging on her shirt. All she wants to do after her children go to bed is put her feet up and rest but she spends her "alone time" doing anything else but relaxing because *how else is everything going to get done?*

I'd try sleeping it off.

"I'm going to go to bed an hour earlier," I'd tell Jonathan.

"Sure," he'd answer, snorting with disbelief, knowing how much I take advantage of those precious night hours.

"I mean it. I want to see if I am less tired." I paused, zoning out on the floor. "It's an experiment."

So that night I forced myself to stop scrolling through old photos of the girls and put down that good book I usually read until my eyes started to droop and closed my eyes an hour earlier than I normally did. And the next morning, I still woke up with a level of worn-outness that hurt. I couldn't kick it.

I'd nap at every chance I got during the day. I'd be lying with my girls on the couch watching a movie and nod off for twenty minutes, until Vivienne and Diana started fighting—and still be tired.

No amount of added sleep seemed to fix it.

Because it's more complicated than a tired that can be solved with a nap or a good night's rest.

It's a deep tired that makes you feel alone.

That exhaustion compiled with never getting a break can make me feel extremely lonely from lack of time with friends, and lack of childcare to get things done outside of motherhood causes me to become emotionally maxed out and burnt out.

All I want in those lonely moments is adult interaction or someone to see me as a human and understand what I'm going through. Kids don't see Mommy as human, and it's exhausting being someone's everything all day long without any recognition.

My kids come first, meaning most of the time I come last. My body isn't my own. It's tugged and sucked on all day long. And I don't want or expect something in return. Kids should get to experience a time in their lives when they are taken care of. It's not a child's responsibility to be grateful to her parents for being parents, but sometimes we feel underappreciated. Because as human beings, we all long to be appreciated. It's primal.

That feeling of loneliness is a sad feeling that creeps up out of nowhere.

I move from place to place, room to room, and feel unseen.

That makes me feel sad, I can't help it.

Especially when I'm sick. I fight through the day, and that can leave me feeling alone, too. Because the kids are extra loud. They will still ask for all the things and not notice I'm peeling myself off the couch with 102-degree fever when I get it for them.

A couple of weeks back I woke up with my throat burning and my bones aching. It was the kind of day where if I didn't have kids, I would have called off work and spent the day in bed. But I couldn't.

I went to the bathroom and dabbed water on my face to try to wake up and went downstairs to make eggs and cut up some fruit. I put a mask on just in case I had more than just an allergy-related sore throat. I pushed through the morning. Through shuffling everyone to the bathroom to brush their teeth, get dressed, breaking up the morning fights, and then off to two school drop offs—elementary and preschool. After, Charli and I came straight home, and I lay on the couch, completely undone.

I made myself tea and took two Advil for my raging sore throat and body.

I tried to clear my throat, "Mommy feels like crap, Charli." She smiled. Two-year-olds don't know what that means. She hit my back, "Mama." When I didn't respond, she repeated, "Mama," and pulled me by my hand as I walked heavy footed to our Fisher Price playhouse. I sat there in the tiny house, surrounded by princess stuffed animals, as she handed me book after book to read to her.

"The Itsy Bitsy Spider . . ." I read, but my head was elsewhere. I shifted so that I was sitting cross-legged to get comfortable. All I wanted to do was sleep, and using my voice hurt.

Then at 11:45 AM, we went to pick up Julia at school, came back and I made her and Charli lunch, and I sat down myself as they ate because I felt discomfort everywhere. We played in the playroom and by the time I picked up Viv and Diana at 3 PM, I felt awful. My entire body ached so badly, but Viv and Diana had to go to therapy.

On the way, I called Jonathan. "Something is definitely wrong with me," I said as I made a right turn. We stopped at a traffic light and my eyes squinted against the sun.

"After you drop off the girls at therapy, go to Urgent Care." I put on my sunglasses. I felt like he'd been brushing it off all day. Too busy with work to acknowledge it.

"I don't think I'll have time." I knew from experience how long Urgent Care could take. I once was there waiting for over two hours to be seen.

"Just try." He insisted. My lower back ached as I shifted in my seat.

"Yes. I'll try. I'll go in and beg for a quick throat swab," I laughed, my body feeling like a giant blister, so sensitive.

I ran the big girls into their therapy offices, which gave me forty-five minutes. I sped to the car and buckled Julia and Charli in and drove to an Urgent Care around the corner. I scooped Charli up in my arms and took Julia's hand as I rushed us in. As I opened the door, I saw a woman at the front desk behind a glass partition. She gave a friendly smile to my kids and pushed wisps of hair out of her face.

The sweat lay on my skin as I went to take off my heavy winter coat. "Hi. I know this is going to be a reach. I think I have strep, but my other two girls are at an appointment, so I need to be out of here in half an hour. Is it possible someone can see me quickly?" I said, out of breath. I could hear the desperation in my own voice and felt my eyes widen.

"Aw, poor mom. Yes, let me try to squeeze you in. I know what it's like." She started typing something on her computer.

"Thank you so much. Gosh you are wonderful. How old are your kids?" I asked. I put my hands on the counter. I felt seen by this other mom.

"I have an eight-year-old and a six-year-old." Her chin lifted as she spoke.

"Those are the ages of my oldest two." I smiled under my mask.

"Do they get along?" She narrowed her eyes.

"They do until they don't. Do you know what I mean?" My eyes darted to Julia and Charli, who were pawing at a fish tank across the room.

"Yes, my kids fight all the time." She rolled her eyes.

"It's a lot. They are a lot. But they are cute." I looked at Charli, who made her way back to me and was now pulling at my pants to show me the fish.

"Yes, or we'd give them back." She guffawed.

"Amen to that." I smiled back, my throat too scratchy and my body too achy to find anything funny enough to let out a laugh.

"OK, give me your insurance card and swipe your credit card here—and then you can come in with the girls." I handed her my insurance card and swiped my credit card as Charli said "Up!" in her husky voice.

"Thank you again." I took my cards back and picked Charli up. We headed through the door and followed a nurse to an office in the back.

We walked into a plain room with an exam table, and a computer in the corner. "The walls for adult doctor's offices are boring compared to yours, right?" I asked Julia.

"Yes. There should be animals." Julia said, examining the empty walls with her eyes.

"I agree. Maybe a pig right there and a monkey on that wall." I pointed left than right, and my hand landed back on hers.

"Maybe a dog on the ceiling, too." She pointed up to a blank ceiling. "Then when you lie on the table you can see the dog and not be afraid anymore." She smiled as her nose scrunched.

"What a great idea," I said. "You are very sweet to think of people's feelings." I squeezed her hand. Julia is my child where if a kid in her classroom is crying, she will ask him to play with her. She cares deeply about others.

The nurse took my temperature: 101.2. My stomach flipped.

"No wonder I'm feeling so sick and don't have my usual patience with my kids," I continued. "I'm really sick."

"You are. Moms don't get any rest, though." The nurse shook her head from side to side, knowing how hard it is to be a mom. "Open your mouth, Mom." I opened wide, tongue sticking out.

She then swabbed my throat for strep and up my nose for COVID/flu as I held Charli.

Fifteen minutes later the doctor came in.

"Open wide." He said pointing a flashlight to my mouth. I listened and stuck my tongue out, again. "So, your culture for strep came back positive, but I can see that by just looking at your throat. It's so inflamed, and you have tiny red spots on the roof of your mouth. I'm going to prescribe you amoxicillin." His words dissolved into my skin. "Anything else bothering you?" He asked, with a pleasant smile on his face.

"No, thank you so . . ." I started saying as Julia interrupted, "Mommy, are you sick?"

"Yes, baby. I am. But I am going to take medicine and feel so much better." I assured her as I placed my hand around her shoulder and walked her toward the exit.

We were on our way to get Diana and Vivienne with only five minutes to spare. As I turned into the therapist's parking lot, I started thinking about sick days when I was younger. They were the best days. My mom would take care of me and make me breakfast in bed. I could get back into my favorite pajamas and go back to sleep or hop into my mom and dad's bed and cover myself in a nest of covers to watch movies all day long. Take a break from the stress of school. Then when I was out of the house, it would be a day to hide away—from work and responsibilities and to heal. To lay around the house. While with kids, I had to push through like it was a normal day without anyone noticing I was sick until Julia asked at the doctor.

Because a sick day for a mom looks like a normal day—except mom isn't feeling well. We power through for our family without a sick day. Because we'd rather Daddy use his sick days when he himself is sick or there is an emergency. So we are somewhat functioning through the day. We don't get to relax. We don't get to take a nap on the couch or watch Netflix movies by ourselves. We keep packing lunches, cleaning up Legos off the floor, and giving bubble baths. And man, the pushing through without getting the time we need to get better, can feel lonely.

But for me the not noticing, or not feeling seen as a human, started taking over, when Diana was one month old, and we moved to suburbia from Manhattan. I started to feel lonely often and like a failure. There was a silence that would fill me, even in the baby screams and toddler demands. A thirst for communication. There was a gap from the level of connectedness I needed to what I had. When I was living in Manhattan my first year of motherhood, I'd walk outside and see adults all around me. I had met mom friends in a support group, and we all had babies the same age. We would take classes together and meet in the park or take walks together. But when I moved to suburbia, I'd walk outside and see nothing but trees and empty houses.

And yes, the busy was much more than with only one child. I was always doing something with two children eighteen-months apart, but I was still holding myself to such unrealistic expectations that it was hard to spend a lot of time outside the house. I was tied to our home base— held by a rigid nap schedule, pumping around the clock, and filling any gaps of the day with needs for my children (out of guilt) instead of needs for myself. I was surrounded by my babies all day but didn't have many, if any, adult interactions on most days. I would be running around taking care of the laundry, changing a diaper, playing a game with Vivienne, pumping, and then when I finally had time to sit down to catch my breath, I'd feel an emptiness: loneliness.

I remember, one day, walking into the kitchen and just feeling an overwhelming sadness. It swirled inside of me as I looked at my two babies—Viv tilting her head as she took a sip of water and Diana sitting in a baby bouncer. I was supposed to feel overwhelming joy, right? But instead, I just burst into tears. I felt guilty because this is what I wanted. I was blessed. But there was something missing. There was an ache for more of me in the day. I knew I needed more community. So, I started to make changes to my motherhood.

I started forcing myself out of my comfort zone. To say hi to the nice mom at the park. To take a number. To make sure I got out of the house for a walk even if it didn't directly benefit my kids. To not seclude myself. To have a lot of playdates. To join more classes. And when I felt that ache sneak up, because it always did, and still does to this day, I make sure to take extra time for myself on those days—to write, and to connect with others in whatever way I need to feel whole.

A part of conquering the loneliness was by making mom friends.

I recently met a mom friend right on my street. I was taking a walk with Charli and Viv one Saturday afternoon. It was a nice fall day. A leaf blew into Vivienne's hair, making a home in it. I took it out and showed it to her. It was brown with a tint of red.

She smiled, and took the leaf in her hand, waving it in the wind. Walking toward us on the opposite side of the street was a mom with long blonde hair, pushing a stroller and her almost-three-year-old with brown straight hair and a contagious smile walking beside her.

Vivienne looked at me and touched my elbow, "Let's say hi." I noticed my hand twisted into her shirt, so she wouldn't run ahead across the street without me. I knew she was eight, but it was an old habit. She's my extrovert. She loves to socialize and is never afraid to approach anyone. It's been such a learning experience watching her natural confidence and has helped push me to follow her lead.

We walked up to them and shook hands. The woman with long blonde hair was extremely friendly, open, and kind. We exchanged numbers. Now we meet for playdates, text, and go out for dinner as families. If we hadn't exchanged numbers, we wouldn't have had our friendship, and neither would our kids.

Over the past couple of years, I've met some very good mom friends. And these handful of very close mom friends in my day-to-day life are who I'm most grateful to for getting me through. They're the people that I can send a meme and I know they'll be laughing or nod in agreement on the other end. A friend I can text at night about our kid's bedtimes. A friend I can send a text saying, *Want to meet for a walk?* and she won't mind Charli being DJ with Spotify the entire time. A friend I can call at all hours of the day or night. A friend who has been through the same experiences, joys, and challenges that I have. A friend who we have been our authentic selves with since day one. Motherhood has forced us to be authentic through its highs and lows, and because of that we have developed a beautiful, deep connection. Having these people makes all the difference because they get it. They get me, and that truly means everything.

So, when I'm feeling underappreciated and overworked, I'll send a text to one of those moms who understands:

No one appreciates me ☹

And then I'll hear *same* or *I appreciate you* ☺ and it will make me feel less alone.

Or we'll joke *those little users*.

Another mom will get it, give you support and chuckle. They can identify because they are living the same invisible existence.

The only problem is it's not always easy to get together as moms. Sometimes our chaotic schedules don't align with so many kids and too many activities, and it becomes hard. When we cancel on each other, we don't do it because we want to, but because someone is napping, sick, or has a test tomorrow and has too much to study. It feels painful to cancel or not find the time, but kids are busy, and their needs come first.

So, another way I combat this feeling is by filling the gaps of the days with things outside of motherhood. If I have a spare moment, I will think of a meme or start writing an article on my phone notes. Having something outside of motherhood that makes me feel accomplished has made it easier to combat those underappreciated feeling days.

And when our family undermines or belittles our efforts, we feel even worse.

I'll never forget the time my mom walked into my house at dinnertime. I saw her eyes zigzagging around the kitchen. I could tell she wasn't pleased with how it looked.

"You can't leave crumbs on the kitchen counter all day; you're going to get ants." She took a sponge and started scrubbing them down. She vacuumed under the table. She unloaded and reloaded the dishwasher.

I went quiet and sullen. "I know, Mom; I'm doing my best." I responded. Her judgment didn't include the fact that the kids were with me all day. It's so hard to watch the kids and get the kitchen as clean as I want it. She's able to clean because I'm still taking care of the kids.

I was angry, because I do so much, but quickly I became full of shame, too, because I guess it wasn't enough. Her judgment pierced into my heart as it let out an achy throb.

Before I was a mother, I was a good student. I'd write a paper, edit it until I was happy with it, and get a good grade. I used to go to a job where I was a good employee and volunteer on the side where I was a great volunteer. My coworkers and the people I helped liked me. They encouraged me. I got a high-five for a job well done, or a smile while volunteering.

Staying home and taking care of the kids is very different. By the end of the day on most days, instead of feeling like I accomplished so much, I feel like I still have so much to do, I must be failing, and I look terrible, too, with purple blots under my eyes. All I want to do is plop down on a couch and read a good book or watch Netflix, but I have an endless list of things that need to get done.

My mom doesn't understand how much I'd love to do what she was doing. How satisfying it is when I have time to do a load of laundry or wash some dishes when the kids are awake. It's something I can check off my to-do list. It's something that makes me feel accomplished. It's something I won't have to do later.

Because even though I was busy all day, I felt like I had nothing to show for the rest of my day and no way to acknowledge or measure a job well done because the to-do list wasn't lessening, and my house still had toys, stains, and mess everywhere.

That day, we came home from the park where Charli cried the entire time because she had to poop but it wasn't happening. Viv and Diana played well, while Julia felt left out and spent most of the time pouting. Then I made lunch. Four different meals per child in one sitting. Because Charli said "p" and I thought she meant peanut butter and jelly, but she really meant pizza. The kids ate, and what was left behind was discarded or wrapped up for another day.

Charli finally pooped. I changed her diaper and gave her, Julia, and Diana a bath. Viv let me know she would bathe herself later.

I cleaned, even though my mom didn't see evidence. I cleaned up the dolls, Princess costumes, and makeup spread around the playroom floor. Then Viv and Diana started a puzzle, leaving a half-finished unicorn face on the playroom floor, and then transitioned to art, spreading crumbled paper, markers, crayons, and colored pencils everywhere. I cleaned up again. Charli then decided to throw a tea party for her princesses. I eventually surrendered to the mess or the "good enough" job my kids did when they finally cleaned after I complained, "Why am I cleaning up the mess alone when you guys made it?" as they scratched the backs of their heads.

As I left the room, Viv said, "It looks pretty clean, mom." I didn't have the guts to turn around for a last look, because I knew it wouldn't be clean to my standards, so instead hid the mess in darkness by turning off the lights and walking away.

"Pretty clean" is good enough when you are bone tired.

I fixed meltdown after meltdown.

Charli wanted a popsicle after breakfast. Meltdown.

Diana didn't hit Julia even though Julia said she did. Meltdown.

The kids fought over a nail polish color they both wanted to play with. Double meltdown.

I fixed the emotional seas because my outstretched arms were the only way to calm the stormy waters. But there's nothing to show after you wipe tears away.

And crumbs on a kitchen counter does not mean I failed my day. At that moment I didn't feel that. Now that I have spent more time as a mother, I see this more clearly.

Because even though nothing looked like it got done, I was doing so much just by raising my children. It's the hardest job there is. You receive more criticism than you've ever received in your life. But you quickly learn that you can't measure success by a clean house, how much praise you get from other people, or how many tasks you completed on a check list.

You gain perspective. Because now I know, the same bedrooms with unmade beds also had all my children sleeping safe and sound with my mind at ease the night before. The kid's bath toys left on the bathtub floor after the water drained is evidence of the time smiling and splashing around. The kitchen may be covered in muffin crumbs, and the sink filled with bowls, but those dirty dishes helped me make a special breakfast of Mickey Mouse pancakes.

You can only measure success by the love your kids felt that day. And that love is measured in mac and cheese, in smiles and laughs, in a thumbs up, and in kisses and hugs. It may be measured in bravery: when one of your children tries something she's afraid of, even if she fails. But you loving and caring for your little humans is far from nothing. It's the biggest something there is.

I also have learned what to do when I'm feeling under-appreciated. With little kids, sometimes you need to ask for the appreciation you need.

"Can I have more ketchup?" Diana asks, about to eat dinosaur chicken nuggets. Her wavy hair jounces as she bounces a little in her seat.

"What word are we missing?" I murmur.

"Can I have more ketchup, please?" Diana corrects herself.

"Much better," I say, taking the ketchup bottle over to her and squeezing it on her plate.

"Thank you," she says on her own, and I give her a thumbs up.

"I need water!" Julia's eating in the seat next to Diana, her curly hair has a drop of ketchup on the tip right by her ear.

"Hold up girl. What word did we forget to use?" I take a napkin and get the ketchup out of her hair.

"Thank you!" she screams, sounding like a squawk-ing seagull.

"It's please, but that was very close—great job. I'll always take a thank you," I grab water in a sippy cup and put it in front of her. I wrap my arm around her shoulders, "You are too cute not to hug." She laughs against my cheek.

Though I know they may not always mean that "thank you"—and it feels void of meaning most of the time—at least they are learning their manners. I want them to always go to someone else's house and be polite when ask-ing for anything, and this is a good start.

And one day they will mean it. There will come a time in our children's lives when it's important that they rec-ognize their parents as humans who have feelings and are deserving of appreciation. Encouraging kids to feel empathy for parents, not because they have to but because they want to, is an important step into adulthood. But for now, they aren't supposed to be thanking us, so we need to do things to help ourselves.

The other day, I was walking with Julia and Charli back to the car at pick up from Julia's nursery school.

"Mommy, what are we having for lunch?" Julia asked me. Her big brown eyes met mine. Charli was wriggling, trying to get me to pick her up or go back into my belly, which wasn't going to happen!

"What are you doing, silly?" I picked her up in my arms.

"I got you the special French toast bagels you like." I said to Julia, knowing they are her favorite.

"Oh, yummy. Thank you, Mommy. You are the best!" Her ringlets bounced as she jumped up and down.

And when they say these words without my prompting, it's the best feeling in the world. Because they truly mean it. They are thankful and appreciative, and it's nice to hear.

The same goes for my relationship with my partner. Jonathan calls me a nag at times for my efforts at trying to keep the house together, but he doesn't realize what it's like to have the entire mental load on your shoulders. To be the one that oversees everything. Because when I outsource things to him, he often forgets.

"Jo, did you remember to bring the computer paper home from work and the Post-its?" I asked as I headed to my office, to finally get some work done after putting Charli down for the night, which in our house means until she needs a bottle or has a nightmare and needs me again.

"Oh man," he said, putting his hands atop his head.

"Oh, and Julia's Universal Health form. I asked you to scan the form to send to the doctor because I don't have a scanner here, or else I'd do it myself." I said angrily, knowing what the answer was going to be.

"Babe, work was just so busy." His brows knitted tight as he squirmed. His expression looked guilty—because he was!

"Jo! You forgot again! I texted you. I am going to make a note." My gaze darted his way, and he looked at the floor.

I saw him squeeze his hands together as I grabbed a pen and started making a list of the items I needed.

"You are such a nag. I'll remember on my own." He said letting out a cold laugh.

I looked down at my feet.

Nag. I would love it if I didn't have to be a nag. It would be nice if someone else thought about everything I did—everyone's schedules, making doctor's appointments, packing lunches and snacks, buying gifts for birthdays, keeping track of what groceries and medicines are running low, everyone's mental well-being, vacuuming the crumbs off the kitchen floor—and it didn't all fall on me.

It would be nice if he wasn't so forgetful.

It would be nice if I didn't have to carry the whole family all the time and they could carry some of their own weight without me reminding them ten times myself.

But if I don't do it myself or delegate it won't get done.

And the most ironic thing of all is that when they finally make the bed or clean up their room, it needs to be congratulated or applauded, or they won't do it again. Can you imagine a mom not doing any of what she did again until she was applauded?

And it's frustrating waiting for Jonathan. He doesn't have the same urgency and level of care I have when I ask him to perform a task. Plus, it's tiring telling everyone to do all the things they should instinctively do—the last thing I want to do is micromanage one more person.

I just want to get everything done for the people I love most—my family.

And yes, Jonathan often takes advantage of all that I do, but to be honest we take advantage of each other. That's what people do when they live together. They get comfortable, and we get used to each other's roles. I take care of the kids and do my work, and he loads the dishes and does odds and ends around the house at night. We expect each other to do these things. I often forget that his day is hard, too. He often forgets how touched-out I am by the end of mine and why. How sometimes I just want silence. But appreciation begets appreciation. I have learned to thank him for the little things he does, and he does the same for me, too. I also express appreciation when he shows his appreciation—so he knows it is noticed.

I have become a better mom through conquering these feelings of being invisible. They have forced me out of my comfort zone, to be vulnerable enough with other moms to make strong friendships, to find peace within myself without getting praise or a pat on the back from others, and to ask for what I need in my relationships.

But the bottom line is that being a mom is so hard. You have to remember yourself, what you love, and who you are. Through this realization, I've learned how important it is to let people in. The community you meet and the life you build make motherhood so much better. Having people with whom you can laugh, and cry is truly a blessing. Having that support and love in my life has made me into a better mom and human.

— 9 —

Married Life with Little Children Is Never 50/50

It's 7 PM on a typical Tuesday night.

"I feel like we are going to have a late night!" I say to Jonathan as I scramble around the kitchen, looking over in disgust at the dishes and the cups and sippy cups piled high in the sink left over from the entire day. I really must clean, but I can't right now. Right now, we need dinner.

I open the freezer and grab chicken nuggets. I am not in the mood for the "what do you want for dinner" game that we play each meal, where I try to get my children to eat healthier and it ends in an argument, tears, and no meal eaten at all.

Jonathan starts cutting up strawberries.

"I'm so hungry," Vivienne moans. Suddenly, a rush of water splatters across the table and onto the floor. "Julia, why did you knock my cup?"

Big tears stream down Julia's face as she pushes out of her chair and storms to the other room, her loud wails assaulting my ears.

"Go apologize. She didn't do it on purpose," I plead with Viv, too overwhelmed to go myself.

"She's being a baby." Viv murmurs.

"Be a nice human, please. She's also tired. Go talk to your sister. Now!" I demand, taking a breath and refocusing on the here and now.

"Fine," she hisses, dragging her feet, each footfall chaotically spaced from the last.

I grab paper towels and wipe up the water to prevent another meltdown—someone slipping and hitting the ground.

"No. Not like that. You're making more of a mess," Jonathan says, raising his eyebrows and tone of voice at my quick water wipe up.

"Then you do it!" I say through the raging of my heart.

Charli splatters an apple sauce pack all over the floor next to us.

We both eye it. "I got it, even though it probably won't be good enough for you," I fume as I get up to take the pack Charli is still squeezing out of her hands.

"That's it. There's just too many of them! It's too loud. There's too much chaos. I had a long day at work. You need to find a better way." Jonathan places his hands atop his head. "I'm out!" he barks, followed by a long breath as he rushes out of the room.

What does he mean *you* need to find a better way?

"What do you mean you're out? You can't just leave!" I yell after him, realizing he probably doesn't even hear me because Julia is crying that loudly. My eyes open wide as Charli pulls herself up onto my back, her chubby toddler hand grasping my shoulder.

When everything doesn't go according to plan it becomes my fault. It always falls on me to fix it. It's unfair.

When the kids aren't behaving, instead of disciplining them, Jonathan yells, "Dani!" as if I'm the one misbehaving, and I need to solve the fight or meltdown in front of him.

As far as our mealtime routine, I have tried everything, and every meal seems to be chaos. None of it makes a difference because you can't predict the unpredictable that happens with kids with many different personalities and mood swings. Someone will usually be upset.

There's a small humming of "Mama, Mama," in my ear above Julia's cries. Charli squeezes me, trying to get my attention.

"Ouch, I hurt my toe." Diana frowns, her eyes filling with tears.

"What did you do?" I said pulling one of her socks off her foot and checking her toes.

"I accidentally kicked the bottom of the table," her words come out broken up and all she can make are stuttering sounds.

"Diana, your toes look like toes. Do you want me to give them a kiss?"

Diana's teary eyes meet mine. "No!" she says through choppy breathing and watery eyes as she dramatically falls from her chair to the floor.

Viv sings "Miracle" from the new Matilda movie with a broken British accent. She pulls herself onto the countertop as if a spotlight is beaming from the kitchen lights down on her. You know, when everyone else is having a breakdown, it's the perfect time to break out into a solo.

"Get off the counter, now! Viv, come on!" I say, completely flustered.

Vivienne keeps singing, as she jumps off the counter and does a lap around the kitchen island—being, well, Vivienne.

I rub my temples and look around at the scene in front of me. I feel hot rage rising in my body. But the rage is not directed toward my kids, who are simply being kids. My rage is directed at the person who is supposed to be my partner in all of this—my husband.

I wasn't sure if I was more impressed or enraged—maybe a little of both, because it must be nice to get to leave, to walk out with no worries. I have said the exact same sentence he said—"That's it. I'm out!"—to myself, in my head, in soft whispers, and out loud in screams, depending on my mood.

But I never actually leave. Never. I can't. Who will watch the kids? I don't have backup. I *am* the back up!

I'm the CEO of the household, a position I never applied for, that has no pay or sick days, but falls entirely on me.

So, when I lose it, I just make the situation so much worse for myself.

"You're mad at me," Julia will say, chin and shoulders trembling as she runs toward me.

Tears will start to fill Diana's eyes, too. Charli will get upset from the loud noises and join the chorus of tears, wanting to be picked up.

Because when the room is filled with tears, screaming never seems to make anything better.

Then I apologize and apologize some more. "I'm sorry. I shouldn't have reacted like that." My eyes will sink as my tone softens.

Or "I'm not mad. Mommy's just frustrated and tired because Mommy's human, just like you, and makes mistakes," as I transform into a human tissue, soaked with so many tears from everyone's wet and snotty faces.

I try to reassure them it's not them, and it isn't. They're kids. A lot of the time it's directed at myself, for having a hard day and feeling overwhelmed. Other times it's directed at my partner for not pulling his weight or not having the patience I have.

It drives him crazy. Our daughters have four very different but loud personalities. I get it. It's a lot.

And even though he handles certain chores and can be helpful, if I need anything else from him, I need to ask. I need to tell him whose birthday party he needs to pick up Vivienne from or remind him to pick up milk on the way home from work. I need to tell him about every detail of the day. I am the keeper of all the information, schedules, appointments, and homework assignments. I know how to comfort Diana's meltdowns and how to get Julia set up the proper way for bedtime so that she'll fall asleep without "wanting Mommy." I know everyone's preferences, and because of my role as the keeper, I need to remind him of everything.

And he will constantly say when I get frustrated, "but I was helping you." "But I was helping you make dinner" or "but I was helping you take care of the baby."

"You aren't helping me. They are your kids, too!" I say, entirely at my wit's end. Because sometimes I do feel like they're my kids, and he's the babysitter. But dads aren't babysitters. They are parents. They are supposed to help with their kids, not help me with ours!

It's all not entirely his fault; I am the parent who stays at home—the default parent—so the mental load falls entirely on my shoulders. I am responsible for everything. And truthfully, I can't imagine not having this position, because I care too much not to—but it can be overwhelming.

I'm the one who is up when the baby is fussy all night long, bouncing her as tears fill my eyes from exhaustion.

I'm the one who takes care of Vivienne when she's sick, propping her up on her pillow so she stops coughing and rubbing her back until she falls back to sleep.

I'm the one who combats the monsters that take over Julia's dreams. I come in and check under her bed, in the closet, wipe away her tears and lay down with her until she feels safe again.

It's not his job to worry. It's mine, and it comes very naturally. I can't help it.

It's my job to worry if the kids get to school on time or we get another Tardy because our kids never seem to cooperate.

It's my job to worry if Diana is having a hard time adjusting to school and working with therapists to try to help her through it.

It's my job to make sure all the kids have their snacks and lunches packed with handwritten notes reminding them how loved they are.

It's my job to make sure they are comfortable, confident, and well-adjusted.

It's my job to make sure they aren't falling behind at school.

It always falls on one parent, and that parent walks around feeling like the Leaning Tower of Pisa. She emotionally and physically holds so much; she can't even stand up straight.

I have talked to so many of my mom friends, and they all feel the same. We complain about our partners' lack of initiative.

Michelle Obama has even said she couldn't stand Barack for over ten years. Ten entire years. And guess when those ten years were? When her kids were little. Yep. She couldn't stand seemingly perfect Barack. Because according to Michelle, marriage isn't 50/50.

And it's not. Some days, it's 70/30. Others, it's 80/20, and sometimes, it's even 100/0.

Don't get me wrong. I love that man more than the day I married him. I swore I'd love him for richer or poorer, in sickness and health, until death do us part, and I do. And he's now the father of my children, which means so much more. But let's just say I'm not staring into his eyes and declaring my unending love for him on a regular basis. Sometimes I'm staring into his eyes and picturing ways I'd lock him out of the house and hide his keys.

As I continue to fume at Jonathan for making an exit and leaving me to deal with the mealtime chaos, I'm thinking of a similar situation that happened a few nights before. We were winding down for the night, and I needed to help Diana brush her teeth—but someone needed to keep an eye on the baby monitor.

"Can you watch Charli on the monitor and feed her if she gets up?" I said firmly, making sure he heard me.

"Sure, put it right here." He pointed to the kitchen island as he unbuttoned the top button of his shirt.

"Are you sure you got this?" I pursed my lips, doubting how sure I was. I double checked it before placing it down on the black crumb-filled-and-was-that-red-sauce-from-dinner? surface.

He gave me a thumbs up as I heard his phone buzz.

"Hey bro," he said, and walked away.

I was hesitant but was distracted by Diana's screams of, "Mommy! Mommy!" I went to help her brush her teeth.

I came back down to see an image on the monitor of Charli sitting upright looking around. He had drifted to the other room and stopped looking at the monitor.

When I pass him the baton, he tends to have slippery hands and drop it, instead of making it to the finish line. Not on purpose, but he doesn't handle it with the same sense of urgency and care as I do.

"Good job watching her." I wanted to say more, but I bit down on my tongue so hard, so I wouldn't keep talking.

"Oh man, I forgot. Sorry." He mouthed, and casually went back to talking on the phone like it was no big deal.

But it *was* a big deal.

Now, I had to put Charli back to sleep because she only wants me at night. And that meant me rocking her despite my aching back. Me, feeding her with my tired-from-lifting-her-all-day arms. There just didn't seem to be regard for what I would have to do if he messed up.

And you know what happens when I ask him to try?

The other night when I heard her loud wails through the monitor, I felt like I couldn't do it anymore. Nothing was going to plan. I needed a break—desperately. I was physically and mentally overwhelmed by parenting all day and night long.

"Can you please get her this time? I'm exhausted." I sat on a chair at the kitchen table, wild-eyed, knowing in my beating fast heart that I was going to be the one running upstairs to comfort her, again.

Because 99 times out of 100 I'm met with a variety of these responses:

"I can't. I need to wash my hands. I was just breaking down cardboard."

"I can't. I need to wash my hands. I was eating chips and salsa."

"I can't. I need to wash my hands. I just took the garbage out."

He says these things while looking down at them, like they are the filthiest, sweatiest hands that ever existed.

And my favorite excuse of all is, "She likes you better." Or "I can't. She doesn't respond to me well."

My mind screams: *She likes me better because I am the one doing everything for her. Always!*

"Never mind." I said instead, going quiet to try to mask how frustrated I was. I had no energy to fight.

And then it was the mad dash up the stairs. Out of breath, I picked Charli up and fed her, stroking her head as she suckled. I watched her eyelids close slowly then all at once, and she was peacefully sleeping again. I stroked her head and took in her littleness. Her soft skin, button nose, and wispy hair. I carefully placed her back into her crib, not wanting to wake her, and lay down on my bed, sinking into the puffy white duvet stained with milk. I was beyond exhausted.

Jonathan and I haven't always been this out of whack. When Vivienne was our only child, we were on the same page—and he often took the lead. She didn't prefer me over him. She wanted us evenly, even though I spent the day with her. Then as we started having more and more kids, the mental load increased way past his capacity with work in the mix. I filled in his gaps and tried to lessen his load as much as possible, especially since I wanted a big family, until it all slowly fell on me. He never wanted four kids. He was great with two, OK with three, and wasn't sold on the fourth.

I put it off for a while, but by Mother's Day 2021, I had such a strong desire in my heart for one more child, I couldn't hold it in anymore. It would complete our family. I was ready to start trying, but I was afraid to tell Jonathan. I came downstairs, my brows scrunched, deciding that day was the day. He couldn't be mad at me on Mother's Day—*my* day.

"Happy Mother's Day," Jonathan said, giving me a kiss that tasted of him, chocolate chip muffin, and a sip of coffee. I pressed him closer.

The girls swarmed my body, covering me with hugs.

"Aw, thank you. That was a yummy kiss, too, Jonathan." I gave the girls hugs and smiles. My mouth burrowing into their heads as I covered them in so many kisses.

"What do you want for Mother's Day?" he asked.

"Well, maybe another one of these," I said, voice cracking, whispering so the girls wouldn't hear.

Our eyes met. His tensed.

"You ruined Mother's Day," his voice strained, and he stormed out of the kitchen.

At first, I thought he was joking because, *really?*

But when he didn't come back laughing, a piece of my heart felt torn out, leaving nothing but a gaping wound. I dropped my face into my hands. This wasn't how I pictured that conversation going.

He didn't talk to me for the rest of the day.

Even though the next day he came around to the idea, this is how I picture him. *He didn't want this. Make him want this.* And I put the pressure on myself to make it as seamless for him as possible.

He also works five days a week, leaving early in the morning and not getting home until after 7:30 PM most nights. So, he's not home in the trenches 24/7, and it's harder to handle the noise and chaos when you're not used to it. Some days he doesn't even see Charli. He's tired, too. He puts in a long day just like me, though it's different.

And when the kids finally go to sleep, he wants to spend time with me, but I have nothing left to give on most days. I still have tasks pending—preparing everything for the next day, paying bills, and doing some work. I also like to unwind and recharge in the quiet, writing or reading after a day filled with so much noise. It's hard to find a balance that keeps him happy, too. I think most mothers feel this.

When I'm spent, the shower is the place I find my refuge in the mornings. It's my five minutes to myself, and it gives me an opportunity to think, breathe, or simply just be.

Once in a while Jonathan will try to join me, like the other day. I let the warm water wash over my face, I looked down at my feet and closed my eyes, still wishing I were asleep.

Suddenly, I heard the shower door creaking open, and felt cold air hit my body. I turned around. It was Jonathan.

"No, Jonathan, what if the baby gets up? Please, I only get a couple of minutes." I said, removing his hand from the small of my back and wriggling my body away from his.

"She won't. Relax," he paused. "I'm sure of it," a coy smile clung to his lips. Only as sure as someone who is clearly thinking with the wrong head.

"You don't know that, and none of that is happening!" I said, shaking my head slowly.

"None of what?"

"That!" I said quietly, pointing.

Not even ten seconds later, we both heard Charli's complaints echo through the bathroom.

"Damn, I knew it." I stomped my foot, splashing warm water at him. Not deliberately, but I wasn't mad about it.

It was a standoff. Me, staring into Jonathan's dark brown eyes, wanting him to make a move—but not the move on his mind—the one out of the shower to get the baby. Him, staring at me as if he is still getting some action. Charli interrupted our showdown by dialing up the volume on her complaining, and my heart couldn't take it. And guess who ended up going?

"You can be so selfish!" I mumbled under my breath. A puddle formed below my feet with each step I took because I didn't have time to wring out my sopping wet hair that still had a glob of conditioner in it.

It's Halloween 2023. It's the first cold day of the season.

I'm wearing a winter coat. In my Bjorn is a snotty, cranky Charli who is dressed as Gizmo the gremlin. She looks so cute that I may dress her up in this costume every day just to snuggle, but she's acting like a gremlin I gave water to after midnight because she's coming off a week filled with croup and pinkeye.

The air coolly hits us as we walk down a street closed off for pedestrians for trick-or-treating. It feels nice not to have to worry about cars coming, or an excited kid possibly running into the street without thinking.

"Mom, come with me!" Julia, wearing a pink cupcake costume, pulls my hand to follow her up the stairs of a brown wooden house. A couple of bigger kids push their way around us. I protect her from the aggressive Minion and Super Mario to her right. She grabs a Milky Way and places it in her jack-o-lantern trick-or-treat bag. I grab a Twix for Charli. We walk down the stairs as I see Viv in her blue policewoman dress, leather coat, and handcuffs hanging from her belt excitedly embrace a girl from her class.

They then grab each other's hand and run to a white house across the street. Jonathan is next to me with Diana in the stroller. We are only twenty minutes in, and she's already over Halloween, complaining she's cold, overwhelmed by the number of people, her legs hurt, and she wants to go home.

"I'll follow them. Stay with Julia." I say to Jonathan, as I run after them. Viv is laughing with her friend, who is dressed as a black cat, whiskers painted on her face. As I'm waiting on the lawn, I look up and watch the clouds drift, then back to the girls collecting their candy.

"Dani, come here." I faintly hear Jonathan bark above the crowd. I point to Vivienne.

"Dani, now!" My heart jitters as I run toward Viv and squeeze her shoulder: *We need to go.*

I grab Vivienne's hand and rush her and her friend toward Jonathan. By the time I get to him, Julia's in tears. Her whipped cream and cherry headband is falling off her head. She's crying and saying something inaudible.

"What happened?" I panic and hold her close as she wipes her tears on my jacket.

"I lost her."

My full body stiffens. *Did I hear him wrong?*

"What do you mean you lost her?" My brows tense. I'm angry. I pull Julia into my arms.

"I was following a kid dressed as a cupcake. And then when the cupcake turned around, it wasn't Julia."

"How do you follow the wrong cupcake?" I look Julia up and down. How could this have happened?

"I don't know, it was a freak thing that happened," he says, averting his gaze.

A freak thing.

I look at Julia. "That will never happen to you again, baby." Tears are sliding off her cheeks.

"I want to go home," Julia moans, more tears, bigger tears, are now sliding down her cheeks onto her pink cupcake costume. I feel a lump burgeoning in my throat. I let out an angry breath.

Because gosh, I'm angry.

What if he lost her for longer? If she slipped away into the flood of kids? She's four. How could he even take his eyes off her for one moment? It's not like she's wearing a mask where you can't check her identity. The thought of it all nearly knocks the wind out of me. Because she's our cupcake, with curly pigtails, a cherry on top of her head, and almond shaped dark brown eyes. Our cupcake who we lie with each night as we listen to the stories about her day. Our cupcake who when I check on her each night, all cozied up, makes my heart burst.

My vision blurs from tears. My eyes burn, and my throat tightens thinking about her. I sweep her flyaway hairs behind her ears.

I know he's human and this is a mistake, but I can't help but feel upset. His sense of urgency and protection is nowhere close to my strong mama bear instincts, and it makes it hard for me to completely let my guard down. He's a good dad, but he doesn't think about how someone could grab her and take her away. He doesn't think about the consequences. He just doesn't think sometimes.

And she should never feel unsafe. And right now, she does, and wants to go home.

"Why don't you choose a piece of candy to eat, and Mommy is going to stay with you the rest of the time." She quickly picks Reese's. I peel the wrapper off, and she smiles as she takes her first bite, still breathing heavy.

"Better?" I ask. She gives me a thumbs up. Her eyes are still damp.

Everyone who I repeat this story to since then thinks it's hilarious. I mean, it could be an episode of Full House. Danny Tanner is following the wrong cupcake while trick-or-treating, thinking it's his youngest daughter, Michelle. When he realizes it's the wrong cupcake and Michelle is fine when he finds her, it's a funny and cute story. They end up hugging and it's a heartwarming episode. It's so nice that daddy went trick-or-treating. What an involved dad.

But, I bet you if Aunt Becky lost Michelle, it wouldn't be seen as humorous or heartwarming.

Because if a mom or any female caretaker did the same thing, everyone would be coming down on her. They would automatically label her as a bad parent or caretaker. How can you lose a child? How neglectful.

And this double standard applies to everything. If a dad makes dinner, does the dishes, changes everyone into their pajamas, he's the best dad in the world. But if a mom does the same thing, she's met only with criticism. *She should potty-train her three-and-a-half-year old already.*

Or, why did she make her kids pizza and chicken nuggets for dinner? She's lazy. People pay more attention to the nitty-gritty details when it comes to moms. When Mom makes a mistake, everyone has an opinion, and she's so easily reduced to a bad mom. But when Dad does, it's met with so much grace. All he needs to do is show up with love, and he's magical.

And it's unfair.

It's time for moms to be looked at with dad goggles—because it doesn't matter how she does it, if she shows up with love, mom is magical, too.

After the Halloween incident, I decided it was time to talk to Jonathan about how we could better support each other at home. I was at the end of my rope, and I knew something needed to change.

That weekend we took a walk with the kids down our street. It was a sunny day with a refreshing yet cool breeze. Charli was in my Bjorn with a wool hat, her button nose running from a cold. I tucked her hands into my coat to keep them warm and placed my hands in my jacket pockets.

Vivienne was scooting ahead of us, her long hair blowing under her helmet. Julia and Diana were following us in a remote control hot pink car.

The leaves rustled below our feet with each footfall. I decided on this beautiful fall day—it was time.

"Our life is crazy right now, as you know. I know you work hard and are tired, too, but I need you to step up when I ask you to try. I don't care if you fail, just trying instead of making an excuse makes a difference to me. Never getting a break is exhausting. Some nights I feel like I'm breaking." I stiffened, afraid he would get upset at my criticism.

"I will do better." He glanced at me and let out a cold breath.

"Thank you. And if I hear about your hands being too dirty one more time, I may end you." I snorted.

"But these hands need a lot of care," he said smiling, as I rolled my eyes.

"And you know what I want from you—more time as a couple." Jonathan's smile faltered.

"I will try to be more present with you in the moments we do have together. I have a million things going on, so it's hard for me not to feel rushed and overwhelmed, but I'll work on it. I know you miss me mutchering you, too . . ." I took one of my hands out of my pocket and placed it on his hand.

When we first got together, I couldn't keep my hands off him. My mom would joke, "Stop mutchering him!" I'm a touchy-feely person—and "mutcher" means to bother in Yiddish. Jonathan loved being "bothered" by me. I'd always have an arm around his back, or be sifting my hand through his hair, grabbing his hand, nuzzling into his neck, and stroking his face. But now that the kids are in my lap, wanting to be picked up, and touching me in some way 24/7, I'm touched out by the time he gets home.

"I do miss the mutchering," He swallowed. His eyes flashed and then found their way back to mine. He smiled.

"We will both do better." I said as the cold breeze pushed my hair off my forehead and his hand laced into mine.

Since that conversation, we started having dinner every night without phones in front of us, so we could catch up on everything we hadn't talked about already during the day without distractions. It became more challenging when I was writing this book, but he was incredibly understanding and supportive. He has even taken over bedtime with Diana, Julia, and Vivienne, which lets me get a head start on everything I have left to do with work and writing. He has tried harder with the baby, and as she's getting older, she's more receptive to him. Even when he fails, the effort is seen and appreciated. I'm very grateful for him and all that he does.

We're far from perfect, but it's a start. We truly are best friends who love each other. That foundation means everything.

And no, we haven't found the magical balance yet in our household—but I think most families can relate to this. Marriage with little children is just hard.

But I'm not here to give you a solution. I'm here instead in solidarity with the mothers or fathers stuck in the 90/10 or 60/40 who hold most of the load. I know how you feel. I know the frustration, and I know it's not OK. I know, society needs to do better.

But at the end of the day, we really are both doing our very best with the resources we have and everything we have on our too-full plates.

Besides, Jonathan is a light in our household.

When Daddy comes home, his footsteps echo off the house announcing his arrival.

Diana's ears perk up, and she runs down the stairs and leaps into his arms, eyes lit with happiness and pure love.

He puts her down and she clasps her hand in his, leading him upstairs. Then it's straight to playing before bedtime because there's not much time.

"Giddy up, horsey!" I watch Diana bounce up and down on Jonathan's back, shaking with laughter. Her brown hair windblown.

"She's going to fall! Careful, guys!" I nervously smile as I enter the password in my phone, wanting to capture this moment on video.

"I want a turn!" Julia moans.

"Me too!" Viv begs.

In these moments, I beam. He's such a great dad.

He's the main source of laughter. The thrower of children into the couch for them to only appear later with a huge smile on their faces and the sound of laughter. The flipper of them upside down as their eyes flash. The favorite for bedtime tuck-in because he reads stories in silly voices. He can bust a move during our family-wide dance parties like no one else. He's the man they can count on to be at every dance recital, sports game, or school event, recording them in awe. He's someone they can always count on, besides me. And that means everything.

A couple of days later after Halloween, we're at our good friend's apartment. It's our first time out as a couple since Charli was born 17 months before. Ben, the birthday boy, is turning 42.

We walk in the apartment, and I look at the shelves covered in framed pictures of their children from when they were babies. I stop at one of the entire family together and smile. I hear banging in the kitchen, and of course, being a mom of two, Arielle's towel-drying dishes as she takes them out of the dishwasher. She's wearing black shorts and a gray t-shirt, sweat glistening on her forehead.

The first thing that comes out of her mouth as we hug is, "I got hot while putting the kids to bed, and I didn't change back." Society has clearly made her feel like she needs to explain her attire—yes, she's not in a fancy dress for her husband's birthday, but she's at her apartment with good friends and doesn't need to be. Besides, this mom doesn't play by those rules either.

"Bedtime is a full contact sport. I get it. Plus, you look great," I assure her. Also, I am her. I have my sweats on, hair frizzy, wild, and down, and a Mickey Mouse shirt on that I wear so often that my husband threatens to hide it.

It's just so darn comfy. I always counter that I'd cut his ties in half. Every single last one of them. He hasn't called my bluff . . . yet.

"Where's the birthday boy?" He gets a hug too, as he pops out from setting up the kitchen table.

Other friends show up. A tall man with scruff and glasses comes in with a gift in his hands. We talk about an art piece hanging on the wall of the different cereal characters from the nineties sitting at a long black table and bond over the role sugary cereals played in our childhoods.

"My favorite was Cinnamon Toast Crunch," I say, thinking about the cinnamon and sweet goodness and eating them with my mom for dessert at night while we'd catch up on the day.

"I was a Tony the Tiger guy for sure," says the man with scruff.

"Well, they're g-r-r-r-eat for a reason!" I smile awkwardly.

"Yes, they are." He chuckles.

I make my way to the kitchen where everyone gathers. I see my husband standing there. I soak him in. The white shirt he wears with slim cut black pants. He's always so put together and smells like Tom Ford cologne. He looks cute outside the house. He's far less irritated, and it's weird seeing him without furrowed brows or a cocked head. I go up to him and lean into him for a hug, wrapping my arms around his midsection feeling the warmth radiating off him. He kisses the top of my head.

"Wait, you guys still hug and kiss after four kids?" One of the guests asks, eyes wide.

"I guess we do," I say. We both share a look as a smile touches my mouth.

Because the truth is my love for my babies overshadows my marriage most of the time, and we do take each other for granted. With the chaos of life, it's hard for us to nurture our marriage like we used to—to find the time to go out on dates or not be too worn out at night to enjoy each other's company.

We are in perpetual survival mode right now, trying not to drown in the day-to-day life of parenting and adulthood.

But at the same time, we love each other more than the puppy love, the butterflies, and infatuation that started our relationship. That faded, but our love is so much deeper. We have been by each other's sides through so much.

He picks me up on the days I'm feeling sorry for myself, crying into a pillow that I'm failing as a mom, wife, partner, and as an employee.

I place my hands over his on the days he's feeling every emotion under the sun and chewing his lower lip hard out of fear.

We have been through hard pregnancies with sleepless nights, morning sickness, swelling, so many aches and stressful moments between doctor's visits where we weren't sure everything would be OK.

We have been through deliveries where we were overtaken by fear, on our knees with red and puffy eyes praying for my life and the life of our unborn child.

And no one knows our kids like us.

No one understands quite like us the sheer volume of Julia's cry, the funny and way-too-sassy words that come out of Vivie's mouth that make us both laugh and cringe, and the dark humor of our sweet Diana.

We both live and breathe these children, each other, and our family of six.

A couple of weeks later, he went away for four days to a wedding in San Francisco.

The days he was gone, the creaks in the house were louder at night after the girls fell asleep.

The house was a lot messier with more dirty dishes in the sink and crumbs on the countertops.

But worst of all, I'd roll over to hand Charli a bottle and his side of the bed was empty and quiet in the middle of the night. I didn't feel his feet touch mine under the covers. I missed his touch. His warmth. His company. I missed every annoying and not-so-annoying thing about him, because gosh, I love that man.

He's my best friend—the first person I call each time I get into the car—and I am his.

This parenthood thing would be so much harder without him.

So, yes, we fight more about the dumb little things. We're touched out and drowning in baby cries, tantrums, and mess. We spend most of our time resenting each other. Our patience isn't as high as it used to be. And we get on each other's last nerve more than we like to admit. But our love has only become stronger through everything we've been through. There is no doubt in my mind this is the person I want to grow old, gray, and wrinkly with. To visit our grandchildren with and to look back on a not-so-easy life filled with so many blessings—because we're unconditional, we are family—and we're better together.

— 10 —

There Are No Bad Kids,
Just Bad Behavior

V IVIENNE HAS A wild heart made of fire and fierce
determination. And I love how that strength flows
through her veins and fills her little body. She's been a
wild spirit since she first began to show her personality as
a toddler. Her chubby feet were always planted on the
ground, unwilling to budge unless it was to take her shoes
off and chuck them across the room, no matter what
I said. And she hasn't changed.

She's a force to be reckoned with.

I have always encouraged her to explore her world—to
climb on things that were meant to be climbed and to
find out for herself what's frustrating or fun. I want her
to feel her big feelings. Even as I want to be the calm in
her storm. I want to support her through those meltdown
moments, not make them worse.

I'll never forget one day when Vivienne was five and
she was being difficult. She was continually hurting her
younger sisters despite my repeated warnings. She
wrecked her sisters' Magna-Tile castle they were building
for their Paw Patrol and Peppa Pigs, the thud causing

every muscle in my body to tense as it scattered debris and unloosed a flood of big wet tears and screams from her siblings.

She wouldn't get her glasses from her room, and after I caved and got them for her, every time I looked at her, they weren't on her face.

She didn't want the scrambled eggs she asked for during breakfast, and when I made the bagel she "really wanted," it was met with the same response.

"Fine, then you won't have dessert later," I said, angrily taking the bagel off the table.

"Fine, I don't care," she tipped her head back, equally angry. That's the frustrating thing about her—she's willing to suffer the consequences just to prove she is right.

Never more so than on this day. I kept my cool for the most part, even though at times everything in me pushed me closer to losing my mind. But by 10 AM I was at my wit's end, trying to keep it together. And then it got worse.

We were cleaning up the playroom, getting ready to leave the house for the playground, when Vivienne said, "I'm going to pick up the puzzle pieces behind the doll house." Eyeing her from across the room, I said, "No," immediately recognizing the danger—Julia was behind it and Vivienne could cause the house to fall on her.

"Stop," I said, but Vivienne kept going.

"You better not." I warned her again. She paid no attention.

"I mean it. Stop. No. NOOOO!"

Four times. I couldn't have been clearer. As if in slow motion, I saw Vivienne wedge herself in behind the doll-house, and I watched as it began to topple—the mini fridge, bathtub, bed, all the contents, falling on my Julia. Quickly crossing the floor, I was able to push the small building back up, injuring my hand in the process. It still hit Julia's head, though, and her eyes welled with tears. Her tiny mouth quivered, and she gasped for air before the flood came.

I glared at Vivienne. How could she not get it? Why couldn't she listen? Why does it always have to get to this point?

The inevitable questions roared through my mind, dragging angry heat, and it was in that state of mind that I turned from comforting Julia, my hysterical child, and stormed over to my strong-willed daughter. Grasping her hands, I began shouting at her, unleashing on her the brunt of my fury and panic.

"I am done with you!" I heard myself say, and ordered her to go to her room. *Done with you? Why would I say that?*

Vivienne cried as my hurtful words hit her ears, and watching her leave the playroom, I was shaken. She could have really injured her sister. Her behavior had certainly injured me. I didn't recognize myself in that moment when a red rage overtook me. It doesn't happen often, but when it does, I feel full of shame and regret. But Vivienne's behavior can do this to me at times. They say parenting is all about picking your battles, but "they" weren't parents to Vivienne or another strong-willed child. A day doesn't go by without her battling me. Now, at eight years old, it is more filled with eyerolls, big emotions, and a disrespectful attitude.

It used to take me over the edge, to a place where I was just done. Broken. And sometimes at that point, I'd lose it. I'd let it consume me.

Returning to Julia, I brushed her tears away. Once she was calm again, feeling at a loss, feeling like a failure, I went upstairs to Vivienne's room and apologized for my overreaction and the hurtful things I'd said.

I never want to discipline her fire out of her, but I also want her to stay alive, keep other people alive around her, and make sure she becomes a good human. And most of the time while considering all of that, it's a challenge not to get mad. I know one day she is going to do great things, but she's hard to parent.

The day only got worse. Because a bad behavior day by one kid makes everyone behave worse. When Viv has a bad behavior day, it trickles down to all the kids who become extra sensitive and whiny. It feels like Julia is crying most of the day while Diana becomes irritated with the loud noises around her. Everyone starts fighting and no one is having fun. It impacts the entire family.

Later at the park, when Vivienne knocked Diana to the ground on purpose, twice, I lost it again, and in a barrage of "What were you thinking?" I put her in time-out.

Moments later, as I comforted Diana, I lost the battle fighting my own tears, and once the first one broke, a torrent followed. What was I doing wrong that caused Vivienne to behave like this? I hated the way I was reacting to her. It was disgraceful. I couldn't keep my cool that day.

I'm such a bad mom, whispered a voice in my brain. Because, gosh, I felt guilty. For my own and my daughter's behavior. And I don't ever want her to feel like a bad kid, but all I was doing that day was disciplining her with "no" and "stop" at every turn. She must have felt it, too, I thought as I shepherded the girls from the park.

While I do tell Vivienne how wonderful she is, I knew days like that must take a toll on her. Piling everyone into the car, I felt defeated by motherhood. I wanted to roll up in a ball of exhaustion. But motherhood doesn't allow downtime. I had to mom on, regardless. Who else would watch my kids?

Driving away, tears flowed some more, racing down my cheeks, dripping onto the wheel.

"Mommy, what are we having for dinner tonight?" Vivienne asked, unaware that I was breaking down.

I tried to answer her, but my words broke into bits and all that came out were stuttering noises. I gulped in a breath and refocused my gaze on the road ahead. I needed a moment to sit in the tangled mess of my emotions. I knew I couldn't laugh the pain away. I couldn't ignore it either. I needed to feel it. Because even though I'm Mommy, I'm also human. And that's more than OK.

Because sometimes moms need to break to feel whole again.

Vivienne caught my gaze in the rearview mirror again. "Mommy, are you OK?" she asked, forehead wrinkled, and eyebrows raised.

I wasn't surprised she was the one who was asking. Because she does care, and she does love me. She is a good kid.

The truth is that there are no bad kids, just bad behavior, and there's usually a reason for it. Shortly after this challenging day, Vivienne was diagnosed with ADHD, which explained her impulsive and hyperactive behaviors. She wasn't using her hands on purpose. She didn't ignore everything I said on purpose. She couldn't help it. This empowering diagnosis helped me change my perspective on everything. I now don't consider bad behavior days to be "bad days."

At Julia's ballet class recently, I saw a little girl with blonde hair hit another little girl with red pigtails on the head with a Hula hoop to get her attention. I overheard her mother talking to the other little girl's mom, apologizing, and saying that her daughter was just diagnosed with ADHD and can be impulsive. No one understood that better than me who overheard it.

Another time, I had a friend come over with her six-year-old. He was having a meltdown like a toddler, kicking and screaming about a toy Vivienne wasn't sharing. That friend had a new baby at home, and her son had been having difficulty adjusting.

The little boy who interrupted his mom's conversation with a friend by jumping around and screaming for her, yelling, "Mom, Momm, Mommm!" at school pick up acted like that because he didn't eat his lunch and was starving for a snack from his mom's diaper bag. I found that out shortly after she yelled at him, and he responded with big tears in his eyes, "Mommy, I am just so hungry!"

When Julia is acting out, most of the time it's because she wants attention. The other day she threw an iPad at my head. That is not typical Julia. But every time she came up to me that day to sit on my lap or give me a hug, Charli would scream and cry with envy. Charli was extra needy. Julia throwing the iPad at me was a sign she needed some one-on-one time.

Because most of the time, they're kids being kids, learning how to deal with big emotions, navigating this big world for themselves, and making mistakes along the way.

Back in the car, I forced a smile and looked at Vivienne. "Yes. Mommy is just a little sad, but I'll be OK." My reassurance was offered through fresh tears. I've learned it's OK to cry in front of my kids. It wasn't necessary to wait until I got home and hide in a closet or go into the bathroom and lock the door.

If we show our kids our tears, they will come to us with theirs, too, instead of trying to fight them or hide them. And then we can be a supportive shoulder to cry on when they don't have the will to fight their battles alone. So, as I let all my tears come out on that ride home, I didn't feel bad about it.

When I looked in the rearview mirror at my children that day, I saw them acting normally, playing with their iPads. I heard their laughter and chatter continue, and I was reassured that they, and I, were OK.

As I tucked Vivienne into bed later, she looked up at me. "Mommy, can you lie with me?"

And though our day had been hard, as much as she had frustrated me, and as much as I wanted to have some "me time," her little voice, asking, melted my heart and I nodded: yes.

Not long after she snuggled in close, draping herself around me, I heard her breath slow and, carefully lifting my head, I studied every feature of her face, admiring how she'd changed since she was a small baby, how she's grown before my very eyes. And I couldn't keep my eyes off her because she will always be the newborn who stole my entire heart and changed my life—and I love her more with each passing day, even the not-so-great ones.

Later that day, I was talking to my mom about my strong-willed girl and our day. I was obsessing, because that's what I did frequently when Viv was that age before her diagnosis. I went on and on about everything I was doing wrong, how I was worried about her, and how I was a terrible parent.

"But you aren't," protested my mom. "You're the best mom because you love those kids with all your heart. And you know what? You're going to try again tomorrow. That's all you can do. They're just bad days. Every good mom has them."

Something clicked when she said that. Because she was right. Bad days happen to everyone.

Vivienne's not the only one with bad behavior days of course. Each of my children's bad days look different.

Julia's are dramatic, sensitive, and filled with "Mommy you hate me!" or "You don't love me!" She will lose it and hit me with fury and then cry from shame for at least a half hour. She is so hard to calm down because she's so emotional. I must reassure her on repeat of my love for her until eventually she calms down. Every child has these days.

But is it just me, too, or do children always seem to be held to a higher standard than everyone else?

Think about it, can you imagine being punished because you woke up feeling "blah" and snapped at those closest to you?

But children? They're punished.

Children are people, too. They're little humans who are learning. We need to give them grace.

So, we can't take our children's "bad behavior" days personally. It's hard to remember that, like us, our kids are human. They hurt. They have days when they're grumpy, when they don't feel like dealing with anyone, and when they don't have a lot of self-control. They either can't express their feelings yet or, if they can, they don't always understand them. They act out in other ways, like refusing to listen or fighting or throwing non-stop tantrums. Their emotions are valid. And it's OK for them to feel them. Because none of us is perfect.

Look at me that day. I was trying hard, but I messed up and yelled at my child multiple times in one day. All moms do this. It's human. We yell when we're overwhelmed, when no one's listening, and one of our kids is about to get hurt at the hands of another, or they're just plain stubborn for no reason, or willful and argumentative for even less provocation. We get pushed closer and closer to the edge.

We don't want to get to that point. We hate when it happens. But just because we lose it doesn't make us bad parents. We're just humans who care more than anything in this world about our children and the type of humans they'll become, all while wanting to keep them safe. During this often-messy process, we get frustrated and mess up, sometimes as badly as our kids.

We don't want them to be brats. We don't want them to hurt their siblings. If they do that to each other, it's possible they'll do that to other kids. So, on occasion, we yell.

We care so much about our children that we get run down from running interference, keeping the peace, helping them learn—we try hard all the time, so of course we lose it on occasion.

And on those days where I lose it because I am not perfect, I try to give myself grace, not a lecture. Because we need hugs and understanding. We always have the gift of tomorrow to make it up to them. To not be so hard on them. To point them in the right direction. Because we can apologize, and we always have tomorrow when we can do better.

So, every day, I try to teach Vivienne and all my girls how to handle those very big emotions, like sadness and anger, instead of yelling at them.

And every day I wake up trying to become a better mom—a more patient, more forgiving, and stronger mom, too. A mom who doesn't let the insanity get to her because she understands her kids are human, like her.

And now, eight years in, I don't consider this type of day terrible—it's just everyday life with kids. They all have bad behavior moments, and that definitely doesn't make them bad kids or mean I am a terrible mom. They are human and learning how to navigate so many emotions. I now consider bad days the days I'm filled with anxiety and struggling at every turn or am pushing through depression. The days when something I am working on fails or something bad happens to one of my friends, children, or a family member. I am more likely to break on those days that are not based on my children's behavior. Learning this distinction has been life-changing.

— 11 —

It's OK to Set Boundaries

S WEAT IS POURING down my face. As I literally push
through labor, I am shaking and I smell like throw up.

And I am also completely surrounded by bystanders.
An audience, watching.

I hear my mother-in-law say, "She's coming. Is that a
head? I see her head!" to my mom.

My father is on one side of me, his curly hair wild as
he holds my right hand. My palms are sweaty from his
tight grip—or is it my tight grip? Jonathan is on the other
side of me, holding my left hand. They can't see what's
going on down below, and I prefer it like that.

"One more push," Dr. Ng says.

I push and scream as my cheeks flush with color, and
Vivienne slides out.

Everyone is trying to get a good look at Vivienne.
There are so many people in the room, between family,
nurses, and Dr. Ng, there's an echo of voices, and I can't
see Vivienne's face.

"Aw, she's so cute," Jonathan says.

"Such a beautiful baby," my mom beams.

I am moving my head around but can't get a good look over everyone gathering around her. I am feeling overwhelmed as I hear her cry. I bat my lashes against a wave of emotions. My hands are twisted in my hospital gown. My dad takes a picture of her being weighed and shows it to me. I take his phone and zoom in on Vivienne's face. She has a full head of hair, a button nose, and big eyes that take up her entire face. She looks like a doll. I am sharing this moment with her grandparents and there's something special about that, but I also secretly feel like this should be mine and Jonathan's moment with our baby.

My delivery room feels like a party, and I don't love it. But I invited all of them, so what did I expect? I didn't want anyone to feel left out. Like, sure, let's all watch me maybe poop instead of push out a baby, it will be a great time. I'll supply the drinks. I mean, we should have installed strobe lights and hired a DJ at this point.

"I'm feeling a little exposed," I whisper to Jonathan.

"It's a lot, but you wanted this." He laughs uncomfortably. He wipes some sweat off his forehead and his eyes close.

I nod my head. "Yes. I wanted this." I repeat, looking around. I am shaking with adrenaline.

But did I? Often in my life, things that "I've wanted" were really things I thought other people wanted, and I took them on as my own wants to make those people happy. I really didn't think about what I wanted. I never made myself a top priority. But maybe it was time for me to be, since I'm a huge part of this family.

My thumb grazes Vivienne's forehead as she's put on my chest. I trace her little face with my fingers, taking in its details.

"Smile, Dan," My dad says, trying to get my attention to take a picture.

As I give an unconvincing smile, all I can think is, *he's ruining our first mother-daughter moments.*

"A more natural smile," he then says. My mouth hitches up a bit more. I want to kill him. That's probably the vibe my unnatural smile is giving off.

"Much better." He has tears in his eyes, which is sweet, so maybe I won't actually kill him.

Deep breaths, Dani, I think to myself, and go back to taking in Vivienne.

Asking to plaster on a fake smile instead of authentically taking in my baby was the moment I decided that the next time I gave birth, I was going to do things differently. I was going to start saying no and think *What is best for my family?* over *What would make everyone else happy?*

Same thing with visitors. It was a revolving door those first couple of days, my parents wanting to introduce their first grandchild to their friends, the cousins, and the in-laws. And what I realized was that I had a million things to do as a new mother, and entertaining just added on to that.

I would try to get something done, and then the doorbell would ring, and my parents' friend Susan and her husband, Mark, would be standing there, smiling.

"You look amazing. And let me see this baby?" She came bounding into the apartment, a blur of curly hair everywhere.

"Oh, my goodness, Dani, she is beautiful. And she has a great head of hair." She grabbed for Vivienne's face, and all I could think was, *Wash your germy hands!*

"I know; it looks like she's wearing a toupee." I gave an involuntary snort of laughter.

She looked at my mom, shaking my shoulders so much that Vivienne and I shook back and forth. "I know this one is going to be a great mom like you," she said.

She then threaded her arms through my mom's, and they headed toward the couch in the living room to sit down.

Mark and my dad were opening cans of beer in the kitchen, my dad's booming voice talking about the birth. Dad's dark black curly hair bobbed as he let out a hearty laugh.

I took Vivienne to the bedroom and shut the door, taking a deep breath. The swing in my chest swung back and forth. I was overwhelmed. I wanted everyone to leave.

All I really needed was one-on-one time with Vivienne to learn how to breastfeed, to heal, and to learn how to be a mother to her. But I had to force a smile on my face—to make people believe I was the overjoyed but not overwhelmed mother they wanted me to be, and that I was genuinely excited to see them—which in all honestly, I wasn't. It wasn't because I didn't like them, it was because I had so much emotionally and physically going on at that moment. I just wanted to be alone with my family.

When I was pregnant with Diana, we let everyone know that we were keeping it much more low key. And we kept it that way for Julia and Charli. So, every birth after Vivienne, I had no one in the delivery room other than Jonathan, and at home, we had no visitors besides my parents, in-laws, and other close family. My parents watched my older children while I was in the hospital, which gave them an important, key role. I spent no energy on who wanted to visit us and take a picture with the baby. I spent no energy buying food to put out for visitors, and instead, spent all my energy on my family because I knew how hard the transition could be on everyone. It was OK to take the time we needed.

I did have the "hard talk" with my parents about how we weren't having visitors right away outside of direct family. And they were very understanding of our family's needs because we set those boundaries in a kind and respectful way. Plus, by baby number two, I noticed the excitement from friends died down. With Vivienne, every item got purchased from our registry. By Diana, I purchased every item on the way to the hospital while having contractions because no one bought anything we needed, and she was coming a month early. For Julia and Charli, I didn't even make a registry.

If you're anticipating your first birth experience, please do yourself a favor, and make your needs clear. Do what is best for you as the mother, not what your mom or mother-in-law want you to do. You are the one working the hardest, and your job is to show up as your best self for yourself, your baby, and your partner. To do that, you have to put your need for space and peace ahead of others' feelings—you're already putting a newborn first.

You'll never regret having set that boundary during the fragile moments of delivering a newborn and postpartum when your world feels like it's bursting at the seams. But you will regret having a visitor in your face as you're pale, in pain, and holding back tears.

It's your life and your baby. This time is sacred, and you deserve to experience it in a way that feels right for you. If someone doesn't understand, that's on them.

Diana was in the NICU for her first eleven days, but Julia spent the first few days of her life at home in the arms of Jonathan and me, and getting introduced to her siblings. We spent that time adjusting to our new normal and the new dynamic. Because bringing a baby home isn't just hard for Mom but is a big change for everyone in the family, especially older siblings, too.

Right after we brought Julia home, Diana spent the first couple of days extra clingy, always needing to be touching or hanging onto me. She didn't like when I held Julia and would often cry to be held at the same time. My arms were almost as tired as my eyes by the end of each day. Vivienne surprisingly had a hard time adjusting, too, even though she was always far more independent than Diana.

Vivienne was having issues separating at school for the first time. Yes, the same kid who waved goodbye to me, smiling, as I walked away crying on her first day of school, was now clinging on to me.

"Don't go!" she hissed. Tears started pouring out of her eyes as her loud cries spilled into the room, filling it up completely, making my ears ring.

She'd wake up at all hours of the night screaming, "I want Baby Bheem!" And demand to watch a Netflix show about an adventurous Indian toddler, Mighty Little Bheem, stomping her feet and crying at all hours of the night.

I'd be up feeding Julia, or rocking her because she had terrible colic, and suddenly, I'd hear, "I want Baby Bheem! I want Baby Bheem!" on repeat through the monitor, until I'd storm into her room.

"Vivienne, what's wrong?" I'd say, my voice hoarse from exhaustion.

She'd look up at me blinking rapidly, big tears falling down her face, "Baby Bheem!" She'd stomp.

"Vivienne, no. It's the middle of the night!" I'd rasp raggedly.

She didn't take well to that and started to jump up and down on the bed, "Baby Bheem! Baby Bheem! Baby Bheem!" she'd chant.

"Vivienne, I am with Julia. Daddy will lie with you, but you have to go to sleep. No more of this." I tried to grab her hand to help get her settled in bed again.

"*Baby Bheem!*" She'd scream pulling her hand away and continued jumping.

Jonathan would then charge into the room, exhausted, and yell "*Go to sleep! This is ridiculous!*" Vivienne would instantly burst into tears.

My voice quavered from the two of them. "I—I—don't know what to do right now. Jonathan, I need you to calm down and comfort her. She needs positive attention right now, not to be yelled at. You are going to sleep with her. Viv, I love you sweet girl, but it's time to sleep." I spoke fast and started to set up the bed for the two of them, all with newborn Julia in my arms.

Vivienne was still crying as I passed Julia over to Jonathan, and he continued where I left off.

I stroked Vivienne's head, "You can't watch TV in the middle of the night, silly. Why don't you go back to sleep with Daddy, and I promise we can watch Baby Bheem tomorrow, and we will also have special mommy and Vivie time. OK?" I held her in my arms until she calmed down, wiping away her tears. She was still a baby herself, only three years old. She was just my oldest baby. This was a lot of change for her.

I took Julia back from Jonathan.

"Now, you snuggle her and make her feel important." I whispered to Jonathan.

"Happily, I don't care what I'm doing as long as I'm sleeping right now," he said and lifted the blanket, tucking her against his chest.

"Goodnight, I love you both," I said with a deep sigh.

Then I left to put the baby back to bed. Can you imagine a visiting human watching this exchange? They would be like, *Is this interaction real? What is a Baby Bheem?* So many questions!

Because a family needs time to come together and marvel at tiny toes and small cries, to let everyone feel their feelings, to have their meltdowns and regressions, to heal, and not have the eyes of others watching and judging making the transition harder. Because what I've learned is the newborn isn't here to please others. She's here to join our family.

So, if a mom says no and needs some time before she wants visitors, don't take offense. Think about me dealing with Vivienne and Baby Bheem, on top of her body healing, all while learning her newborn. I hope you understand—she's overwhelmed!

She's doing what's best for her family right now, and that's more than OK.

"Danielle, wait up!" The director of Julia's preschool chased after me, her blonde curly hair down past her ears, her glasses sitting on the tip of her nose. I was really happy with Julia's Threes class, and Diana was going to the same school and having a great year in kindergarten.

"Yes?" I stopped, sweat brimming along my forehead. Charli is in my Bjorn, holding a bottle. Someone opened the door and the cool breeze hit my skin. My ears rang as all the chatter around us muffled together.

"We were hoping you'd join the Board of the school," she said, clapping her hands together.

"Oh." I paused for a second, my gaze flashing toward a cubby in front of me, and I got lost in thought.

I used to struggle with saying no to things like this. I always wanted to help as much as I could. It's who I am at my core. Even the things I don't want to do because I have no interest, I want to do if it helps someone else. The people pleaser inside of me also wants to be liked and accepted. And what if people think I can't handle the pressure of everything? That I'm a bad mom? I could do it all, sure! So, I said yes way too much.

"Will you bake cookies for the bake sale on Friday?" Sure, I'd say, even though I don't bake well at all. I'd just add it to the endless list of things I needed to do.

"Will you be a class parent?" Yes, and I'd be so overwhelmed sending emails, planning the details of class events, and attending meetings, when all I really wanted to do was show up at class events for my child.

When I start saying "yes" too much, I become burnt out, exhausted, and don't have time to put my energy into things that matter more to me and my family. Now I know saying "no" to other things is saying yes to my children and my own needs. Because when you say yes to something, you inadvertently say no to something else.

"I think right now, I unfortunately need to pass, as much I'd want to. But thank you for thinking of me," I said.

Her eyes connected with mine, with warmth and full understanding. "Don't worry, maybe next year."

I nod. I felt some guilt. But as I walked out the door with Charli into the cold air, I knew I had done the right thing. I was proud of myself. This was growth.

As I walked to my car, I thought about my growth as a mother in setting boundaries for myself and my kids.

Before I had kids, I would do anything anyone asked. I had no boundaries when it came to pleasing others. I was always willing to help, and I wanted to help. I was also afraid if I said no, they wouldn't like me. I struggled to make decisions. And I wanted to make everyone happy. I would take everything on and give myself more and more to do until I took on too much. I was filling everyone's cups around me while I was running dry. People took advantage of my kindness, and I lost who I was and became resentful of the people in my life. This led to burnout and a huge struggle with my mental health. I was miserable until I hit rock bottom with my eating disorder and decided to change my life— I needed to live for myself, not just for others. But it was easier said than done.

It was my kids who gave me the backbone to bring more of what I wanted into my life and let go of the things that didn't give me happiness.

I looked up at Julia and Diana's school, in a beautiful church close to our home. It was a school Diana's therapist recommended, and she came out smiling on most days. A school I couldn't be more grateful for because our journey to get to this "happy place" was hard won. I thought about all the times I had spoken up and advocated for Diana, another important skill I needed to hone in on, no matter how uncomfortable it made me. I had to fight hard to get her there. I learned to say no to people who had given me or her a hard time along the way.

It started when she was a baby. She'd cry every time we'd go into a music or sports class with Vivienne, as I'd wear her on my chest. It was nonstop until she left. Any class with other kids would overwhelm her, and she'd want to leave. She also had a speech delay, which made it hard for her to communicate how she was feeling. I knew her strengths and weaknesses better than anyone. And I knew I could come off as pushy or would feel like I was crossing a boundary at times, but I quickly realized I was responsible for getting her the help she needed. If I didn't speak for her, no one else would.

I remember going up to the director of Vivienne's preschool a couple of years before on a cold winter day and having a conversation about Diana attending the same school the following year. The director was older with glasses and short dark brown hair. She was wearing slacks and a blouse with purple and white flowers all over it. She pointed for us to go outside to the playground so we could have some privacy.

"She gets afraid when she's in a room with other kids and cries nonstop and hides behind me. We have been doing exposure therapy, but she still won't stop crying the entire class. She would need a lot of support in the classroom. I could go in with her and then transition out, too," I said over the roar of the wind, my eyes focused on her as I spoke.

"Well, we have siblings that go to different schools than their other siblings all the time." I was taken aback at her dismissal. She didn't want my kid in her school. She basically said she would keep Vivienne, the typical student with no known issues yet, but Diana and her needs were too much work.

For an awkward moment, I went pin-drop silent trying to take in what she said. Uncomfortably quiet. "OK. Then that's all I need to know." I snapped my fingers. "She will go to a different school. Thanks for the conversation." Anger rushed through my veins as I stepped back into the school. The warmth seeping through my skin. I hated the school for rejecting my kid because she had differences. I was disgusted. But that doesn't stop a mom, it lights her up to find somewhere better. So, that's what I did. I found her a special program that had occupational therapy, speech, and was a mommy-and-me program, where I stayed with her in the class. And then when she was finally doing well in that, COVID happened and she was out for a year and a half, which was a huge setback.

I learned to step up and find her the help she needed during and after COVID. To get her into the right programs, it took a lot of advocating, IEPs (Individualized Education Programs) and therapy but we found her the right schools where she thrived.

Advocating took me out of my comfort zone because I don't like "bothering people." But when it comes to my people and getting them what they need, I don't care what other people think. I don't care if I am a bother. My kids' needs are just way too important to me. And now, I will do that for anyone in need, not just my family. I am a fighter for what's right, and my kids have brought that out of me.

Prioritizing my kids was one boundary that came easily to me. The moment my kids were born, something clicked where even if I felt bad and had to disappoint people, my kids would always come first. I'd swallow that guilt for them. As I moved through motherhood, I have started feeling less and less torn and guilt-ridden over these situations. It's just life as a mom.

"Ugh, I think Julia is sick, babe," I said on the phone with Jonathan, feeling her head with my lips. "Wow I think I just kissed fire." I went to get the thermometer. She was lying on the couch, and her cheeks had a crimson red sheen.

The seesaw feeling rocked through me because I knew I wouldn't be able to go out for dinner. I was not going to leave her if she was sick. I just wouldn't, and I knew this would disappoint Jonathan because he craved adult alone time with me and friends.

The digital thermometer beeped. "Crap. 102.4. I'm not surprised. I will call you back."

I soaked a towel in ice-cold water and placed it on her forehead, trying to cool her down. I brought up some Motrin and water, begging her to take it.

"Bubba, this is going to make you feel so much better," I said as I rubbed her back.

"Is Julia sick?" Diana asked. Her hair was slightly wavy from wearing it in a braid all day long. She was wearing Pikachu pajamas.

"Yes. I'm afraid so," I answered, my gaze dark and steady.

I watched Charli dancing around to *Moana* out of the corner of my eyes. Her arms were swinging like a monkey and her smile was big.

I shifted Julia to help her sit up and encouraged her to drink the medicine. Tears filled her eyes. "I don't want to, Mommy!" Her big brown eyes were zoned out, and she seemed defeated.

My phone chimed. As I broke eye contact with her, I pulled it out, and read a new message from Jonathan: *Should I cancel dinner tonight?*

I texted back, *I'm sorry, I think so* ☹. I put my phone down and looked back up at Julia. "OK, let's take this medicine. How about a big sip in exchange for a piece of chocolate?"

Julia just stared at *Moana* on the television as I kissed her forehead.

During winter sick season, the more kids you have, the likelihood that you will have a child sick at all times increases. With four kids, it feels like someone is always sick in our house. We hardly have more than a day with a completely healthy household. And I'll never go out for dinner with a sick kid at home. I won't. Because my kids need me, and they come first—so winters can be antisocial for me. Jonathan will go out for boys' nights, but it's rare we get out together for a date night in the winter since our kids are small.

Recently, we tried to go out when Charli had a cough. We strategically went to a 9:45 PM movie so we could leave after the kids were asleep. We picked up our friends, Arielle and Ben, on the way.

Arielle was wearing sweats like me, and her curly hair hit me in the face as she gave me a warm embrace.

"I just woke up from a nap, since it's a late show and I want to stay up," Ben informs us as he buckles himself into the back seat and rubs his eyes.

"Gosh, we are getting old," I said. His eyes flashed as he started to laugh.

We talked on the way about our wild kids, and I made fun of the ridiculous list of make-up I had to get for Vivienne's upcoming dance competitions.

"Can you believe they want me to get her concealer?" I said peeling my pants off the leather car seat. "She's seven years old, what is she concealing?" We started laughing at that truth.

Jonathan and I hadn't been out to a movie on a date in a while, eight years ago to be exact—and this theater was the perfect romantic movie night experience. We walked into a room with big chandeliers, and a restaurant with a full bar in its center to the left. I felt like I was out for a nice dinner, not going to a movie. It was kind of magical.

"Wait, this is what movie theaters are like now? We have been missing out, Jo," I said, touching his arm.

"I mean, we have been missing out on a lot of things, Dan," he said, his eyes meeting mine.

"But we aren't missing out on watching our children grow," I said on purpose, knowing he would think I was cheese city.

"Thank goodness for that," he said sarcastically as he squeezed my hand.

"Right?" I said with a flippant wave of the same hand he squeezed.

"The food is great at the restaurant here," Arielle said, interrupting our banter. She played with her ringlet curls with one hand and pointed to the restaurant with the other.

"It looks good," I said, my head tucked beneath Jonathan's chin as we went up the escalator to the second floor.

We'd heard about these types of movie theaters, little rumblings here and there, but we had never made it out into the wild to experience one for ourselves. And so far, it was living up to all its glory.

Do you know that game where you read the fortune out loud from a fortune cookie and add "in bed" to the end of a sentence to make the results funnier? Well, if you add "in a movie theater" to the end of my sentences everything will sound so much cooler when I'm describing it to you.

So here goes . . .

We entered our theater. Jonathan and I had our own pod that came with a table in the center . . . in a movie theater. I even got my own blanket . . . in a movie theater. I looked over the menu and felt so fancy as I ordered spicy tuna on crispy rice . . . in a movie theater. It was heaven . . . in a movie theater.

As the previews finished and I was finally settling into the seat, I got a call from my mom.

"I'm so sorry to be calling you, but Charli won't stop crying. She's been crying for ten minutes and only wants you." I heard Charli's loud screams in the background, saying "Mama," out of breath.

I popped up.

"Jo, I've got to go. Charli won't stop crying. Can you call me an Uber?" I was panicking, as I apologized to our friends and ran down the escalator, past the restaurant, and out the door into the cold air to a red Uber. My heart was screaming just thinking about her so upset.

I got home in ten minutes and rang the doorbell. No one answered, so I ran to our garage and entered the code. I ran up the stairs, nauseated from the car ride. I stormed into my room where Charli was still crying in my mother's arms. My mom looked so upset. Her shoulders were slumped, eyes dull. Charli reached for me, and I held her close, comforting her for two minutes as her heavy breathing slowed, until she fell asleep on my shoulder.

She needed her mommy. And yes, I heard the movie was good, and I would have loved it. It would have been nice hanging with adult friends and watching a non-animated movie, but I'll never regret leaving to take care of Charli or any of my babies. Plus, if I had stayed, I would have been too worried about her to enjoy the movie, the spicy tuna over rice, the romantic little pod—all of it.

I'll also never regret having to say no to a coffee/lunch date with a friend instead of showing up for my kids in any way they may need. I know I get made fun of behind my back about how I am with my kids, and how much I worry. I know some people think of me as "too protective," that "she'll just cry and be fine eventually," but I just don't function like that when it comes to my children. I honestly don't care what anyone thinks, too. My kids will always come before any plans.

And my kind of people will understand why I would have to leave and say no to whatever we are doing, even if they wouldn't, because they respect who I am as a mother in the same way that I respect their parenting decisions. We accept each other's boundaries.

When Vivienne was born, I said yes to going to a close friend's wedding across the country three months after I gave birth. I initially thought I'd just fly there with Jonathan early that morning, and we'd take a night flight home after the wedding. We'd be in and out, no big deal. I didn't even see taking her with us as an option at the time because I was told the plane had too many germs for a baby.

But I quickly found out how hard it was for me to leave Vivienne. I felt this terrible guilt in the pit of my stomach like I'd be leaving my heart behind. She needed her mommy. She depended on me. Mom guilt is the worst like that.

So, I chose Vivienne.

I called my friend and told her I couldn't make it.

Silence.

"It's fine," she said tersely.

I knew she was mad, and I hated upsetting people, especially people I care about. My heart was beating in my head so loudly I could hardly hear anything else she said. But with my track record as a friend at that point, I couldn't blame her. Because I blew off everything in my early twenties. I was too sick to be anyone's real friend.

My anxiety, eating disorders, and depression kept me away. My invisible illness told me I didn't belong, that I was damaged and unlikeable, and I'd cancel constantly thinking that if someone got to know me well, they would figure me out.

She must have gotten off the phone and said to her fiancé in a huff, "Of course Dani blew my wedding off." I could imagine her in a long black sweatshirt and leggings, color rising along her cheeks. There would be a look of vulnerability in her eyes. No hope, just pure disappointment.

The thought of it hurt my heart.

And I was trying to do better with my friendships—I was in recovery and was working on my depression and anxiety, but it felt impossible to choose a friend over my child. I was always going to choose my child.

Now, as a mother of four, I see I could have easily taken her on that trip with me, and things could have been different. But I do give that new mom me grace. She had to say no, and that's OK. But I now know newborns don't break. It's different with every child after your first because, unlike with your firstborn, you have no choice—you can't isolate them. Diana was at a play space and classes for her sister one month after she was born, and Julia was at school pick up the day after she came home from the hospital.

One of my essays was included in an anthology and all the writers chosen to be in the book were meeting in Nebraska for a book launch party in April 2023. I wanted to go more than anything. Over the years I have met such wonderful supportive women writers online. We've talked over Zoom and texted, but I never got to meet them in person—because I couldn't leave. My kids were always too young, and I felt a mix of guilt and FOMO because I would feel like I was missing out on moments with them. So I watched over the years as these women went to retreats together and meet ups. I was happy for them but as I scrolled through Facebook and Instagram photos, I was also jealous, wishing I could be in two places at once.

I finally said yes to going—yes to me. Charli had just turned one, Vivienne was seven, Diana almost six, and Julia was about to turn four. They could spend the night with Jonathan with the help of my parents.

But I couldn't leave them with four kids, especially a baby who was all about mommy, without feeling incredibly guilty and worried, which I know is "my own stuff" that I need to get over, but it just wasn't something I could wrap my head around. I also felt extra attached to Charli after her time in the NICU. So, I decided to take Charli with me to Nebraska.

Charli had quite the twenty-four hours. She went on her first flight, slept through a lunch meet up, attended a book launch party, and walked around Omaha. I had the best time meeting wonderful women who weren't only accepting of me, but loved Charli. The best part was that Charli wasn't the only baby; there were two others.

Charli and I had our tougher moments. We walked back to the hotel after the book launch in a rainstorm. I wore her in my carrier under my blue raincoat, with my dressy outfit underneath, and shielded her from the water the best I could, but it didn't stop rain from soaking us because we didn't have an umbrella. We walked into the lobby dripping water, a cold breeze from the air conditioner wriggling through my wet clothes. But it was worth it. The entire trip was me saying yes to myself, and my soul needed that.

The point is, you do what is best for you as a mother.

People had opinions when they found out I had brought Charli to Nebraska for a twenty-four-hour trip.

The main one being that it was crazy to take her with me, but I didn't care.

I want to note that it's more than OK if you can easily leave your kids to go on vacations. It's very healthy. Moms should never feel guilty, and we deserve a break, too. You are a great mom, too. These are just things that I have struggled with as a mother that I am speaking to.

Learning to say no and set boundaries has helped me become more than the mother I wanted to be. It has helped me become the mother my family needed all along—a happier mom, who trusts herself and gives herself grace. A mother who doesn't stress as much, because she won't put herself in situations that make her or her family uncomfortable. Parenting isn't about people pleasing. It's not about doing what my mother-in-law, my mom and dad, or cousins want me to do, or the mother my friends want me to be so we can go on girls trips together. It's about raising the best humans we can.

So, yes it is difficult to tolerate others' disappointment, but we have to so we can show up as the mothers we want to be. It's the only way we can take control of our own happiness. Next time you get nervous before setting boundaries, remember that doing what's best for you and your family by setting appropriate boundaries will change your life.

— 12 —

Empowering Resilience
in Our Children

I AM AN EMPATH, so bad news seeps into my soul and impacts my entire mood. When I feel this way, you can see it in my frazzled face. My eyes wide, head shaking, deep in thought. My fears and anxieties completely taken over. And when it comes to news that could affect my kids, it's not, "will I spiral?" It's a matter of when.

I hear about a school shooting, and I want to home-school them. It takes me back to Sandy Hook, and I can't breathe. I cannot believe people are crazy enough to kill little kids—to go into an elementary school just like the one where I drop off two of my kids every morning.

It gives me so much fear that my heart becomes raw, tender, so delicate like an open wound, and I need to protect my babies at all costs. I need to protect my family. Anything can happen, and it's terrifying. My heart can't take it.

The other night, I couldn't fall asleep. I read something disturbing and was spiraling about our world. I heard the rain and the claps of thunder and flashes of lightning, but I couldn't seem to find it soothing like Jonathan. I looked over at him. His eyes were closed, and he breathed heavily. Charli was sleeping sideways, her head by my neck and her feet touching Jonathan's stomach.

I tiptoed out of the bed and softly closed the door behind me. I walked down creaky steps to the kitchen. The lights were dim. I grabbed the bag of pretzels from our snack cabinet, and filled a sandwich bag to take upstairs. Creak.

I heard something. I jerked forward, afraid.

I heard footsteps getting louder and closer. Then a crack of thunder so loud. I grabbed the pretzel bag just in case because my thought process was to hurl the bag of pretzels at the perpetrator and run to save my family.

"Hello, hello, *hello!*" I shakily echoed, jumping back, hitting the cabinet, convinced I was about to come face-to-face with a perpetrator who probably had an axe.

I let out a scream as Jonathan appeared in the kitchen, disheveled.

"What's going on?" He jumped and looked puzzled and frightened.

"Why are you creeping around? You gave me a heart attack!" I could hear my heart in my head, it was beating so loud.

"I saw you left our room, so I wanted to make sure you were OK." He started laughing. "And what were you going to do, throw the bag of pretzels at me?"

I cleared my throat, "Obviously! And then run." Adrenaline was shooting through me from how scared I was. I was wide awake with butterflies in my stomach zooming around and my heart jittering.

The bottom line is we live in a scary world. And all I want to do is protect my family, and sometimes because of that I live in fear.

When the kids were little, I was overprotective. I'd helicopter around them to prevent a fall, or comfort tears right when the first drop fell. We'd go to a park, and I'd hover. There were just too many places they could fall and get hurt. Too much risk.

And yes, I'm still there every second I can be—inspecting every bruise, analyzing fights and tears, helping with homework, and leaving outlined details of directions if I have to leave the house—but I now know I can't protect them from everything. I can't make sure the girls at school will be nice to Diana. Or that someone will be able to calm Julia when she's hysterically crying at school.

But I can empower Diana to stand up for herself or tell a teacher when other kids are mean to her. I can teach Julia to cope with her big emotions.

I believe in empowering our daughters. When I say "empowering," I don't mean toughening them up to become who they're not. I don't want sweet Diana to go around pushing other kids to the ground or to turn her into someone hard and closed off, constantly thinking everyone's out to get her. I don't mean she should become cruel and fight back with the same hurtful words that are thrown her way.

When I say we need to empower our daughters I mean, we need to empower them to be brave.

When Julia was two years old, she was playing in the basement with Vivienne and Diana.

Diana and Vivienne were coloring, while Julia was trying to get their attention.

She went up to Diana and tapped her back. Diana didn't move. She tapped it again.

"Stop!" four-year-old Diana said as she frowned. She looked behind her, glaring at Julia, and settled into the chair again.

Julia ran away, smiling because she got a reaction.

"Julia," I said, frustrated with her. There was always fighting. I couldn't get one moment of peace without pulling someone away crying.

Julia blinked at me, and then ran over to Vivienne and grabbed her pen out of her hand and started running. Vivienne ran after her, chasing her around the room, Julia laughing, me screaming at Julia and Viv, "Stop!" Suddenly, she accidentally jabbed the pen right above her eye.

For a second there was silence.

Then Vivienne let out a scream. Julia started screaming and crying as blood fell onto her face. I grabbed her and screamed, "Jonathan!"

He came racing down the stairs, fumbling on the last few steps, and his mouth fell wide open. Julia's eyes were blurry with tears and blood.

I grabbed tissues and applied pressure on the area.

Diana was crying in a corner, so afraid. Vivienne was crying, too.

"I need to take her to the emergency room," I said to Jonathan, gathering Julia in my arms to go.

"Wait!" Jonathan said, his eyelashes fluttering, as he became the voice of reason. Jonathan's best friend is a plastic surgeon, so he sent him pictures of the wound.

I heard on speaker phone, "Bring her to my office now. I will stitch her right up."

My heart dropped . . . stitches. Poor Julia. I didn't want her to do something hard without me, her mom by her side. She was too young.

"I will take her!" I ran out the door with Julia in my arms, only turning around to blow a kiss and assure the girls she would be OK.

I took Julia over to his office, and I held her down, her small body on top of mine, as he gave her a shot to numb the area, and then stitched above her eye on an office chair. Julia's wails filled the room, and her quivers made me shake with her, as he put in seven stiches. I was afraid but my love for Julia made me hold her down strong. I was brave for her, so she could be brave, too. Because I want her to always look at me and see a strong woman who can handle anything that comes her way.

I want my girls to be unafraid to be themselves despite what everyone else around them thinks. To wear what they want and do their hair the way they like. If a "cool and stylish" kid with a trendy outfit rolls her eyes at her outfit, I don't want her to think twice about it. I want her to still wear it, loud and proud.

When Vivienne was in kindergarten, she loved wearing pigtails. Every day she would analyze the part I made in her hair, making sure it was even.

She'd look in the mirror, smiling at her reflection with such a natural confidence. It made me feel so in awe of her.

One morning Viv woke up a bit crankier than normal. I helped her pick out her clothes and chucked her pajamas into the laundry.

"OK, so let's do your hair," I said as I took the comb in my hand, getting ready to part it.

"I don't like pigtails anymore." Vivienne got quiet and sullen. I touched the spot where her dimple belonged, trying to get her to smile.

"Why?" I nudged.

"Because Peter told me they were ugly." Her voice was low, and her hair was messy, tucked behind her ears.

"Oh baby, we are not going to listen to Peter or anyone. When you get older, you will learn everyone has an opinion, but you wear what makes you feel good and don't care about anyone's opinions but your own." I touched Viv's elbow, making sure she was listening. "Now do you want to wear pigtails?" I looked up into her face, searching for any clue of what her answer would be.

There was a beat of silence.

"Yes." She said leaning forward and flashing a thumbs up.

"Then we are wearing pigtails." I flashed a thumb back at her. I parted her hair and started making the first pigtail as my mouth quirked into a smile. Then the other. I ran my hand over my jaw as I said, "What do you think?"

She smiled as she looked in the mirror.

"Remember that smile. You like it, and that's all that matters."

She nodded.

I also want them to be unafraid to take up space and accept compliments. To be confident in what they have and not try to downplay it for anyone.

One morning, Vivienne looked at me and said, "Mommy, you look pretty."

I was taken aback. My hair was unwashed, milk stains on my shirt from Charli, and a tiredness loomed over me that not even a strong coffee could fix. I had run around all morning, and so far, there had been no time for me to look like a person. I felt anything but pretty.

I was about to say, "no, I don't," and cringe out of habit, but I stopped myself.

My usual response to a compliment is never just a thank you. It's more like a "not really" or a return of the praise like it's a hot potato: "No, you look amazing." Like, "Stop, I can't handle it."

Also, an insecure part of me thinks if I say thank you, it sounds like I agree with them, like "yes, I'm hot." A woman is supposed to be modest and humble. That's what I was taught.

But as much as compliments make me cringe, because of what I grew up thinking, the thought of Vivienne or any of my daughters shrinking themselves down to make other people comfortable makes me cringe more.

Because I want my daughters to be able to give themselves credit where it's due and be able to own their achievements.

I want them to be comfortable enough in their own skin to handle nice things being said about them. And though I'm affected by our culture and struggle to take a compliment, I don't want to teach my daughters to do the same.

Besides, when my daughters look at me, they see the most beautiful woman around. They see my heart: my strength when they're weak and their beautiful mother.

And that's a compliment I always want from them.

"Thank you," I said, forcing my awkwardness into a smile.

And yes, it was uncomfortable coming out of my mouth, but I won't give up. Because the more I say it, the more I'll believe it, and so will my daughters. And they deserve not to have to downplay themselves.

Because our kids become the air they breathe. If we want that air to be kind, authentic, honest, and confident, we must be, too. They are always watching and listening to us. They see how we handle stress. They observe how we eat. They hear us apologize when we mess up. They soak it all in like little sponges. Kids repeat what they hear and imitate what they see.

Since recovering from my eating disorders, I do keep the compliments about appearance to a minimum. I want them to know they're so much more than their appearance. I work hard every day to do that. I compliment them on their intelligence, their kindness, their resilience, and their creativity. I want them to know that those things matter more than anything.

We don't own a scale, and I won't talk about body size in our house. When one of my kids gains weight, I don't say anything. If I mention it, she will only assume something is wrong with her when it's not. I will not perpetuate that feeling of shame and "not good enough" onto them. I will always stress how every size is beautiful.

Since they were little, I started teaching them that pretty is surface-level and about their appearance.

When Vivienne was as young as three years old, she loved putting on a princess dress and twirling around in circles. "So pretty," she would beam. And she did look pretty as she gracefully twirled, her slinky-like curls bobbing along with her blue Cinderella dress. Her crown shining, matching her smile.

One day, while browsing the toy section during a Target run, Vivienne saw Disney Princess dolls—Ariel, Moana, Belle, and Snow White dolls lined up. She picked up a Snow White doll, and the first thing she said was "so pretty."

"Yes baby, she does look pretty." I nodded in agreement.

In the late afternoon, she saw four-year-old girls that she labeled as "big kids" in ballerina costumes, a sea of tutus flooding both of our visions, before a ballet class. "So pretty, Mama," she pointed to them. I did a double take.

"Yes, baby they do look pretty," I said. Because they did.

But beautiful, we only use beautiful on select occasions.

Because beauty is deep.

Beauty is beyond the physical. You can have a pretty face, but it is your soul, your passions, and what you do to make others and yourself better that makes you beautiful.

When Vivienne finished working on a painting in the basement and showed it to me, her face lit up with pride.

"So beautiful," I said. I looked at the red, green, blue, and purple spotted masterpiece she created on a blank sheet of paper.

Creativity is beautiful.

When the girls were taking a bubble bath together and Vivienne shared a toy with Diana, she handed her a Rubber Ducky to play with.

"So beautiful. Sharing is beautiful," I said. Because it is.

Being kind is beautiful.

When Vivienne and Diana would comfort each other when they heard the other cry.

"So beautiful, you guys are good sisters," I'd say.

Empathy is beautiful.

When Diana kissed me and said, "I love you so much."

"I love you so much too, baby," I'd say back, and add "showing love is beautiful."

Showing and giving love is beautiful.

This definition of beautiful is what I have been teaching my daughters since they were toddlers. I am trying to get it to sink into their heads, so they believe that what they do and who they are is what makes them beautiful.

Because I don't want them to think you become beautiful by dieting until you are "thin" and therefore beautiful by society's standards. We don't talk about dieting in our house. We don't label foods as good or bad; all foods are good in our house. We just eat everything in moderation. We listen to our tummies.

And I, too, need to continue working on being unafraid, so they are unafraid.

They have given me courage, and strength to pursue my dreams because I am brave for them.

All so they can be, too.

Because I was afraid for way too long, and I don't want that for my girls. I don't want them not to kiss the boy or girl they have a crush on because they fear they'll be a bad kisser. I don't want them to hold back raising their hand in the classroom when they know the answer because they are afraid of what their classmates will think. I don't want them to feel like there is only one path to success.

I don't want them to be how I was the first twenty-six years of my life before I hit rock bottom. Afraid to breathe wrong, to feel anything, so obsessed with trying to be perfect, and how I came off to others. I want them to learn how to cope and feel their entire range of feelings instead of looking for unhealthy ways to numb out.

I want my kids to be everything I was afraid to be—which is basically myself. Real me wasn't perfect enough. She's not fashionable; hell, she's lucky if she matches her sweatpants with her T-shirt. She's not popular or naturally brilliant—but you know what? She's good enough. She is one of a kind. And she shines as the person she is, because that's when she's at her happiest.

Every day is a chance to empower them.

One warm February day, we went to the park to meet friends because the weather was in the 50s, so we took advantage of it. I followed Charli as she walked around unsteadily. She wanted to do everything her sisters were doing. I smiled to myself as the wind blew a wisp of hair across my face.

I looked to the left of me. Diana was playing tag with two of her friends. I admired how fast she was as a flurry of chatter and laughter passed by me.

I looked to the right of me. Vivienne was playing on a twirly green slide with her friend, Luna. Vivienne threw her rainbow jacket off the side.

"Vivienne, why would you just throw it?" I said.

"I'm warm." She screamed. She and Luna let out a laugh. They had the sillies and were too busy acting crazy and having fun to think.

"You don't just throw it on the ground, Viv," I whispered under my breath, as I picked it up off the muddy ground, and placed it on a bench.

They played as I talked to one of Diana's friend's moms with the usual interruption of Charli wanting a snack or pulling me here and there. After an hour and fifteen minutes of playing, the wind started picking up, and Julia was becoming increasingly sulky and tired, so we decided to leave.

We got in the car as Viv moaned, "Why can't we have a playdate?"

"It's almost 6 PM. We are going to have dinner. Tomorrow is school." I repeated for probably the fifteenth time as I started buckling everyone in. As I fastened Diana's seatbelt across her body, I said, "It looked like you guys had an awesome time."

"Perry was kind of mean to me," Diana raked one hand through her hair and shrugged.

"What did he do?" I hated it more than anything when someone was mean to her—or any of my kids.

"He called me rude three times and told me to go away." She started playing with her hands.

"Did you tell him to stop?" I asked.

"No." She turned her eyes downward.

"Why didn't you tell me?" I squinted at her in total bewilderment. We have the type of relationship where she can come to me with anything and everything, and normally she does.

"I don't know." Her eyes were glued to the ground, transfixed on the smooshed Ritz crackers and gummies below her feet.

"Diana, if someone is being mean to you, you tell them to stop. If they don't stop, you come to Mommy, or a teacher if you are in school. You don't just let them continue to be not nice to you." I explained. "If no one knows, we can't help you. I thought you were having the best time."

The whole exchange bothered me because I knew if she didn't come to me today, she wasn't going to turn to a teacher at school if someone was making her feel bad there. But in that moment, I empowered her. I told her that she needed to speak up for herself.

She nodded.

I hope these conversations sink in. She also sees me speaking up to her daddy or any of her siblings when they say something that bothers me, all the time.

Because I'm empowering them in small exchanges and by being a role model, in my everyday actions. I show them how to support other women by bringing women together. I am the mother at drop off talking to everyone, I don't care who you are. If you are a nice person, we are talking. I include everyone. I don't talk negatively about other women. I will always stand up for what is right.

I want them to know friends don't talk behind your back. And if you hear other women talk negatively about others, they are likely also saying not-so-nice things about you.

I had a "friend" who would nonstop talk badly about other women who were her friends.

I wouldn't engage in the negative talk. I'd just listen as our kids played, making mental notes about the kind of friend she was being.

I started to distance myself from her because I knew she would never be a true friend. My theory proved itself true on a couple of occasions. One being when she didn't talk to me for a week when I cancelled dinner plans because Julia was sick. There was too much drama all around. I don't do drama. Life is too short.

True friends genuinely like you and want the best for you, and that's the kind of friend all our kids deserve.

Earlier in her second-grade year, Vivienne ran into a situation where her best friend since kindergarten, Alex, wasn't being nice to her. She honestly didn't realize it, or maybe she did but didn't want to see it, but I did and I needed to force her eyes wide open.

I saw Alex laughing with another friend as Vivienne tried to get her attention after school.

I saw Vivienne try to FaceTime her from my phone and her just text back: *I'm busy.*

I saw Alex moan as I tried to make a playdate with her mother. And that was it, I was done with Vivienne trying.

"She's not acting like a friend right now, so she's not your friend. If she decides to act like a friend again then you can be friends with her again. But you don't hang around someone who isn't nice to you. You deserve so much better." With little kids especially, you can't judge someone by their actions, so I didn't completely write off this child, who is still learning. At that moment though, Alex was not acting like a friend.

I encouraged Vivienne to play with other kids and not approach this girl again, set up playdates with other kids, and she made new friends. She moved on. But it hurt her.

For months she would ask me for playdates with Alex.

"Is she being nice?" I asked.

"No," she groaned dropping her forehead to the table.

"Then I don't think she's a friend to invite over right now." I gently broke the news to her, grabbing her hand. "But why don't we invite over Ella?" I forced a smile out, trying not to grimace, because her hurt is my hurt.

"Yes!" She said jumping up and down.

My face softened.

After some time, she stopped asking for Alex, but it took a while. This was a girl I had over at my house multiple times a week. The previous year, their teacher was happy when Viv brought home another girl to play with her after school, because they were attached at the hip. It was a huge loss for her, and I was sad for her during this time. But she will have many friend losses in her life, and this was a learning experience. She learned resilience, and realized she was OK without her.

Vivienne has been that fickle friend before, too, like Alex, especially when she was in kindergarten. She was much younger at the time, and it was more innocent, but she is far from perfect. She has always been a strong personality and impulsive, so if she didn't want to play with someone, she'd let them know. She'd say whatever was on her mind. If she didn't like your artwork, she'd let you know. But I always set her straight. I didn't let her get away with mean girl behavior, even when she was young and it was unintentional. It's up to us parents to hold our kids accountable. To make sure they're includers.

Vivienne has gotten better as she has gotten older. She's a very nice kid, and I'm proud of her, but she still tends to follow the crowd and make mistakes. She's only eight, she will get there.

"I haven't played with Ella for a week," Vivienne said at dinner one night while taking a bite of her lo mien noodles.

"Wait, why?" I asked, as I helped Charli into her chair and put a bowl of noodles in front of her.

"Well, Liz was mad at her, and I wanted to support Liz." She kept eating her noodles like it was no big deal. In her mind, she was being a good friend to Liz. Ella was one of Viv's nicest friends. She would never do anything with the intent of being mean.

"OK. First of all, you use your own brain. Second, you don't ignore someone for a week. Ella is such a good friend to you. You are going to talk to her tomorrow and stop this. She must be so upset." I put my arm on her loosely around her shoulders.

"OK." She pulled me against her side.

"Promise me." I took her pinky in my pinky.

"I promise. I didn't know what I was supposed to do." She slurped another noodle into her mouth.

I took out my phone and texted Ella's mom. *Hey, Viv told me she hasn't been talking to Ella. I made sure she knew that wasn't OK. I'm so sorry that happened. If it ever happens again, please let me know.* I looked at Viv. It's so important to me that she and all my girls know that strong girls empower other girls. They aren't mean, petty, and jealous of each other. They don't fight over boys. They don't gossip. They uplift each other and support each other's dreams.

She texted me right back. A splash of anxiety washed over my face before I picked up my phone, and my mouth quirked faintly in anticipation. *Yes, Ella did mention something but has been playing with other kids. She was upset, I didn't want to make it into a big thing. Vivienne's young and I wasn't sure how you'd react too, to be honest.*

I thought for a second and then texted. *Always let me know. I want to correct her behavior. Viv is young and makes mistakes. I want her to learn from them and do better.* I read it over once more and sent it.

Same. She texted back with a heart emoji. I felt relief as I sent a heart emoji back.

These kinds of conversations are what we should do with each other to hold our kids accountable. That mom is an includer like me. We should all want that for our children. It's not a reflection on us if our kids do the wrong thing, it doesn't make us bad parents or them bad kids. It gives us an opportunity to teach them and help them to do better.

Because that's who I want my daughters to be. If there isn't enough room for one of their friends at their lunch table, I want them to move somewhere else with that friend, not laugh with mean kids at their table, and stay put. I don't want them to let their friend's heart sink, hands get clammy, and feel rejected.

I had a friend say to me recently that she didn't know her friends were not actually good friends until she was in her twenties. They would leave her out a lot and make fun of her in front of her. But she thought that's just what girl-friends do. I don't want my daughters to think that. I don't want any of our daughters to think this. This is why we need to talk to them about what makes a good friend.

But we all make mistakes, of course. What matters is how we try to not repeat those mistakes. I am not perfect in my friendships, and I will teach them they don't have to be, too. I will also teach them that I'm not perfect in any aspect of my life, so they don't have to be as well. That mommy cries, she has bad moods, and bad days.

The other day I was having a day. The kind of day where I just couldn't get it together. And every parenting decision I made seemed like the wrong one. The kind of day where all I wanted to do was hide under the covers, but I had to parent. The kind of day where my mental health was not OK, but I had to keep going. I was feeling depressed.

On top of that, it was the kind of day where we were constantly running late because Charli pooped or had a tantrum at all the worst times, and everyone was nonstop fighting with each other. It was to the point where I was questioning if I was doing a good job raising my kids—they were so mean to each other. The kind of day where we weren't just late, we were also sweaty and cranky, and Diana was crying.

And that's how we showed up to the birthday party we were invited to that day.

Emotions were tangled in my throat the entire party. I felt like I was one more mishap away from tears.

We got into the car to go home, and Julia screamed, "Ow Vivienne that hurt. Don't hit my butt!" Her voice was husky and low.

"Viv, cut it out!" Heat rose to my neck and ears, as if I were dynamite and someone lit me up.

"She's being a baby. I was joking," Viv moaned.

"Viv, you are making me sad," Julia pouted as big tears started to fall down her cheeks. Julia and her big emotions. Once she gets started, she has a hard time stopping. She's the energizer bunny of tears. We always wonder if she feels dehydrated after one of her crying sessions. So, the rest of the way home my ears were filled with loud screams and sniffles.

My teeth skated over my bottom lip.

I was just over it. Over the noise. The fighting. The feeling like no matter what I did it wasn't enough. I couldn't make anyone happy. Someone was always crying no matter what I did. Normally, it wouldn't bother me, but I was depressed. *Why was I sad?* I couldn't exactly put my finger on it, but I couldn't get rid of the feeling. That's how depression goes. So, I broke down in the car in front of them, which was okay because I knew I would show them that they could do the same.

One day, I walked into the kitchen to Diana having her first sad feeling day. She was lying on two chairs in the kitchen.

"What's wrong?" I asked, concerned. I kneeled next to her.

"I just feel sad today, and I don't know why," she said. I started stroking her brown hair.

"Did anyone do anything to upset you?" I hated that she was sad. I continued stroking her hair as she dangled her long six-year-old legs off the chairs.

"No." She moaned, then groaned, and then complained, "I don't like feeling this way." I clutched my heart, acid rising through my stomach.

"I know, baby. I don't like it for you either. But this happens to Mommy sometimes, too. It happens to everyone. It's OK to feel this way. You'll feel better soon." I stroked her head again, reassuring her. I traced the outline of her ear.

"That tickles," she let out a laugh and paused for a minute. "When will I feel better?" she then asked, flashing her gaze toward the space under the vent.

"It will pass soon, and if it doesn't, we will talk to Dr. Yun (her therapist) about it." I stood up.

"What do you do to feel better, Mommy?" Diana tipped her head back.

"I spend time with you and your sisters because I love you so much. Sometimes I write or go for a walk." I gave her a big kiss on her forehead, then her nose, until she smiled so hard, revealing her dimples.

She was able to come to me because we are open about our feelings.

Talking about our negative feelings with children can achieve several things. For one, it normalizes them and shows children that it's OK to acknowledge and express them. Secondly, when we talk to children about dealing with uncomfortable feelings, they learn how to cope with them. Lastly, communicating our negative feelings ensures that our children know that we aren't having those bad feelings because of them.

Will I tell them about how when I was twenty-six, I woke up in a hospital from a seizure caused by years of eating disorder behaviors? Yes.

Will I tell them my entire history with anorexia and bulimia from day one? Yes.

Will I mention how I used alcohol and pills to numb myself during those sick years and kept it up through early eating disorder recovery, too? Yes.

Will I mention we have a history of drug abuse on my husband's side, and how we need to be careful? Yes.

We teach our kids to brush their teeth, wash their hands, eat balanced, get enough sleep, and shower. We need to do the same with their mental health. It's so important for them to identify their feelings and talk about them without shame. Going to therapy should be cathartic, like going to the gym, writing, or reading. There is truly nothing more important than mental health.

My kids know there is nothing shameful about having a therapist or a diagnosis. A diagnosis is empowering. We then know what we can do to become our best selves. They don't think something is wrong with them. They know they are learning new skills that will help them throughout their life. We have made it a normal thing in our house. It's getting a brain checkup and my kids like it much more than a physical checkup. We want to give them the confidence to take control of their thoughts and emotions without substances or bad habits.

I have already spoken to Diana about my anxiety to help her work through her own. I try to show her what works for me. We started seeing Diana's therapist weekly at the start of kindergarten when she was struggling to adjust to a new school—though she has seen her on and off since she was two. Vivienne sees a therapist every other week for her ADHD, which she was diagnosed with in kindergarten.

For Vivienne, her ADHD diagnosis was extra empowering. For years I worried about her behavior. But then COVID struck, and she wasn't in a classroom for a year and a half. Her first week of kindergarten, she left the room to fill her water bottle without telling the teacher on multiple occasions, wasn't listening to the teacher, and punched a kid in the face. We were called in, and that's when we got her tested for ADHD. That diagnosis made me understand her better. A lot of those impulses that made me crazy over the years, she couldn't help. I was then able to give her more grace and find different ways to parent her.

She practices coping mechanisms with her therapist. If I had healthy coping mechanisms the summer going into third grade, I wouldn't have found comfort in my eating disorder. So, I'm giving them these tools young.

Julia is even jealous she doesn't see a therapist. When she asks why she doesn't, I say, "I'm sure you will one day" as I "knowingly" smile because we all have stuff to work on or work through at one point or another.

And I'll show them how every night before I go to sleep, I take a small pill, an antidepressant, that has been helping me for years.

I don't have shame about my past. I will openly admit, "I have a chemical imbalance and this pill helps me repair it." I fought taking an antidepressant for years. But medication was part of my agreement shortly after my seizure, if I didn't want to go to hospitalization or a residential treatment center. I remember sitting in Dr. Blatter's office days after having my seizure. I was wearing a red sweater, which covered my black tights down to my knees. I had a green scarf around my thin neck, another layer that made me look less sick. My mom blew my hair out that morning to cover my bald spot, from the years of starving my body and making myself sick.

"I know we have been talking about medication for years. What are you afraid of?" he asked. He was jotting some notes on a small yellow note pad in front of him.

I looked down at my feet, trying to avoid eye contact, "I don't want to turn into a robot. I also don't want to become fat. But since I'm going to become fat anyway, I might as well take it. Plus, I have no choice, or I'll be hospitalized," I admitted as tears welled in my eyes. I was nonstop emotional during that time—sad for where I was in my life and afraid of what I was going to become. I hated myself for caring about something so superficial as weight gain when I couldn't care less about those things in other people. I had never been the person who cared about things like clothes, cars, any of it. But I was starting to learn that it was the illness, not who I was. I needed to stop hating myself.

"It won't make you feel like that, and if it does, we will switch medications. I promise." He blinked as his brows tensed.

There was a long pause that was filled with my tears.

I nodded. Now that I wasn't allowed to starve, I had to feel, and feeling was so hard and painful.

And now it was time for me to succumb to change. To do the scariest thing I ever had to do in my life. They asked me to eat and gain weight, but the illness was making me feel worse, not better about that. I was fighting my own brain, and it was the hardest fight of my life. So to help me in that fight, I took a little white pill.

And ten years later, I'm not sure I'll ever stop taking it. And that's OK—it doesn't mean I am weak. It means I am strong for getting the help I need.

Being a mom who takes an antidepressant doesn't make me a bad mom. There's still a stigma around these medications when there shouldn't be. Because the truth is I'm a better mom for taking antidepressants. I'm a better mom for taking charge of my mental health. There are so many reasons to be on them—maybe life has thrown too much your way, maybe you have terrible anxiety that keeps you inside and antisocial, maybe you have been battling with a mental illness like OCD or an eating disorder. Medication for mental illness is necessary to survive just like insulin is for a diabetic. As moms we need to be OK, to take care our kids. They need the best version of us and sometimes that takes a little pill.

They help me not obsess in a loop. They help me not to worry about what everyone else thinks. They help me keep everything in perspective. Everything doesn't have to mean something, and the small day-to-day things don't seem as overwhelming.

And through my battle with mental illness, I became empowered. I now know I am capable of really anything because I went through something so unbelievably hard and came out on the other side. Since I came so close to wanting to end my life, I now know how fragile life is, and it has given me the power to try. I am no longer afraid. I no longer care what people think. I didn't truly live the first twenty-six years of my life. I was paralyzed by my all-consuming illnesses. The perspective those years gave me, and the fight for my life, is a blessing in disguise. I have found such strength and purpose in it—in helping others feel less alone in their struggles. So I will live a full life the rest of my life to show my children how to live theirs. I am confident in myself to do that. I will never sit on the sidelines again. I made a pact with myself the night I asked for help, that I would change my life—and I will never go back.

So, do I think it makes me weak to have a mental illness and actively manage it? No, I think it makes me incredibly strong.

Because even when my depression is so awful it feels like it's pressing down on me forcing me to stay in bed, I rise. Some days, I don't want to move because the day before was tough. It was the opposite of happy kids on an exciting outing. Maybe it was a boring monotonous day of unhappy kids, just like the day before. Motherhood can be very repetitive and that can get to you at times. And behind the smile, I sometimes feel a deep sadness that continues into the next day—like I am stuck in quicksand and slowly sinking, and I can't get out. But if Charli's wails echo through the silence of the room, I take the blanket off my head, toss it to the side, and roll out of bed.

Because anything with my children would get me out of bed. If Diana and Julia come in complaining "my tummy is so hungry," I'd throw the covers off me and go make them eggs, pancakes, and cut up some fruit. Even something as simple as Vivienne not being able to find a shirt she was searching for would make me jump out of bed and help her frantically search her drawers for that one shirt on her mind. They make me stronger. For them, I keep going.

Above all else, I want my kids to always feel like they can come to me as they are. Because I'd understand what they are going through no matter what it is. There will be a time that they'll disappoint me, they'll disappoint themselves, they'll make big mistakes, but I will always be in their corner during those scary and confusing times where they feel lost. And having someone in your corner is empowering. Knowing you are loved unconditionally and not judged for your mistakes makes it easier to keep on going during those hard times.

I want a lot for my girls. I do. But don't we all want more for our kids?

I want my girls to be loud and messy because that's how they will be empowered.

I want them unafraid to be imperfect. To try new things without being afraid of failures and struggles. To be OK with being a "work in progress."

Unafraid to take ownership of the space they take up in this world and the dreams they have to make it better.

Unafraid to ask for help or put their mental health first.

Unafraid to prefer real as beautiful. To be proud of stretch marks, to resist self-deprecating remarks, and to know their self-worth.

Unafraid to go against diet culture. To know how strong and capable their bodies are.

Unafraid to be kind in a world where it's easier to be mean.

Unafraid to set boundaries.

Unafraid to have real conversations about the world around them. The kind of powerful conversations that can light the fire that drives them throughout life.

And in this world, they'll be much better off.

— 13 —

The Enduring Strength
of a Mother's Love

"WHAT DO YOU want for breakfast?" I asked two-year old Julia. Her curly hair was in her face. I wiped down the sink area of the kitchen and then washed my hands while waiting for a response.

"Eggs, pwease," she said, pounding on her high chair with her turtle WubbaNub pacifier.

I opened the fridge and browsed around. I moved the strawberries and the Paw Patrol yogurts, and looked in the drawer where we keep the apples and oranges. "Darn, we are out of eggs. I'll get more later. Julia, what else do you want?" I shut the fridge. My eyes dropped to orange crumbs on the floor. *What were those from?* I examined closer. Maybe Cheetos from the night before. *Ick.*

She shrugged. Her cherub cheeks were extra red from running around with her sisters.

"Pancakes!" Five-year-old Viv started dancing around. Her arms swinging from side to side.

"Are we doing the pancake dance?" I said, as I paused to watch.

Diana got out of her seat and joined her as they spun around and around. Viv sped up and fell to the ground as a roar of laughter filled the room.

I smiled at how cute they can be. "I dig it. I'll make pancakes." I swept my hair back from my neck and started taking out the ingredients.

After breakfast, I took the girls to the park because it was a nice sunny-but-not-too-hot-yet summer morning. They ran around for an hour, red glistening faces, going down the slides, and playing a game of house, until the clouds started to turn grey, and the air turned humid. The entire sky was tar-black by the time we got to the car. On the way back home, when I wanted to stop at the store, it started to pour.

As the cold droplets hit my front window, I decided to call my mom, who was coming over later anyway, to see if she had eggs instead of dragging everyone out in the rain.

"Hey mom, it's really pouring," my windshield wipers were rapidly swishing back and forth as raindrops steadily hit the window.

"Yea, it's really coming down," she said. I saw lightening streaking down in the near distance.

"Do you happen to have eggs in your fridge? I was going to stop at the store, but I don't want the kids to get soaked," I asked, as I turned on my street, a puddle splashing up onto the hood of my car. The roof of our car became heavy with rain—so much was falling that the sounds became one whirring noise. I pictured us running from the parking lot as our umbrella wobbled in the wind, all of us getting drenched, and Julia crying in my arms as I tried to shield her. It wasn't worth it for some eggs.

"Of course, I'll check," she said, pausing for a couple of seconds. "OK, I've got to go finish something up, but I'll see you soon." And that was that.

It rained all day, so we spent the rest of the afternoon inside. When she came over for dinner, she handed me the carton of eggs in a plastic bag. "Thank you so much. I'm glad you had these. Very clutch," I said, placing the bag on the counter and opening the fridge. "Oh, I didn't. I went to the store and bought them for you." She admitted as her eyebrows lifted a little. Vivienne was skipping around the kitchen, her nose wrinkled as she laughed each time she passed us. "Oh my goodness, you didn't have to do that. That was so unnecessary. We could have gone tomorrow." I placed the carton of eggs in the fridge and gave her an around-the-neck hug. Her hair was down and long, and she wore jeans and a royal blue blouse. "Yes, I did. I couldn't bear to think all my babies didn't have what they needed," she said matter-of-factly, like it was no big deal.

And that's a mother's love.

It goes above and beyond and shows unconditional love. And a mother always takes care of her babies even when their baby is a mother, too. A mother never stops worrying about her children.

My mother has said that now that I have kids, she has more people to worry about, but her heart has never been so full of love. Because her grandkids remind her of her own children—me and Erica, my sister. And it's like getting to love that version of us all over again. It's also her baby having babies. She is all heart with them.

My mom says to me often, to explain her love for my kids: "Imagine if Vivienne or Diana had kids." I can't even put into words the big love I'd have for those kids —I feel it already as just a thought. So, I can imagine it.

I ordered a pizza to the house the other night from a new place, and the rain-speckled box came with a pizza with arugula on it. Diana refused to eat it. The corners of her mouth twitched, and her gaze dropped to the table. She crossed her arms over her chest and shook her head. My mom sat there picking the arugula off the entire pie.

She put a slice in front of Diana, and Diana looked at it, spun the paper plate around, and pushed it away "I don't want it." She sulked.

"It doesn't have the arugula on it anymore," my mom pleaded with her. I could tell she was more annoyed than she was letting on.

"But it tastes bad," Diana said, looking down at the slice again.

"Diana, it does not taste bad. You didn't even try it," I argued. I stared at her throughout this entire interaction, and she in no way took a bite of it. She glared at the plate, like its presence offended her, sighed, and pushed it away.

"Yes, I did! It's so gross." Her voice cracked when she said "gross," as she shrugged and stuck her tongue out.

"Fine, what else do you want?" My mom shook her head and removed the pizza from the table.

"Are you the same mom we grew up with?" I let out a breathless laugh. This was insane. My eyes widened at how my mom let her get away with that.

My mom was strict with me and my sister growing up. I remember sitting at the table with Erica admiring her long blonde locks that were held together in a low ponytail. My hair was wild and curly, with frizz. My mom placed a chicken and pea dish in front of us.

Erica and I gave each other a look.

My sister took a bite and instantly spit it out. "Ew, this is terrible," she murmured. "I can't even pretend."

My mom gave her a sidelong look, the corners of her mouth tense. "Then don't eat it, and there will be no dessert." My mom was tough. Fair but tough. She never gave second chances.

I took a bite of it. It wasn't my favorite, but not terrible. I scratched the back of my head.

"It's good," I forced out, trying to be nice. I knew my mom worked hard making it.

I ate it bite by bite, as my sister sat there her arms crossed, taking the stance of a hunger strike.

And now, here she was letting Diana get away with not even trying her pizza after she picked the arugula off one by one.

But it's just different when you are a grandparent. She now just gets to enjoy her precious girls, instead of carrying the mental load. She lives more in the moment with them, and it's beautiful to see.

She spoils them with love, as good grandparents do. And she would do anything for them. She wants to protect them. To love them. To hug and kiss them. She would do anything for all of us. Sometimes, she shows that love by helping us with struggles that feel impossible to overcome, and other times she shows it in small ways, like buying us a carton of eggs.

And I will be this kind of grandma, too. I know it, and it will happen before I know it. The days are long, but the years are short. People said that phrase to me before I had kids, but I never understood it until I became a mom. Now the years are flying by. We blink and our kids are grown. I am constantly missing the babies they were while still celebrating their growth.

I look at Vivienne on the stage dancing, and I can't believe that eight-year-old with so much confidence in a green puffy dress is mine. Vivienne taught me that things were going to be done her way, not mine. She is now at the age of eyerolls and letting me know I embarrass her. She doesn't need me to put her hair up or help her in the bath. There's a slow loss of innocence I am seeing that frightens me. She wants to chew gum and says, "shut up," for "no way," even though she gets in trouble. She's growing more into herself and wanting less and less of me. As much as that hurts my heart, it means that I have given her enough confidence in herself to start to soar on her own. And seeing her become the person she is, is magical.

Especially when I watch my kids overcome obstacles and gain resilience themselves.

Diana is afraid of flying. The first time we flew after the pandemic, the flight home had terrible turbulence. She came home from the airport saying on loop, "I'm never going on an airplane again." She even had a nightmare that night that she was on a turbulent plane, waking up screaming and crying and covered in a cold sweat so sure her dream was a reality. Since then, if we'd even mention the word "Florida" or "vacation" she'd burst into tears and go into a corner, head tucked between her knees. I'd sit next to her, and her forehead would lean against my shoulder and her tears would soak my shirt until I'd convince her we weren't going anytime soon.

So, for our most recent trip to visit my grandma in Florida when Diana was six, we worked with her therapist trying to desensitize her to the plane. We took a bus in preparation, trying to get her to see public transportation isn't scary. We talked about the steps we were going to go through at the airport: arrive at the airport, check in, security, go to the gate, get on the plane, takeoff, and land. We designated prizes for those stops as well, to get her from one location to the other without throwing a fit out of fear.

She went on the plane knowing what to expect and was looking forward to the prizes more than her fear was holding her back. She couldn't have done better. Yes, she got introverted and sad when I tried to support her through her scared moments, but she did well. She even said, "I'm not afraid of planes anymore." But the return flight was another story.

As we got closer to New York, the pilot made an announcement: "Please sit down and fasten your seatbelts, we are going to experience some rough air." I saw the flight attendants disappear to get into their own seats. Diana was on her iPad holding onto the seat arm for dear life. Charli was in my arms, looking around. I looked out the window. We were in the clouds. I let out a breath.

The plane started shaking a bit, and it dropped. Chari clenched onto me tight and started to wail and quiver with terror as I rocked her back and forth in my seat. Diana propped her head up in her hands, swallowed then murmured, until she got extra quiet. I prayed that this would end soon but remained calm, focused on the two of my four girls who needed me most. Diana stared at the back of the seat in front of her as we continued being rocked by the "rough winds."

"It's just like the bumps on the road when you're in a car," I whispered to her as I grabbed her hand. Charli was now snuggling into my chest, frozen.

"But we aren't on a road," Diana said, her heart in her throat making it difficult for her to speak. Her hand was now squeezing my leg a little too hard.

"Ouch Diana. That's tight." I cringed as she popped her hands back to her armrest. "But that's not the point silly. Just close your eyes and pretend we're in a car instead of a plane." She nodded and closed her eyes. She breathed through the bumps.

The truth is, I don't love turbulence either. When I was little, I too was very afraid of planes and remember shedding many tears on flights. I never loved being 36,000 feet in the air and bumping around. It never made me feel safe. So, each time we dropped, my insides fell a little, too. My heart was in my throat like Diana's.

But I didn't let her see that, because in this case seeing me afraid wouldn't help her. I stayed brave for Diana so she could muster every ounce of bravery inside of her. And soon the turbulence subsided, and we were in smooth air again about to land. My vision blurred with tears, I was so proud of her. She got through a hard flight. And she's come even further since then.

Diana had her first field trip to see *The Very Hungry Caterpillar* show close to the end of her kindergarten year. She couldn't even go to a local Nature Center the year before without her anxiety taking over to the point where she was on the ground in tears, leaves threading her hair, sniffling while begging me to stay to the point where the teacher wanted me to, so she would stop.

Also, we haven't been able to get into a movie theater with her, even with her noise-canceling headphones on, because of sensory overload and fear of the unknown. The last time I tried, she wound up outside the movie theater, with her hands over her headphones, crying ugly gasping breaths, her voice croaking while begging to take her home. This was all without making it into the movie to hear if it was "too loud" for her or if it was all in her head. I eventually gave in and took her and her sisters home.

When her school scheduled a field trip to see a live show, I found out there were no parent chaperones allowed on the trip. I was nervous for her but was working to prep her to feel comfortable. I talked to her teacher, who was going to sit with her on the bus and in the theater. Diana seemed most nervous for the bus ride without me. So, I promised her I'd wait outside until she was on the bus that morning.

Of course, that morning didn't go smoothly because that's motherhood. Charli had a 102-degree fever the night before and Vivienne bruised her ankle against her bedframe doing a cartwheel on the bed before she went to sleep. It was also the weekend of the dreaded Daylight Savings Time. Everyone struggled to get up that morning from a rough night.

When I finally woke up Viv by pulling her entire blanket to the floor after attempt three and me screaming, "We're leaving in ten minutes for school. Get up or you have to go to bed at eight tonight!" She stretched, moaned, and buried her face back into her pillow. Trying to push up from the pillow she murmured, "I can't move my leg!" She limped over to her closet and leaned against the wall, catching it with her shoulders and very dramatically melted into a puddle of tears. "Oh my gosh, I can't move my leg!" she repeated.

"What do you mean you can't move your leg? Do you mean your ankle?" I moved toward her, hesitating for a second.

"I don't know. It hurts so much." She crossed her arms and continued to cry. She flicked her head back to get her tangled brown bedhead hair away from her face.

"Then we need to go to the doctor and maybe get an X-ray." I cut her off, thinking this may have been a ploy to try to get out of school.

"I don't need an X-ray. Can you pick me up?" I scooped her into my arms and brought her downstairs.

I examined her bruised, black, and blue ankle and determined she wasn't lying, though Jonathan kept whispering to me, "She's putting it on." Jonathan stayed with Vivienne and Julia—it didn't matter if Julia was late for PreK—while I brought Diana and Charli to school so Diana wouldn't be late for her big trip.

On the way, I called and scheduled a doctor's appointment for 9:30 AM for both Charli and Vivienne.

As I picked up Charli out of the car seat my lips started to chatter. It was freezing out for mid-March.

"Let me zip your coat," I said to Diana before she got out of the car.

The wind was howling. I held Diana's hand, and Charli snuggled in. On the way to Diana's classroom,

I kept thinking about my 9:30 AM doctor's appointment for the girls, and how freezing it was for Charli, who wasn't feeling well.

"Diana, are you OK if Mommy leaves or do you still want me and Charli to wait until you get on the bus?" She fell into silence and looked at her feet as a gust of wind made her hair blow.

Then her gaze lifted as the quietness bubbled over. "Wait," she said, as she gave me one last kiss, and ran into her classroom.

"Awesome," I said under my breath, looking at Charli. So, we waited outside for twenty-five minutes in the cold, the wind blowing as I tried to entertain Charli by playing a game of chase with her. When I'd catch Charli, I'd breathe into her hands to try to warm them up as she'd let out a laugh.

But that's what we do as moms. We are there for our child who needs us the most. We make sure they're OK, even if it's a wild morning, we're freezing, and we have somewhere else we have to be soon. From my experience, that reassurance is always worth it.

As I waved to Diana through the window of the school bus, she grinned crookedly, waving back. I saw her teacher sit next to her and dimples appear on her cheeks before it drove away. I knew she was in good hands, and my heart fluttered with so much pride knowing how far she had come, how well she was doing, and what a big accomplishment this was.

She is overcoming so much with each passing year and experience. Her teacher sent me a selfie of the two of them. Diana had her headphones on and an ear-to-ear grin on her face. I saved it to my camera roll and sent it to Jonathan. These moments of growth fill me up with so much pride.

And gosh, a part of me wishes they could stay little forever. I swipe through my camera roll at night and stare at photo after photo on my phone. Because, for a moment, they are babies again. I can smell the tops of their heads and feel where they fit into the crook of my arms. Now they're starting to need me less. They spend more time at school, with friends, or in after-school activities. When I ask Viv how her day is, she often answers with grunts. No, not Diana, Julia, and Charli yet, but I know it's coming. Even with their grunts and eyerolls, I love them more as I get to know the people they're becoming. And I know I'll always be there no matter their age.

I have seen this growing up with my mom. Every time I have needed her as a kid and even more so an adult during the hard times, she's been there. She found a way. She always seemed to have a sense if something was wrong, an intuition.

Moms just know some things from living our own lives before kids, hearing about the dangers of the world, and making so many mistakes along the way for ourselves.

And if we miss something because we aren't perfect—we are human after all—all our kids should have to say is four words: "Mom, I need you," and we will show up.

Because showing up matters so much in motherhood. And if you ever doubt it does, the next time you're at the basketball game cheering in the bleachers or a dance recital ready to snap photos, look at your kid's reaction when they first spot you.

Their entire body and face will say, "I'm so happy to see you."

Because when you're there, showing up for them, they light up. It truly means the world to them.

Even if you're late, they'll only see you made it, running as fast as possible, ensuring you don't miss one more second. And when your eyes connect, joy will fill their face. And it means everything.

So I will show up emotionally and physically even if I'm tired, if I don't have to, if I'm busy, if I have an excuse, and if I won't get recognized for it anyway. Because they'll remember I was there, and if they don't, their heart will, and that means everything.

Because I remember it all . . .

When I didn't have my best game of soccer, or we lost because I missed a penalty kick and I came home disappointed in myself, feeling down, and really beating myself up. My mom always made me feel better by taking my hand in hers and saying, "You tried your hardest. Not every day will be your best game," and I felt her love even if I didn't play the best game of my life. It was comforting. She didn't give up on me.

When I was in my sophomore year of high school and lost a lot of my middle school friends to parties and drama I wasn't keen on participating in, I spent most weekends doing homework by myself. She encouraged me to invite another girl I talked about from school over who would then become my best friend for the rest of high school into college. She didn't give up on me.

My junior year of high school, I had memorized an entire presentation from start to finish for Spanish class. I was called up to make my speech, and while looking at my classmates faces, my mind went blank. My heartbeat thumped loudly in my chest. I felt like I couldn't breathe from an intense pressure in my chest. I was sweaty and lightheaded. I wasn't sure what was happening, but I ran to the bathroom, looked in the mirror, and completely broke—descending into tears until I was lying on the dirty bathroom floor. When I got home from school that day, my mom was there to comfort me, and to help figure out ways to prevent it from happening again in the future. She didn't give up on me.

When I was twenty-five on the tile floor in my bathroom at 5 AM, eyes blinking, and vision in and out, so down, and close to death, I could see the vultures, circling, getting lower and lower, because I wanted to die— my first thought when I was sure I wanted help was to text my mom. And she came right away, threw a bunch of clothes into a red Kipling suitcase, and took me home to get me the help I needed. She didn't give up on me.

A couple of hours later, when I had fallen sideways off the kitchen chair, my body alternately contracting and relaxing, she'd pinned me down and dialed 911. She rode with me in the ambulance as gibberish came out of my mouth instead of words. And she waited by my side through all the tests and held my hand. She didn't give up on me.

She has been there through times in my recovery when I couldn't take it anymore. When I sat in front of my food at twenty-six years-old and my anorexia possessed me. I wanted her to tell me I wasn't worth the fight. I wanted her to give up on me so I could give up on myself. That would be my excuse to self-destruct. But she didn't give me that. Yes, I got to her. She took me to the back door in her house and threw me outside as I screamed louder and louder "*I hate you. I hate you!*" Then she pulled me back in and hugged me. She knew it was the anorexia hating to be fed, not me. She didn't give up on me.

The time I snuck laxatives into the house while in recovery, I was so ashamed of myself. When I hid away from her in my childhood closet, paralyzed, not wanting to face what I did. Through the vents I could hear my parents talking. Then they shouted "Dani!" and I stayed in the closet of my room, under hanging clothes, squishing old dress shoes, and wiping tears from my eyes. I made them nervous. I heard, "Did she leave the house?" I heard the front door open, and slam shut with a loud noise. When I finally came out and apologized through broken tears, my parents both took me in their arms. I cried into the warmth of my mom's body. She didn't give up on me.

And I am alive today thanks to her. She didn't give up on me at eighteen. She didn't give up on me at twenty-six. I felt hope to keep living on my darkest days because deep down I knew I was loved. I knew if I died, it would destroy her and my father. I needed to be OK for her. Then when I was in a more solid place of recovery, I started wanting to be OK for me. If someone chooses you every day, you want to be the best version of yourself for them. I hope my kids feel that from me.

Because a mom never gives up on her children. That love doesn't have a time or distance limit. It also never stops. I have heard the beauty of motherhood isn't only in those early years when we're raising little ones, and I have seen it in my relationship with my own mother. It's just different now than it used to be—but it's arguably better. My mom is my best friend.

So, a mom will check her weather app or tune into the news every morning and text her twenty-year-old child, letting him know it's going to rain and not to forget an umbrella and a raincoat.

She will call to see how the first day of school separation went for her grandkids, and if her daughter made it to the car before tears streamed down her face.

She will watch her grandbaby so her daughter can take a nap and rest her postpartum body. And she will also clean up the house, cook dinner, and do as much as she can to make her daughter's life easier when she's done resting.

She will text her forty-year-old son, making sure he's home safe from a wedding, and making sure he had a nice time. Because knowing that her child is happy and safe is still the only way she can sleep well. She will buy her thirty-four-year-old daughter Wetzel's Pretzels when she goes to the mall because she knows how much her daughter loves them.

And she no longer needs to do these things, but she does them anyway. Because a mother always wants to make life easier for her kids when she can, even when they're capable, responsible humans and can do all the things for themselves.

Every night before I went to bed as a little girl, my mom would tuck me tightly under my blanket. She would remove any stray hairs from my face and pull me into a hug where I could relax in her arms. Then she'd kiss me on the top of my forehead or cheek. "Goodnight, I love you," I'd say as we drew apart.

"I love you more," she'd say, giving me one last kiss.

"That's impossible." I'd throw my arms out of the blanket. I'd watch her walk to the light and switch it off and as she'd leave the room, she'd say one last thing: "You will understand one day." I could almost hear her smiling through the darkness as I listened to the door shut. I couldn't understand how she could love me more. I am an empath who loves hard and feels everything hard, and I loved her that much—more than anything in my life. My mom was my world.

But now that I'm a mom, I know she's right.

Now when my mom texts me, "I love you more" each night, I don't argue. I know she's right. No one could love more than a mom.

Because my love, now that I'm a mom, is a different kind of love. It's a love that prioritizes their well-being above my own. It's a love that's loud and so strong that at times I ache. It's a love that protects and supports. Because I fell in love with each of my kids when they were just a thought, before I even met them, before they were small babies who fit on my chest.

It's the kind of love that will make me conquer anything and everything. It's strong and unconditional. As long as I'm alive, I can't help but put them first no matter their ages. It has given me purpose and has made me so much better. And I wouldn't be the me, I am today, without each version of my kids at every age and stage.

Epilogue

The Hard Grows Us
into Better Moms

I WAS ONE OF those little girls who always dreamed of being a mother. I didn't think about being a wife. I never dreamed of my wedding dress, or where I'd honeymoon. I'd never pictured how I'd wear my hair, but I always imagined myself with a little girl or boy in my arms. I was going to labor and cry and give my whole heart and soul to my children.

In 2012, I joined my parents, aunt, uncle, and much younger cousins in Disney World. I was nervous because I hadn't been around people during meals in a couple of years. I had made myself so isolated that I wouldn't have to eat with anyone. I made sure of it.

I would make every excuse and find every fault on blind dates because deep down, I felt too damaged for someone to love me. I was embarrassed by my behaviors. I knew I wasn't normal. There was too much shame for me to be in a relationship.

But this trip, I wanted to go. I loved my younger cousins and hadn't seen them in a long time, between college, starting work, and my eating disorder, depression, and anxiety taking over. And my uncle and I had a great friendship. I called him Big Pal and he called me Little Pal. I always looked up to him, like a big brother.

He lived with us when he was in college and my grandma died of ovarian cancer. I didn't understand the devastating reason why he was there at the time. That he just went through something awful, my mom too. It was something my four-year-old mind couldn't even begin to understand, but the silver lining was the relationship we formed. I was so young but remember running into his room every morning and jumping on him, bouncing up and down. He'd chase me and Erica around the house pretending he was a dog, barking at us as we screamed, my fuzzy hair bobbing around, laughing so hard. That time, with him living with us, was short and special.

I wanted to see him and the beautiful family he created. I truly love them all. It was just a hard trip for me because I wasn't in a good headspace. My brain and body were very sick.

During our trip to The Magic Kingdom as we were going on the Dumbo ride, It's A Small World, and meeting Pooh Bear, all I could do was be worried about "the next meal." I'd obsess about what I was going to eat, how I'd distract everyone. So much so that I couldn't enjoy the company.

My cousin Diana was a tween at the time. We walked out of a store, and I saw her head toward me. Her beautiful ringlet red curls were down to the middle of her back and her green eyes looked like a precious stone. She gave me a hug around my hollow, bony chest.

"Why are you so skinny?" she asked, symmetrical dimples appearing on both sides of her cheeks. What she said wasn't meant to hurt me. It was an innocent question by a child. I was abnormally skinny by this point, unhealthy, so it would be normal for a child to have questions about it. But her words made my heart sink and so much shame filled my body all at once.

I was numb. I didn't know what to say. I didn't want to admit why. I wasn't proud of my habits. How skinny I was. I just didn't see any way it could be different.

"Because she works out a lot and doesn't eat anything," I heard in slow motion. I wasn't even sure who said it. I knew it was one of the adults around me, but I was too ashamed to make eye contact. Hearing that out of someone else's mouth made it that much worse. I thought I was a master of disguise. I could push food to the corner of my plate and pretend I was eating like a pro. I should have stayed home. Then I wouldn't have been found out. I felt naked. I wanted to cry and cover up. I hadn't even admitted out loud to myself that I had a problem. I knew what I did wasn't normal and shameful, but that's why I did it in private.

All the panic I felt about the next meal was instantly eclipsed by the next moment. "I wish I were as skinny as you." That, I was sure, was my cousin Diana. Her green eyes were piercing into my soul as she spoke, and I couldn't unhear it. It would forever be etched in my mind. How she looked. How it felt. How time seemed to stop.

"No, Diana, you don't want to be anything like me. Please don't ever say that. You're beautiful." My voice cracked as I said that. I lifted her hands off me, and backed up, trying to create space between us. I didn't want her to be anything like me. I didn't want anyone to be like me. I couldn't breathe.

I walked away. Speed walking from the front of the store as fast as I could. I could feel a warm wind hitting my body. Sweat glistened onto my face.

"Dani, where are you going?" My mom chased me.

I shook my head. I can't, my eyes warned. I couldn't speak. I could only cry. She grabbed my hand and squeezed it hard. My dad ran up behind us. "What's going on?" I heard. My parents' comforting voices muffled in the background of my loud thoughts and sobs. I knew at that moment that I couldn't be a mother. I was unfit, a terrible role model. And for all I knew, I could have destroyed my body from all the binging and purging— but if I shouldn't, meaning adoption would be out of the question for me, too, I'd be losing the one bit of hope I had for myself. Some people don't need to be a mother to feel complete, happy, or fulfilled, but I did.

Kids make you see yourself for who you really are, and I hated what I saw.

I also didn't see a possible way to get better. I was sick for almost two decades. I didn't know another way to live. I wasn't sure I wanted to, either, especially now that I was sure I couldn't be a mother. In my mind, admitting I was anorexic and getting the help I needed would mean I was damaged and unlovable. I still felt like I had to be perfect to be accepted in our world. So, I would have rather died than admit that something was wrong with me. There was too much shame for me to come forward.

Since I started my recovery journey in December 2012, our society has come a long way—we recognize anorexia as the deadly disease it is. It's an illness, not a choice, a way to cope and not feel. The shame around it has lifted. People are now so much more open and honest about their struggles, making it easier to come forward and get the help they need.

This is when I let my eating disorder take me to rock bottom. I didn't see the point in going on. There was no future for me. I didn't want anyone to want to be like me.

I wasn't living for myself at all to make any passion, any anything, worth it. In my mind, the world would be better off without me. So, I let the eating disorder win.

This is why I am extra grateful to be a mom. I have people come up to me in the park or at school pick up and say, "You are so calm. How do you have so much patience?" Or "I don't have your patience to have four kids." Because Diana and Julia could both be crying, Charli insisting on being picked up, her hands pulling on my shoulders from behind, and Vivienne making a face like she's too embarrassed to be related to any of us, and it doesn't bother me.

Nothing my kids do will embarrass me. I am so calm in the chaos because there was a time where I genuinely didn't think I would get to be a mother. I truly have the gift of perspective, so a toddler tantrum or a bad sibling fight doesn't throw me off. I didn't think I'd get better. I almost died, I wanted to die, and I should have died. When you go through something like that and are in such a dark spot where you become at peace with dying, you become grateful for everything in your life after you turn it around.

So, I don't miss the woman I was before kids at all. Because now my days have a different purpose, and that purpose has made me someone that I am truly proud of. This person doesn't have shame and has the courage to live in whatever way she sees fit. It helped having something to live for besides myself, something that keeps driving me to be OK.

Yes, I had "me time," but now I have little feet following my every move, little noses smooshed against the glass while I shower, little hands tugging on my shirt as I brush my teeth, needing something. And as some of my kids get older, they need me for other things like homework help, or to vent to, and sometimes they just need a hug. They have given my life so much meaning.

Yes, I used to sleep in on weekends, but now I wake up to my children's voices screaming *"Mommy!"* at the crack of dawn and morning snuggles, and it's truly the best way to wake up, even when I'm exhausted. Pro tip, hand them an iPad and sleep and snuggle into them as they watch a show on Netflix. There's no shame in my early morning iPad game!

Yes, I used to go for a jog whenever I felt like it, and now I take walks with my children and it's not as peaceful, but I wouldn't trade it for the world.

Yes, I could dine out with my partner on a whim, and now I tuck my kids in and read them a story, but it's the best way to end the night.

Being needed is a gift. Their voices light up my world even in the early hours, seeing nature through their eyes is pure joy, and getting to be the last words they hear before they close their eyes is a highlight of my day.

I know motherhood has made me into a better me. A stronger me. A me, who appreciates the small moments where sticky kisses hit my face and "I love you" fills my ears, where hugs make my heart burst, and where I connect with my mom on a whole new level.

And these moments beat out the ones where I want to run away, am exhausted, and feel like I'm doing it all wrong. This book is about overcoming the hard in motherhood and how we become better through that, but I don't want it to scare away potential parents out of how amazing it can be to be a parent. There are plenty of moments in a day where dreams are made of that make it all worth it.

The other day I was driving my kids home from a play space in the minivan and Viv told me to put on the YMCA song. I did, and she led all my girls in the dance. All of them were dancing in the car, even Charli put her hands in the air waving them around. There were no sibling fights, just pure joy and laughter. At that moment I thought to myself: I love being a mom so much. There are so many moments like this.

So, the truth is, I don't miss the woman I once was because this woman is much better, stronger, and happier than she's ever been.

Two of the hardest things I have ever done were beating my eating disorder and becoming a mom. Two of the most life changing and rewarding things I have ever done were beating my eating disorder and becoming a mom. I don't think that's a coincidence. I believe that most things that are rewarding in this life are hard. Relationships are hard. Motherhood is hard. Accomplishing a dream is hard.

My battle with my eating disorder made me a better and more understanding person. I was much more judgmental before I admitted to myself that I had a problem. I thought I had to be perfect, so I held others to unbelievably high standards, too. It became easy to let me down. I closed myself off to everyone.

When I accepted and overcame my illness, I became very understanding of other people's struggles that I never understood before. For example, I never understood the actions of people with addiction. Going through my own struggle has made me realize that any damaging behaviors is part of their illness, too.

When I first met a relative of Jonathan's who struggled with addiction, I felt such a connection to him. I looked into his brown eyes and saw a deep hurt that I could relate to. It seemed liked he wanted more but was too deep into his struggle to pull himself out of it. It was a realization that there was a good person inside that body from having genuine conversations. So yes, he may have emotionally hurt and stolen from so many people, but it's because all he can think about is his next high. My heart broke into a million pieces for him. I realized we weren't much different. He was sick like I was. His illness killed his shine.

Because the truth is the difference between empathy and judgment is whether you know someone's story, and now I know everyone has a story. All humans do. And that story makes them more lovable.

I realized my past judgments had to do with myself. I was insecure and lacking self-acceptance and self-love for who I really was. I was afraid to do anything that would come off as not the right choice by society's standards. I did what was expected of me. As soon as I accepted my imperfections and saw that I didn't have to be perfect to still be lovable, I was able to do that with other people and live the life I wanted.

My recovery is a blessing. I wouldn't be here today without it. I wouldn't be the mother to my four beautiful children. Recovery has given me so many wonderful gifts—the gift to live and love without fear. And the gift of being a person my girls can be proud of and want to be like.

Motherhood has also been full of so many challenges from the start, as you have read throughout this book. We are always met with situations where we think: How am I going to do this? And once we overcome them, we are empowered.

Each obstacle I tackled head on made me more resilient and more confident in myself as a mother.

Pregnancy and labor show us how strong our bodies and minds are. We may go through complications like cholestasis, gestational diabetes, preeclampsia, and mis-carriage. We deal with all the emotions of feeling over-joyed, overwhelmed, anxious, regretful, and fearful all at once. We may not love everything about our changing body. We may absolutely hate being pregnant or maybe we don't feel energized and glowing, or we don't connect with our baby while pregnant. If it's our first baby, we may worry about how the baby will impact our relationships or our sex life because a baby will impact everything. But we do it. We get through every negative feeling. We learn and adjust.

Maybe our birth plan didn't happen. Maybe we didn't get an epidural, or we had a scary labor where many things went wrong. But we quickly became responsible for another life we love so much, and we're trying to manage everything but quickly realize life postpartum isn't very glamorous. It may not feel like the happiest time of our life, like we expected, though we're grateful beyond words. And between the lack of sleep, hormone changes, taking care of a newborn, the pain from childbirth and birth complications—like needing a blood patch or a stitch coming out—there's no doubt we will get the "baby blues."

On top of that maybe our child is in the NICU. We may struggle with our new body. We may have a hard time bonding with our baby. We may get mastitis when our milk comes in which makes us feel like someone hit us with a truck.

It's a lot to overcome, but mothers do. And through each hurdle we gain resilience. Even if we struggle with postpartum depression, we become stronger through treatment. We feed our baby. We learn to give ourselves grace, we grow and adjust into someone better, stronger, and more resilient.

We are forced to make hard decisions from the start.

We may struggle with breastfeeding, something we so hoped would come easily, but we get through, we learn how with a lactation coach or fixed tongue tie, or we pump or use formula. Each decision is brave.

We learn through each stage.

Like during the toddler years, we learn that toddlers are always testing boundaries. They cry. They have tantrums. They are discovering the world. They want to be independent but are so needy at the same time. They can't speak well, and they are all about the dramatics but that has nothing to do with our parenting. They are supposed to act like that.

We learn big lessons.

We learn not to care what other people think. We learn to give ourselves tons of grace. We learn not to compare. We learn that "good enough" is enough. We learn not to listen to the impossible expectations of motherhood. We learn to say no. We learn to set boundaries. We learn to build our village. We learn to make mom friends. We learn to make "me time" a priority.

We take in all this information through experience, and we become more compassionate toward other moms and kids. Our priorities and perspective shift. Living through the trials and tribulations gives us a greater sense of empathy allowing us to relate to what other families are going through.

We don't judge the mom of the "wild" child who can't sit still during our three-year-old's art class, because we have one of them, too.

We don't judge the mom who has a kindergartner who doesn't want to separate and is on the elementary school grass crying, throwing a fit like a toddler for all to see. We have empathy. We try to make that tantruming child laugh and comfort the parent with a look that says, "I have been there. Hang in there."

We help the four-year-old who fell in front of us and scraped her knee. We wipe away her tears and give her a Paw Patrol band aid.

We step in when we overhear a little boy not being nice to two of his friends.

We mother every kid around us who needs mothering.

I was at Julia's class holiday party and a little boy with buzzed black hair wearing a Pokémon sweatshirt, taking a bite of a chocolate cupcake, sat across from her. I saw the frosting sitting on the tip of his nose and around his mouth.

"Lucas, you are really enjoying that cupcake. It looks so yummy," I said observing his big smile as he ate.

He looked up and nodded his head, and then turned his gaze toward his cupcake.

I squeezed Julia's shoulders as she took the first bite of her vanilla cupcake. Her eyes widened. I softly snorted beside her, thinking that she was just so darn cute.

"Everyone is loving these cupcakes. Good job, mama." I said to a mother next to me who baked them, interrupting her animated conversation with another mother to her side.

Suddenly Lucas sneezed so loud, and snot shot out of his nose toward his lips. Several moms went right into action. The mother next to me with bright red hair who had her red-haired, freckled face son on her lap, picked up her bag and searched frantically through it for a tissue. I heard her mumble "tissue, tissue, tissue . . ."

I shot off my chair and ran to the Kleenex box by the sink on the other side of the room, grabbing a handful of tissues for him. Another mom started scanning the area with her eyes and grabbed a napkin from the table next to his and put it right in front of him, too. He had a pile of tissues to choose from.

"Thank you," he said as he wiped his nose with one of the tissues in front of him.

That pile of tissues represents "mother to one, mother to all." Once you're a mother, you want to make sure all the children around you are taken care of. You help them zip their coats and put on their hats, so they won't be cold. You comfort them when they're crying. You don't want any child to be sad. So, that pile of tissue in front of Lucas is a mother's care.

If it happened again, he sure had a lot of tissues to choose from.

Because we start looking at every person as someone's child. So we lead with kindness and tell our kids to do the same.

The child with differences who often eats his lunch alone in the cafeteria is someone's child. The waitress who accidentally mixed up your order and put a BLT in front of you instead of the chopped salad you asked for, is someone's child. The driver of the car in front of you who accidentally cut you off is someone's child. So we make sure to tell our children to ask the child with differences to sit with them, and we never yell at the waitress who mixed up our order or the driver who cut us off.

Because somewhere out there is a mom who is worrying so much about her children, knows the good in them, and is praying the world will see them as she does. We know as humans we're all trying our best, and once we are parents, we eat a big slice of humble pie, because it is hard and messy.

Mothers are made through every trial and tribulation, and become stronger, more resilient, and braver. So as my kids change, so will I. I will keep evolving as they evolve too. We will keep going through hard things together. And that's the beautiful thing about a mother; she is always getting stronger and better. As her children grow, their needs change, and so do her responsibilities—from nurturing little kids, to disciplining rebelling teens, to being a confidante to grown-ups—but she's learning and changing through all of it.

I know I will keep being made, all because of my kids. And I can't wait to see who I'll become.

Acknowledgments

THERE ARE SO many people I am grateful to for shaping this book.

The first is my agent, Linda Konner. Thank you for believing in me and this book, even when I doubted myself, for guiding me through the publishing world, and finding my words the best home with Laura at Alcove Press.

Alcove Press, thank you for taking a chance on me and this book and for making *Mothers Are Made* everything I knew it would be and more.

Laura, from our first conversation, I knew you would be a fantastic editor to work with. My instinct was right. Your vision for this book, talent, and guidance helped bring the book to life. You're truly a gift.

To Leslie Means of Her View from Home, I wouldn't be here without that first acceptance and your belief in my words. The home you created on the internet of supportive women writers is truly magical. Thank you for everything.

To all my writer friends, you hold a special place in my heart. Thank you for being my biggest cheerleaders. This industry is hard, and having people understand what you are going through means everything. For the friendships we have forged and the invaluable support we give each other. To see busy women taking time out of their lives to champion each other is beautiful to witness and be a part of. There is so much talent in one place, and I will be forever in your corner, too (as you know).

To Angela, thank you for everything. I am so happy I ran into you that fateful spring day.

To my followers on Living FULL, you don't know how much your support and belief in my words mean to me. Each share, like, and message of encouragement has meant the world. I truly wouldn't have this book without each of you. I am forever grateful for this community and hope I help you feel supported and less alone in your lives, too.

To all the people out there struggling, thank you for being brave each day and pushing through. I hope this book gives you the strength to ask for help. Recovery is worth it. You are worth it. You will be better for it, I promise you.

Thank you to the authentic mom friends who keep me sane through motherhood and treat my kids with so much love. You know who you are. There are too many amazing ones to name, but you are all so special to me.

To Margo, my person, my sounding board, and one of the best people I know, thank you for supporting me with everything, from motherhood to this book. Your friendship means the world to me.

To my parents, thank you for everything. Thank you for showing me how to be a loving parent, for your belief in me, and for always being there. I now know you love me more, but gosh I love you so much.

To Beth, thank you for everything: for reading my book, catching some good edits, and most of all, cheering me on. Grateful.

To the rest of my family by blood and marriage, I am so blessed to be surrounded by so much love.

To my husband and love of my life, Jonathan, for your endless support. For putting up with eight months of dirty looks when you came into the living room talking when I was in the middle of writing a sentence. For taking over bedtime with our oldest three so I can write. For letting me write even while we ate dinner (our only sacred time) and putting up with constantly sharing me with my computer. I don't say it enough but thank you. Most of all, thank you for being my best friend and partner and believing in me. You are such a blessing.

And finally, my beautiful girls, Vivienne, Diana, Julia, and Charli. You are my reason. Thank you for being my inspiration to make the world a better place. You make me brave. You make me better. I am so lucky you are mine.